PLASTICITY INTO POWER

Comparative-Historical Studies on the Institutional Conditions of Economic and Military Success

VARIATIONS ON THEMES OF
POLITICS
A WORK IN CONSTRUCTIVE SOCIAL THEORY

ROBERTO MANGABEIRA UNGER

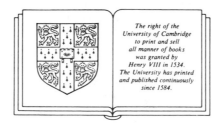

The right of the
University of Cambridge
to print and sell
all manner of books
was granted by
Henry VIII in 1534.
The University has printed
and published continuously
since 1584.

CAMBRIDGE UNIVERSITY PRESS

CAMBRIDGE

NEW YORK   NEW ROCHELLE   MELBOURNE   SYDNEY

Published by the Press Syndicate of the University of Cambridge
The Pitt Building, Trumpington Street, Cambridge CB2 1RP
32 East 57th Street, New York, NY 10022, USA
10 Stamford Road, Oakleigh, Melbourne 3166, Australia

First published 1987

Printed in the United States of America

Library of Congress Cataloging-in-Publication Data
Unger, Roberto Mangabeira.
Plasticity into power.
"Variations on themes of Politics, a work in
constructive social theory."
1. Sociology.   2. Social institutions.
3. Adaptability (Psychology)   4. Necessity (Philosophy)
5. Power (Social sciences)   I. Unger, Roberto
Mangabeira.   Politics, a work in constructive social theory.
II. Title.
HM24.U535   1987   306   86–8232

British Library Cataloguing in Publication Data
Unger, Roberto Mangabeira
Plasticity into power : comparative-
historical studies on the institutional
conditions of economic and military
success : variations on themes of Politics,
a work in constructive social theory.
1. Political sociology
I. Title
301.01   JA76

ISBN 0 521 32976 0 hard covers
ISBN 0 521 33864 6 paperback

Contents

Introduction

THE three convergent essays that make up this book advance a revised practice of historical explanation. They explore through comparative-historical analysis a series of related problems in our understanding of the institutional conditions of economic and military success.

These three studies do not imply a particular social theory. They are nevertheless meant to further both a negative and an affirmative theoretical endeavor.

The negative work is the criticism of the intellectual traditions, including orthodox Marxism and modernization theory, that have dominated our most ambitious efforts at social and historical explanation. This book denies that there must be tightly drawn correspondences between levels of development of practical capability and particular institutional arrangements. It denies also that such arrangements come as stage-ordered sequences or indivisible packages, such as "capitalism" or "the market economy."

The affirmative task is to supply materials for a less necessitarian practice of social and historical explanation. This practice resembles in some ways the theories it criticizes but differs from the positivist social science and historiography that have largely replaced such theories. The approach taken here acknowledges the central importance of the distinction between the formative institutional arrangements and imaginative preconceptions of a society and the routine practical or mental activities that these structures help shape. It recognizes that such institutional and imaginative frameworks cannot be adequately explained as the cumulative results of a society's normal episodes of conflict and compromise. It shows that we do not need to predefine possible trajectories of large-scale, discontinuous structural change in order to understand what happens in history. It severs the link between our ability to explain past or present situations and the premise that these situations were or are necessary. It enlarges our sense of the real and the possible. It places explanatory ambition on the side of an acceptance of contingency and an openness to novelty.

A unifying substantive theme emerges hand in hand with this methodological campaign. In one statement the theme is that social plasticity brings wealth and power to the societies and the groups that achieve it. The benefits of practical opportunism and flexible work relations soon override the advantages of rigid schemes of social control and coercive surplus extraction. But the plasticity that counts is not just anarchy or indefinition. Particular institutions and ideas are needed to attain it. In another, complementary statement the theme is the relation between failures of institutional invention and constraints on collective conflict. Plasticity-producing and power-bringing institutions have usually resulted from runaway social warfare. They have built opportunities for conflict and innovation into the routines of social life.

A subsidiary substantive theme is that the subjection of factional privilege to challenge and conflict has been the single most important spur to social plasticity. Plasticity develops when central governments cease to play their familiar role of helping established elites hold on to entrenched positions. But, historically, the antielitist intentions of the occasional masters of the state have been secondary. More important are the unforeseen institutional experiments that take place when a government-supported structure of social control breaks down and when the powerless, the propertyless, and the prostrate can fight on more equal terms with their immediate social superiors – bosses, landowners, and local notables. A less halting pursuit of the goal of plasticity requires the invention of institutions that turn economies and polities into machines for the ongoing destruction of all privileged claims on the resources – of capital, power, and expertise – with which we make and remake society.

The methodological and the substantive concerns of the book come together. The more successfully we learn and practice the gospel of plasticity, the less suitable we become as subjects of the necessitarian styles of social and historical analysis that the great social theorists have taught us. We can, in fact, raise a storm in the world and still understand and explain ourselves. All we need is a better approach.

Studies like these must depend almost entirely on secondary sources. I see no point in exhaustively rehearsing these sources in notes. The controversial aspects of this book have to do less with historiographic details than with ideas about the connections and the implications of familiar facts. Notes acknowledge direct, individualized debts for insights or observations and signal places where the argument shades into more focused historiographic disputes. Two books published simultaneously with *Plasticity into Power* work out the perspective from which these exercises are written – *Social Theory: Its Situation and Its Task* and *False Necessity: Anti-Necessitarian Social Theory in the Service of Radical Democracy*.

1

The Periodic Breakdown of Governments and Economies in Agrarian–Bureaucratic Societies: Its Causes, Antidotes, and Lessons

A Comparative Study of the Relation Between Failures of Institutional Invention and Constraints on Group Conflict

THE PROBLEM STATED AND THE ARGUMENT PREVIEWED

THIS study explores the cycles of commercial vitality and decommercialization, of governmental unity and fragmentation, that plagued the agrarian–bureaucratic empires – the dominant social organizations of preindustrial history. It also examines the social conditions and the institutional inventions that enabled some societies to escape these cycles and, as a result, to revolutionize the world.

A methodological thesis and a substantive concern drive the analysis forward. The methodological thesis is that we cannot understand the problems discussed here without reorienting the practice of social theory. The substantive concern is to explore some unintended constructive by-products of uncontrolled group conflict.

Throughout much of history a strange event repeatedly cut off the approach toward conditions that might have allowed society to achieve higher levels of productive and destructive capabilities. This event foreclosed the experiments with machines, work, and institutional arrangements that such an advance requires. The foreclosure took place most often and most dramatically in the great agrarian empires that were the largest and most influential states of preindustrial times. But it also recurred in city-state republics that had gained territorial possessions or in agrarian societies that never came under a single government. Its recurrence – and its occasional failure to recur – were decisive for the collective struggles and the material progress of mankind. To understand both the reappearing event and its rare, all-important avoidance is to grasp the most important link between material progress and the fights or the surrenders that give rise to a social world.

There were times in the history of most of these great agrarian societies when money-based commerce flourished and extended to trade in the ordinary necessities of life. The central government could count on receiving a significant portion of its taxes in money. The need to pay taxes in money worked as one spur to extending money-oriented markets far into the ordinary world of work – the work of farming on which both the subsistence and the luxuries of these countries so largely depended. Money taxes usually went hand in hand with the ability of rulers to recruit part of their armies directly from the laboring population of tenants and smallholders. In these favored and prosperous times imperial governments enjoyed access, through direct tax gathering and military recruitment, to the ordinary working population. No cadre of warlords, priests, or landholding magnates held an inclusive stranglehold on the sources of wealth and might. Among the farmers themselves there was a large range of different forms of property and labor. Prosperous but middle-level farmers coexisted with smallholders, tenants, and even slaves. Large disparities of material welfare and autonomy divided this agrarian population as well as the peddlers and craftsmen of the towns. But petty owners or relatively secure small-scale tenants worked a large proportion of the land. Much dependent labor earned money wages. At such times the masses were neither safe nor prosperous, and they were certainly excluded from governmental power. But they held on to opportunities for advancement in the modest affairs of work and trade.

Then there were other times when the roof fell in on this world. The money-using sector of the economy shrank rapidly: monetary trade narrowed down to luxury goods. More important, most of the working population found itself reduced to the condition of dependent labor, paid in kind rather than with money wages. The masses of the people no longer had direct access to markets or to protection (and claims) by officials of state. The central government lost its ability to exact money taxes and military manpower directly from the ordinary work force. The state disintegrated, withdrew, or fell entirely into the hands of military, ecclesiastical, and landholding grandees. The peasantry – now a still larger part of the population as towns got smaller – were driven in ever larger numbers into servile, nonmonetary labor for large landholders. These landholders now ruled, with many fewer escapes or exceptions, the lives of the large mass of dependent laborers.

Sometimes this dependence resulted from naked coercion. On other occasions it came from debt slavery and bankruptcy. At still other times the immediate cause of the peasants' fall into direct dependence on an overlord–landowner was their desperate attempt to escape from the mounting fiscal and military demands the central rulers demanded. The grandees offered protection in exchange for subjugation. Although the triggers of subjugation might differ, the same driving forces were always at work.

In the following pages this condition of relative collapse is called the reversion to natural economy. The name should not make anyone forget that the narrowing of monetary trade always remained just one of the more tangible aspects of this recurrent crisis, and a relatively superficial one at that.

There were preindustrial societies – like imperial China, all the way from the Han to the Ch'ing dynasties – in which this reversion occurred repeatedly, with variations in kind and degree. Some societies – like the Roman Empire in the West – witnessed reversion as a grinding, entropic process, temporarily halted and modestly reversed at times, but finally helping to destroy, once and for all, the order it had tried to contain. In yet other societies, like the Byzantine Empire, periods of reversal of reversion crises coexisted with a long-term disintegrative movement toward the repetition and aggravation of those crises.

The near universality of this event in these agrarian societies remains astonishing. Not only did it recur in countless circumstances over long periods but its recurrence ran contrary to a broad range of interests. There were the interests of the supreme rulers in overshadowing and controlling the grandees and in sustaining the unity, the independence, and the prosperity of the realm. There was also the interest of the ordinary working population in avoiding the total replacement of independent family holdings or relatively free labor by unqualified subjection to an immediate master. Moreover, these vital interests were openly acknowledged; they were widely understood to be at stake in the events that led up to the reversion. The strangeness of the play of unintended consequences is exceeded by the still greater surprise of the repetition of an event that both the highest and the most numerous elements in the society openly feared and often resolutely tried to avoid. The anguish of Romanus Lecapenus (920–944) or Basil II (976–1025) at the height of Byzantine power over the effect that the ruin of the smallholders would have on the military and fiscal basis of the empire did not differ sharply from the warnings of frustrated reformers during the T'ang–Sung interregnum (10th century) – or, for that matter, in a very different setting, from the views of Tiberius Gracchus and his set about the effects of the Carthaginian Wars upon the agrarian foundations of the Republic.

The importance of the reversion cycles for the agrarian–bureaucratic empires hardly needs emphasis. The initial source of transformative economic growth in these societies was the critical difference between agricultural surplus and subsistence. Even more significant was the effect of relations of power and ideas of possibility on the use of this surplus. Moreover, both elite conceptions of conservative or reforming statecraft and the preconceptions of ordinary people about what they could expect from life had constantly to be measured in turn against the overriding realities of day-to-day agrarian work. To whole empires and their masters, as well as to ordinary peasant households, the reversion to natural economy and the ensuing destruction of smallholders and independent tenants and wage laborers were an ever-present fear and an exemplary disaster.

For both the rulers and the ruled, the realism of any scheme of social and economic reform lay, in the long run, in its ability to translate into the daily routines of agrarian life. These routines remained impermeable to visionary ideals like the Chinese "well-field" (*ching-t'ien*) system. Instead of serving as credible guides to reform, such commitments survived indefinitely as rhetorical conceit and confused nostalgia.

Remember, finally, that the agrarian empires represented the largest and most populous societies of the preindustrial world. The fate of smaller trading states was settled in the long run by their relation to these great powers, whose prosperity and influence remained in turn bound up with the vicissitudes of agriculture and of the forms of control over land and agrarian labor. It is less obvious but equally true that an understanding of these periodic breakdowns of premodern governments and economies can make a major contribution to our grasp of later events in world history. For it was by avoiding these cycles or by breaking out of them that certain societies took the lead in the development of the practical productive capabilities of mankind.

The following study of the reversion crises and of their broader significance explores four main theses. The first thesis is that the cycles of reversion to natural economy were central to the history of the agrarian–bureaucratic societies and that they elicited from reforming governments a small number of characteristic policies. These policies, at once varied and repetitious, included the recruitment of a bureaucratic staff from social groups directly below the landowning nobility, the direct involvement of landowning magnates in state service as a condition of land tenure and, most notably, the establishment of a class of government-protected smallholders with fiscal and military responsibilities to central government.

The reversion cycles did not occur with the same severity in all the agrarian societies of Asia: among the great agrarian–bureaucratic states the Byzantine Empire and China before the Mongol Conquest were the most vulnerable. By contrast, the Ottoman Empire, although suffering occasional economic, administrative, and military down-swings, never underwent a wholesale reversion crisis. Many other societies stood somewhere along this spectrum of vulnerability. The central argument of this essay helps explain why the agrarian–bureaucratic societies demonstrated such different susceptibilities to these peculiarly thoroughgoing breakdowns.

The second thesis concerns the reasons for the repeated failure to safeguard the smallholders and thereby to prevent or control repeated economic and administrative decline. The key problem here was the unwillingness of even the most perspicacious and antiaristocratic regimes to court the dangers of revolutionary despotism that would attend any attempt to form a common front with the smallholder class against landowning magnates. Technical difficulties of control and communication in preindustrial societies aggravated the problem. But they were not its essence.

The heart of my argument lies in a third thesis. This thesis deals with the conditions that enabled some societies to escape the disintegrative processes of decommercialization and administrative fragmentation. Two independent historical circumstances – late medieval Europe and Tokugawa Japan (1603–1868) – witnessed institutional innovations that destroyed the basis of the reversion cycle. In each instance these innovations occurred in conditions that enabled peasants to organize and to struggle against their immediate landlords without confronting central governmental intervention in the landlords' favor. But this circumstance took completely different forms in the two cases. In Europe the premise was the nearly complete disintegration of a central state structure. In Japan it was the government-promoted withdrawal of armed landowners from the countryside.

The European and the Japanese experiences did not represent the only ways to break through the reversion cycles. In fact the history of the Asian agrarian–bureaucratic empires shows another, slower and less far-reaching but nevertheless partly successful solution. Several of the agrarian–bureaucratic governments gradually assimilated conceptions and techniques of statecraft pioneered by their occasional pastoral conquerors and rulers. The peoples of the inner-Asian steppe developed, first in their homelands and then in the conquest states they set up, institutions and ideas that more effectively disengaged central state power from private or local privilege. As they learned from the conquered, they in turn taught. Their lesson helped some of the agrarian–bureaucratic empires of Eurasia to perpetuate a commercialized economy that retained a varied spectrum of small- and large-scale landholdings. The steppe peoples as conquerors also pioneered a style of centralized administrative structure which avoided the more conflictual social experiments that Europe, to a greater degree, and Japan, to a lesser extent, had undergone. The Ming–Ch'ing and Ottoman empires represent the most important examples of this administrative style. But as the means in these two states were less radical the results were not as successful than in either Western Europe or Japan. These reformed agrarian–bureaucratic societies went much less far than North-Atlantic societies toward a practice of permanent organizational and technological innovation and a cumulative weakening of rigid social roles and hierarchies.

The fourth thesis of my argument is historiographical. Both Marxist and liberal views of European history have been dominated by a stereotyped image of the modern English road to worldly success:

relentless agrarian concentration and the triumphal march from domestic production and the putting-out system, through centralized factories, to mass production. The political counterpart to this economic picture is the gradual enfranchisement and assimilation of the working classes on terms that make possible the reconstitution of a ruling and possessing elite. Whatever departs from this English stereotype is made to appear a deviation, qualifying or delaying an inexorable developmental tendency. But the argument of this essay turns this prejudice upside down. It suggests that the English stereotype – to the extent that it accurately describes even the English events – represents the least telling and distinctive aspect of the European experience. The English route is the closest Europe could come to Asia – that is, to the situation of the agrarian–bureaucratic empires – without falling back into the Asian cycles. The supposed anomalies were and are the real Western thing.

WHY THE REVERSION CYCLE HAS NOT BEEN WIDELY DISCUSSED AND WHY ITS THEORETICAL IMPLICATIONS ARE FAR-REACHING

Despite their astonishing recurrence in so many different societies, over such extended periods, the cycles of reversion to natural economy have rarely attracted comprehensive study. The neglect becomes all the more surprising when you remember that the problems presented by these perennial breakdowns were no secret affliction that a speculative mind must retrospectively diagnose. They were the obsessive concern of the most articulate reformers. The records that historians most like to examine are full of talk about them. Even the continuing predominance of national historiography over comparative analysis fails to account for the disregard of such manifest and pervasive apprehensions.

A more persuasive explanation is that an approach to the problems occasioned by reversion requires a mode of understanding able to combine two sets of qualities habitually opposed in the available forms of social and historical analysis. On the one hand, the approach must be bold and comprehensive. It must enable us to identify formative institutional arrangements and influential preconceptions about the possible and desirable forms of human association. It must show how such basic preconceptions and arrangements shape routine social conflicts and social policies. And it must explain how changes in those institutions and beliefs can alter the standard policies and conflicts of the societies in which these changes occurred. The escape from the reversion crises of the agrarian–bureaucratic empires did not merely replace some routines with others. It diminished the sense in which social relations and struggles were routinized at all. The societies that emerged from the European and Japanese escapes were not just different; they stood open to more variations and combinations of forms of work organization, resource use, and public policy than had previously been possible. Only in the traditions of speculative social theory can we find habits of mind that make it possible to address such conceptual concerns.

But these traditions lack the antinecessitarian and antiteleological skepticism that an adequate account of the reversion crises must also possess. The approach we need must dispense with the idea of a predefined and limited set of possible trajectories of institutional change or with the appeal to the evolutionary laws that can generate them. The present study suggests reasons to believe that we cannot identify such possible transformative routes. In fact, we do not need to determine the range of possible transformations in order both to explain the transformations that actually took place and to recognize alternative pathways to similar outcomes.

An adequate treatment of the problems examined here refuses to invoke a closed set of possible sequences of institutional change and acknowledges instead the ability of central governments and social groups to respond to their circumstances in surprising ways. Revisionist tendencies within the Marxist and liberal traditions alike have already emphasized the relative independence of politics from social structure, taking politics in both the narrow sense of conflict over the mastery and uses of governmental power and the more inclusive sense of fighting over all the terms on which people can make claims on others.

But it is one thing to define the autonomy of politics as a limited margin of variable response; it is another to say, as we must, that neither prospectively nor retrospectively can we ever know what the limits of variation are. It is one thing to claim, as the revisionists do, that there were several forms of passage from feudalism to capitalism; it is another to recognize, as we must, that concepts like feudalism and capitalism are only summary allusions to unique, institutionally codified social settlements that resulted from unique sequences of practical and imaginative strife, underdetermined by the prior settlements they disrupted. The argument of this essay hinges on the latter, stronger set of claims.

Thus, an adequate account of the reversion cycles and of their supersession has to anticipate, in fragmentary and implicit form, a revised practice of social and historical analysis. It has to show how we can combine skepticism – about historical laws and evolutionary sequences and about the finality of the constraints that social structure imposes on politics – with the explanatory ambitions the skeptic seems to renounce.

THE AVOIDANCE OF REVERSION

The most concrete requirement of the avoidance of reversion to natural economy – so concrete that it fades into the definition of the outcome to be explained – is that the magnates of the realm not be allowed to gain unrestricted control over peasant land and labor. Whenever they gained this control, they destroyed the sector of the agrarian economy given over to smallholding, independent tenancy, and wage labor. They turned their estates into kingdoms within the kingdom.

Three more particular conditions have to be met for the reversion to natural economy to be stopped or postponed long enough to make possible a revolution in production and productivity.

First, and most important, there must be a large amount of independent, local collective organization by the people occupied in agricultural work. They must be able to draw together closely and long enough to deal collectively with their immediate superiors: the bureaucrats, captains, and landowners with the power to push working people into unmitigated subservience and into a lifetime of confinement on a large estate ruled by its master's will. The organizational practices the peasants adopt must be consciously suited to the needs of contentious collective self-defense rather than just accepted as the way things are. This joining of forces presupposes neither equality of circumstance and community of affect among the workers nor a master strategy of collective advancement pursued over long stretches of time. It does require that threat, disruption, and organization combine in the proportions necessary to avoid a disastrous tilt of the balance of power between the strong and the weak in the countryside. It turns out that the successful exercise of this capacity by smallholders, laborers, and petty traders is in turn connected with the existence of other sources of constraint upon the magnates' greed. These alternative constraints may be set by policies of central rulers or by the realities of military danger and labor scarcity.

The second general condition for avoidance of the reversion to natural economy is that the power of the state – if a central government exists at all – be partly screened from the influence of any unitary or single-minded elite. Central government may have disintegrated altogether. Then what matters is that its disintegration occur in such a way that peasants have a fighting chance in their collective deals with local magnates and warlords. If, however, a central government does subsist, it must combine a special kind of strength with a particular sort of weakness. It must be strong enough to resist the triumph of any unified class of warriors, bureaucrats, and estate holders. But it must also be too weak to transform the part of the peasantry not already under magnate domination into a helpless source of taxes and soldiers and thereby deprive these peasants of any independent organization of their own.

The third condition for the avoidance of reversion is an extension of the second. The elites must be so fragmented that they cannot present a united front against the peasant mass. Different groups must answer for distinct governmental responsibilities. The military, the ecclesiastical, and the landowning grandees do not wholly merge, by identity or alliance. Their squabbles give both rulers and workers an opportunity for independent action. The peasants and the imperial staffs then have a chance to make something of their minimal common interest in holding the grandees at bay. If no central state exists, the necessary fragmentation is more likely to be geographic. The elites that count are then the great landowners who, on their separate estates, become little princes, trying to concentrate all mastery in their own hands. They will want to hold as much economic, military, and religious authority as they can. Each will keep rival claimants to dominion at a distance. At the very least, if the peasants are to have a fighting chance, local potentates must remain at odds with one another. No higher institution must stand ready to weld them into a single force in the contest with the peasantry.

Before this initial account of the conditions for the avoidance of reversion to natural economy is developed through comparative example and argument, it can be pushed to a further level of generality. What these different requirements share for the avoidance of reversion and what, together, they point toward is a heightened condition of plasticity in social relations. This plasticity counts for most in the relations that concern the routine affairs of power and production. In some higher measure, these routine dealings must be lived out as possible objects of a transformative will and imagination. For all their weight and inertia, they must be treated as realities whose nature is both revealed and changed by conflicts among collective forces and visions of the ideal.

The joint effect of peasant self-defense, of the partial independence or disappearance of the state, and of the breakup of elite unity is to perpetuate conflict and to make its outcome uncertain at the ground level of daily life and labor. The outcome gives the peasant household a chance to hold out, and to hold out in a way that helps keep the monetary commercial economy from periodically vanishing. It also prolongs the uncertainty about how the surplus over subsistence will be appropriated and what it will be used for.

Continued material progress in an industrialized or industrializing society may demand a constant transition, back and forth, between a condition of heightened conflict and innovation and a state of relatively vested rights. The access to permanent technological and organizational innovation requires that the social forms of power and production be even more constantly and consciously subject to struggles of will and imagination. At this more advanced moment of material progress, the theme of the plasticity of social relationships – of their indefinite susceptibility to penetration and revision by individual consciousness and collective effort – gains relief. The theme of plasticity stops being a remote, vague background to more immediate conditions of material progress. It takes on a new degree of immediacy and concreteness. It works through a vastly enlarged range of possible forms of organization at the workplace and in society at large.

The imperative of plasticity, which comes to play so central a role in social life after the industrial breakthrough, is prefigured, indirectly but unmistakably, in the development of the conditions that make the breakthrough possible. This foretaste of the most revolutionary aspects of the outcome in its distant genesis finds analogies in aspects of the history of politics and character that at first seem to have nothing to do with changes in material life.

The utopian element in politics lies in the ability to disentangle the image of possible human association from forms of life that make people's material and moral availability depend on their acceptance of predetermined hierarchical and communal divisions. The struggle of this visionary politics is to deny the identification of society with a limited repertory of social forms. Such a repertory imprisons all experiments in practical collaboration, in self-expression and reconciliation, within a determinate scheme of ranks and divisions, of authoritative ideals, and of accepted contexts for the realization of these ideals.

In another realm, the indispensable instrument of a visionary politics is collective mobilization, which brings people together in ways not foreordained by the established structure or the prevailing dogmas of society. The weakening of established hierarchies or, more generally, of the ruling ideals and practices of association is mirrored in the activity that destroys these forms of social life and reinvents them.

Or, again, the same circumstances that see men and women accelerate their experiments with the disentanglement of associative possibility from the hierarchical and communal examples of association already available to them are also likely to witness experiment with the assertion of their personalities beyond the limits drawn by their routines of conduct and vision. Such experiments encourage the individual to treat his settled character as the incomplete and corrigible expression of a self. The stratagems of imagination and activity by which he carries out such experiments already involve a partial victory over the automatisms and rigidities of a closed character. To come out from under the protective wall of role, habit, and frozen perception, a person must throw himself into a situation of heightened exposure. He must put himself at greater risk to the harm that other people may do him and to the destructive influence that enlarged experience may have on what he had previously regarded as his enduring core of identity.

The analogies between process and outcome in material progress, visionary politics, and personal experience are more than superficial parallels. The further you go in the understanding of any one of these lines of movement, the more clearly you see how such experiments connect and how they all give practical significance to the idea that, in politics, means create their own ends.

From this point on, this discussion of periodic breakdowns in premodern economies and polities moves forward in three stages. First, I refine the initial crude idea of the natural and the money economy, of the process that leads from one to the other and of the driving forces behind this process. Then, the analysis turns to two situations that satisfy the conditions for postponing, for a crucial period, the reversion to natural economy. The comparative study of European and Japanese experiences make it possible to enlarge an understanding of these conditions. Finally, the argument takes up a number of cases that exemplify a more gradualistic and equivocal route of escape from susceptibility to reversion crises.

THE CONCEPT OF REVERSION REFINED

Start by returning to the contrast between the natural and the money economy in a preindustrial agrarian society. Under the money economy, a sizable part of the countryside remains under cultivation by relatively independent proprietors and tenants. When large estates prevail, many of the agrarian laborers are salaried and mobile. A major cut of the agricultural produce is sold. The cash proceeds of these agricultural sales are used to pay off landlords and governments (rents, tax, and tax rents). These agricultural profits also support, directly or indirectly, a flourishing urban life, manufacture and trade in luxury goods, and even the decentralized mass production, in the cities or the countryside, of basic necessities like clothes and tools. Such an economy is thoroughly monetary; in it, coerced labor and barter play only a subsidiary role.

The political precondition and counterpart to this money-oriented economy is that the imperial government manage to keep landlords and warlords from engrossing the greater part of peasant land and labor. The rulers of agrarian–bureaucratic societies repeatedly moved among a small number of strategies for holding the magnates back without courting the dangers of revolutionary despotism. The connection between the economic and the political aspects of the situation is brought out into the open by the organization of state finance and military strength. The conditions under which an imperial government can hope to be something more than a listless tool in the hands of rival aristocratic factions broadly overlap with those in which a commercialized, money-based economy is likely to prevail.

In principle, the government might get its revenues and its soldiers directly from military colonies and state farms without contesting the engrossment of land by the magnates and the magnates' ability to coerce most of the peasant masses into dependent and forced labor, out of the reach of any market. But, in fact, this policy of agrarian dualism is never likely to be enough for long – especially, when the state-supporting sector of small farms and military colonies loses access to monetary transactions.

To obtain the resources and the soldiers it is likely to require, the central government could not limit itself to setting up military colonies on the frontiers of the realm and a few isolated public farms within it, to be administered by agents. If the ruling household were truly forbidden to take men and money from all estates, large or small, that were not under its direct control, it would have to place a major portion of the countryside in its own hands. To do this, and to do it in a situation in which neither the state nor the nonstate sectors are commercialized, is almost sure to be impossible.

For one thing, as the size of the bureaucratic apparatus needed to manage huge estates and supervise multifarious transfers expands, the opportunities for plunder of government by officials increase. Large private landlords continue to exist. The ambition of every bureaucrat is to become a landholding aristocrat in his own right. To remain effectively in charge of this huge management operation the central rulers would have to choose at every point between an all-out campaign against private magnates and terroristic intimidation of the servants of the state.

For another thing, by bringing a large part of the countryside under its immediate and visible exploitation, the government casts itself as a threatening rival of the grandees and the independent cultivators at the same time that it tries to coerce the labor of a huge peasant mass. The potential war on two social fronts is all the more dangerous because it is likely to take place when the state is least able to wage it. When a military and fiscal emergency occurs and the burden on the state-protected peasantry goes up, the incentive to flee to the nonstate sector will increase. The charge on the remaining population of the state farms and military colonies will be aggravated.

If, however, the agricultural economy is largely monetary, the central government can more easily restrict its fiscal activities to collecting money taxes and overseeing certain limited transfers in kind, such as grain provisions to large cities and strategic supplies to the army.

Public officials can be made more accountable, and their number more readily limited. The starkness of the contrast between the state and the nonstate sectors can be effaced as transactions between them are encouraged. The dealings of the government with the small cultivators on which the state depends for much of its wealth and fighting strength can be redefined in less exploitative, costly, and destructive ways. Trade with partners beyond the political borders can be fostered.

As soon as the problems of fiscal and military administration are understood, it becomes clear that the devices by which the central government of a preindustrial, agrarian society can avoid both the rise of magnate influence and the disintegration of the realm into hostile aristocratic strongholds are inseparable from the conditions for commercializing the agrarian economy. This inseparability appears even in the tactic the government uses when it relies directly on the output and manpower of part of the peasantry while abandoning the remainder to the magnates (the policy of agrarian dualism). It is even more true of the other available strategies by which central governments might contain the powerful: the direct involvement of the landholding nobility in state service and the constitution of a career bureaucracy as a counterweight to the landholders. With no part of the ordinary, working population directly responsible to it, the central government must be all the more careful to keep officials and grandees from gaining absolute dominion over peasant land and labor. For such control would enable the magnates to deny the central rulers any flexibility of finance or recruitment. It would consume the efforts of organized government in an indefinite number of costly transfers. The profits of these transfers would easily stick to the would-be intermediaries. The losses would fall on the treasury above and the masses below.

The distinctive traits of the natural economy are the reverse of those of the money economy. The part of agricultural production sold for cash in fairs and towns declines. The class of minor independent cultivators – small-scale proprietors, sharecroppers, and tenants – loses ever larger parcels of its independence to the greater landholders. Money rents and wages are broadly replaced by rents in kind and in corvée labor. The large estates are economically sealed off from each other. Urban trade and manufacture shrink; a major segment of the artisanal class shifts to the countryside. To be sure, these processes usually remain incomplete. There are forces operating to counteract them. The towns almost never disappear. Part of the harvest continues to be commercialized.

The shrinkage of the commercialized, money-based economy, like its growth, usually goes together with a characteristic change in the dealings between state and society and in the relations among the classes. The ascendancy of landholding magnates, warlords, or ecclesiastical estate-building accompanies the emasculation of the state and the heightened subjection of the peasant plot to landlord power.

The career of taxation clarifies the link between the economic and the political aspects of the reversion to natural economy, although it does not explain their common origin. In the more moderate forms of economic naturalization, the central government gives up trying to tax the whole of agricultural output directly. The state allows the prosperous and powerful men of the realm – within or outside its official bureaucracy – to become the exclusive intermediaries of its taxes and rents. The tax, convertible into money and paid in the city, gives way to the tax owed by some local potentate on behalf of the people under his direct control or in his sphere of influence. In the more virulent forms of naturalization of the economy, the resources that the state can effectively extract from these intermediate powers both diminish in volume and assume an increasingly nonmonetary form. In the end, the treasury runs dry. The warlord armies take over.

In all the great agrarian empires of antiquity, the monetary economy periodically broke down. At these times, economic life became largely or significantly naturalized. Even when the breakdown did not occur, statesmen and publicists would be very much aware of tendencies afoot in that direction. A great deal of effort or luck was required to set these tendencies back.

The frequent return to natural economy opposes the fundamental interests of the central government. It brings added oppression to the vast masses of the population. It denies them the hope of independent petty proprietorship. Only when the state has already been weakened by the factors responsible for starting the naturalization of the economy; only when it has allowed the magnates to shift the fiscal and military burden onto the semiautonomous village and thereby ruined the peasantry and driven it into revolt against officialdom; only when the rulers and administrators of the realm have given up the attempt to impose order and to ensure prosperity or have wholly identified the interests of the state with those of the great landlords; only then will the peasant abandon his independent plot and seek subjection to the landholder as a lesser evil or an imperative of survival.

Yet this recurrent transformation, which jeopardizes workers and rulers alike, cannot easily be attributed either to the independent breakout of conquest and insurrection or to the workings of a spontaneous economic logic. In some instances, it occurred in the absence of generalized fighting. In others, it was itself largely responsible for the weakness that made invasion by the foreigner possible or that unleashed warlord factionalism and peasant revolt. It has even happened that the consolidation of power following a time of troubles, which was itself already preceded by a long-drawn-out naturalization of the economy, reestablishes the conditions for a dramatic reversal of this economic breakdown.

Nor is it possible to discern any universal reason of comparative efficiency capable of explaining a reversion to natural economy that occurred with such persistence in such varied conditions and that remained a real and acknowledged peril even when it failed to occur. You might think that the link between the naturalization of the economy and the growth of coerced labor could explain the economic advantages of naturalization, not only to the landholders but to collective output and productivity. The hypothetical cheapness of slave labor, however, could not account for the constancy with which the reversion to natural economy took place.

Full-fledged slavery was rarely a concomitant of economic naturalization. On the contrary, in most preindustrial agrarian societies, slavery, when it was important at all, flourished at times when money-based markets were strong and widespread. Even then, slavery often took root in the most commercialized and capital-intensive parts of agriculture. The slave was expensive, the supervisory burdens were enormous, and the work incentives were minimal. Above all, slavery usually turned out to be a wasting investment. People do not thrive outside families; one of the most sensible ways to distinguish slavery from other sorts of dependent labor is that, in slavery life in the work gang almost or wholly replaces life in the family. These economic facts were likely to be reversed only in exceptional circumstances when, for example, conquest or civil war threw large numbers of slaves on the market.

Nor did nonslave coerced labor have a better claim to foster output and productivity. Forced labor in the lord's demesne required perpetual vigilance over a reluctant work force. The extraction of rents-in-kind from surrounding plots became more unwieldy as the estate grew. The demands of the peasant plot and of corvée labor on the desmesne tended to undermine each other. The peasant resented each moment given to work on the lord's field. The lord's exactions repeatedly drove the family plot below the size or the level of investment at which it was viable.

The basic causes of recurrent economic naturalization lay elsewhere: in the repeated failure of either the central government or the independent peasantry to keep magnates, warlords, and concentrating landholders under control. When the crunch came, the autocracy proved unwilling to place itself squarely on the side of the peasantry. This unwillingness reflected either a more or less deliberate rejection of the dangers of revolutionary despotism or an identification, in interest and outlook, with the magnates themselves. There was little hope of carrying through any of the policies that could both reconcile the claims of magnates and autocrats and stabilize the place of the peasantry (e.g., agrarian dualism, independent bureaucracy, service nobility). Either the effort to hold the landlords and officials in check would fail, or its partial success would destabilize the government. The inability of the dynastic state to ensure the continuity of a strong political will helped deny antimagnate policies a fighting chance.

A crucial feature of the situation was usually the capacity of the magnates to frustrate the application of restrictive agrarian and fiscal laws. They imposed such obstacles either through their hold on officialdom and its courts or through their effective dominion over the countryside. This capacity gave them a crucial edge at times when emergencies forced the central government to step up its fiscal and recruiting demands or when crop failure weakened its ultimate resource base. The magnates could see to it that the burden would fall on the weakest shoulders. As the peasants rebelled against tax collectors or central armies, or were forced by debt and danger to throw themselves under the protection of the greater landlords, these grandees could build up their holdings and their military strength even more.

The mere ruin of the smallholder and the small-scale tenant was never, in itself, enough to characterize the process of reversion. Two examples make the point. One is drawn from the history of a society that did in the end undergo this special type of collapse. The other example comes from the history of a country that avoided such a breakdown until – through other intervening developments – reversion crises could no longer occur.

Part of the sequel to the Roman–Carthaginian wars was the decline of the independent peasantry in most of the territory directly or indirectly under the control of the Roman Republic. This decline testified to the disruptive impact of long-term conscription upon peasant agriculture. The ruin of the smallholder also resulted from the ability of the reconstituted Roman oligarchy to manipulate the exploitation of the vastly enlarged *ager publicus* in a way that favored the large estate. Yet the result, in context, was not the naturalization of the economy. It was the promotion of a still more remorseless commercialization of Roman life. Slavery itself worked in this direction. Although slave labor displaced the wage relationship in many areas of the economy, it flourished most in the more highly capitalized and commercial sectors of Roman agriculture.

That the oppression of the smallholder did not precipitate the kind of collapse described in the preceding pages may be attributed to the larger political setting in which it took place. The fiscal and military disintegration of a central government, to the advantage of landowning, military, and priestly magnates, did not occur at this stage of Roman history. Instead, the decisive events were the long-drawn-out realignments, through sizable payoffs and civil war, that allowed a self-confident oligarchy to strengthen its hold on the state and to strike up alliances with its counterparts in the new ecumenical order it was helping build. The Mediterranean world into which Rome expanded had already become a highly commercialized and integrated economy. The defeat of the Roman smallholders was connected with the particular ways in which Rome made an empire out of these Mediterranean surroundings.

The effective expropriation of a large part of the Italian smallholders had enduring effects. These consequences ranged from the immediate crisis in military manpower that served as the background of the Gracchan conflicts to the consequence that the buildup of fiscal and military demands in later imperial history left the magnates in many areas of the empire as the only class with the power to resist the exactions of the central government and to benefit from its failure. The narrow options open to the post-Diocletian emperors in the West in their dealings with the magnates reflected the fragility of independent small-scale property, tenancy, and wage labor in the western parts of the empire. Thus, though the doom of the peasant household need not, by itself, have precipitated the reversion to natural economy, it created a structural weakness – an impoverishment of alternative ways of meeting emergencies – that later crisis broke open.

Again, in late sixteenth century England (at the time of Thomas Cromwell and Somerset), the decline of independent peasant farming was not followed by the typical pattern of reversion. On the contrary, in context, it became part of a process by which a breakthrough was achieved that ultimately foreclosed, once and for all, the possibility of such a reversion. To understand why this result could happen, it is necessary to explore, at a later moment in the argument, what it was in the larger and earlier context of Western European agrarian history that, by the sixteenth and seventeenth centuries, made the avoidance of reversion to natural economy compatible with either the flourishing or the ruin of family-size agriculture. The failure to consider this earlier experience produced a mythical history in which relatively late developments in English agrarian history were mistaken for the supposedly necessary stages of agrarian revolution: from the combination of small-scale agriculture with petty-craft production to large-scale "capitalist" farming.

Whenever it occurred, the reversion had a specifically economic aspect which further aggravated its characteristic perils. As the economy became naturalized, the relative prominence of long-distance transactions in the remaining monetary sector increased. Naturalization strikes first at the bulk trade in mass-consumption manufactures and food staples. The situation of partial naturalization was usually one in which the monetary economy was more exclusively occupied by the interregional exchange of luxury goods, foreign trade, and specific fiscal transactions with the state than it had been at times of more widespread commercialization. The value of the goods money could buy rose relative to the cost of dependent labor. Money itself became scarce. The landlords had an interest in reinforcing their effective class monopoly on access to trade in the monetary sector. They could use their profits from that trade to strengthen still more their control over the dependent peasantry and to reduce still further the varieties of labor or commodities for which they had to pay cash.

There were nevertheless countervailing forces that often set limits to economic naturalization. First, to the extent that the whole process involved the weakening and disintegration of central political authority, it put everyone at risk. The splintering of the larger order created the opportunity for invasion from abroad or power seizures from within. Unregulated aristocratic factionalism was, after all, as much a tacit limit of the system as revolutionary despotism. If central authority was not soon reasserted, the conflict between landholders and collectively organized peasants might shatter the agrarian society's whole logic of closed political options. Such a shattering actually happened in early medieval Europe.

Second, the large estate resembled the empire it sought to replace in one respect: expenditure tended to increase disproportionately to size. The same facts that caused this cost rise on the larger scale of the empire reproduced it on the smaller scale of the estate. To the extent that the estate relied heavily on corvée labor, growth in size would increase the danger of losing control over the costs and the loyalty of both the work force and the supervisory staff. To the extent that rents-in-kind from independent peasant plots were preferred, the landholders would find it hard to produce the raw materials or cash crops demanded by the remaining monetary trade, for these usually required large-scale, organized production, and the landholder would often be reduced to skimming off the variable surplus of the peasant plot.

Third, the destruction of peasant independence, the aristocratic and peasant–landlord warfare surrounding this destruction, and the lord's constant struggle to squeeze his dependents of land and labor would help bring the economy to ruin. It would undermine minimal standards of security and welfare. People of every rank would then become available for contests of force and imagination that might create, very quickly, another social reality.

Any of the forces that tend to limit the decline into natural economy could and sometimes did combine to reverse the process decisively. The centralizing monarch – a foreign invader, an upstart warlord, or the determined scion of a weakened dynasty – might reestablish both the social conditions and the fiscal and military devices that favored a return to an inclusive, commercialized economy. The luckier or more organized parts of the peasantry or of the class of agents and foremen might seize the opportunity to reestablish links with markets. Merchant groups from within or from abroad might seek the support of the strengthened government. Their gains might be partly turned into rural investment. When interest on capital that seeks the countryside fell enough to undercut the eventual advantage to be gained from the nonmonetary payment of labor and the avoidance of monetary investment in improvement, agriculture would indeed be commercialized. To prosper, landlords then had to broaden their participation in the market for commodities and labor and their capital investments. But the likelihood of any of these reorientations of advantage and attitude was wholly dependent on some change, achieved through will or conflict, in the power relations that shaped the naturalized, magnate-dominated economy.

So the whole dynamic of occasional declines into natural economy, limits on this decline, and reversals of it, grew out of a characteristic situation of group struggle. This situation has to be understood in its unity if it is to be understood at all. Even the aspects of the process that seem most narrowly economic had no life apart. They, too, were politics.

THE ANTIREVERSION POLICIES

The effort to avoid the reversion cycles ranked as the most persistent concern of the most lucid rulers and reformers in all the societies that remained vulnerable to these recurrent crises. A small number of policy responses were repeatedly tried out and combined in the most varied circumstances. These attempted solutions moved in a space defined by two excluded limits: revolutionary despotism, by which the autocracy would ally itself with the peasantry against the magnates, and aristocratic factionalism, by which the imperial order would degenerate into the untrammeled and unstable sectarianism of magnate warlords. Revolutionary despotism is a manifestly unpromising venture: if the autocrat is not smashed by his lordly enemies, he will be undone by his own peasant allies. Aristocratic factionalism invites the foreign invader, opens the way to the seizure of central power by one of the contending families, and weakens the shared power and authority of the landholders over the peasants. Within the boundaries defined by these two limiting situations, the autocracy and the magnates must be reconciled. The number of possible deals is severely limited; the same compromises recur constantly, though in varying combinations, throughout the history of the large, enduring agrarian states. Looking at it from the viewpoint of the autocrat, there are only three choices.[1]

First, recruit a bureaucratic staff from men below the magnate class who will owe all to you. (This was a formative principle of Chinese statecraft, at least since the rise of nonaristocratic officials in the centuries preceding the imperial unification of 221 B.C. It was also central to the Ottoman palace system and, in a radically different setting, to the state-building efforts of European absolutism.) You must then constantly shake up your own administrative apparatus in order to call up new levies of recruits; otherwise, the bureaucrats will merge with the magnates or become magnates in their own right.

Second, you may try to turn the magnates into a service nobility by involving them directly in the running of the state. By making land tenure dependent on office, you bind them to you. But, unless you are ever vigilant to beat them down, they will gain independence. In the end, to keep their allegiance, you will have to give them absolute dominion over the larger part of the country's land and labor. They, rather than you, will then be in direct control over what goes on in the countryside. (An example was the gradual assimilation of *pomestye* land, held during a lifetime in return for service to the tsar, to the status of *votchina* tenure, inheritable and assured dominion, during the period from Ivan the Terrible to Peter the Great. Petrine absolutism was founded on the consolidation of precisely the type of ownership that Ivan's scheme had temporarily unsettled through his conditional land grants to the subaristocratic gentry. Early Yi policy in Korea suggests a variant of the same trend: at first, only the Merit Subjects (kongsin), to whom the Crown was beholden for special services, were allowed hereditary land; as officeholders managed to wring agrarian privilege out of administrative power, this favor lost its exceptional character.)

Third, you may set up a dual agrarian order. Alongside the large hereditary estates, there will be a special class of landholders who will owe you direct funds and recruits, or who will be granted claims to part of the land tax in exchange for their military readiness. (Remember the Byzantine *ktemata stratiotika*, the Ottoman *timariots*, the Mughal *zamindars*, and the Aztec military life-tenants.) This solution fades into the previous strategy to the extent that the nobility under that other policy is held to no more than occasional army service or assistance in tax collecting. This special class of state–serving landholders may be made up of village communities and smallholders

---

[1] Most of the remainder of this section is transcribed from Chapter 2 of *False Necessity: Anti-Necessitarian Social Theory in the Service of Radical Democracy*, Cambridge, Cambridge, 1987.

who are expected to provide the government with wealth and soldiers. (Think of the Byzantine peasant freeholds and military farms – the *ktemata stratiotika*. The failure of Romanus Lecapenus and Basil II to save them had issued in the final triumph of military aristocracy and monastic landlordism.) You may resort to both powerful men with conditional land tenure and village communities with army and fiscal obligations. (Consider, for example, the land policies of the Toba Wei Empire (386–535) in China and the sequel of experimentation with agrarian and military reform during the early T'ang dynasty, 618–907.) When the military or economic pressure on you mounts, and you try to increase taxes and recruitment, the magnates will be able to defend themselves unless you humble them; the brunt of the burden will fall on the smallholders themselves. Impoverished and decimated, they will seek protection from the aristocrats and, in the next round of the contest, you will end up worse off than you were before. (This tendency became a familiar problem for the rulers of the late Roman Empire in the West; it had its counterparts in several periods of Chinese dynastic decline, in the subversion of independent peasant proprietorship during the final centuries of the Byzantine Empire, and in the collapse of the Islamic Abbasid regime in the Near East and northern Africa, when the ruin of many small farmers helped the central government lose control of tax collection and military power alike.)

In a social world marked by the repetition of the reversion cycles and by the continued deployment and frustration of these antireversion policies, there are only a few ways in which ordinary people rise collectively to the surface of history by dealing actively with the chief power blocs in the country.

First, they may rise as a privileged urban mob, distinct from other, larger segments of the population and country. This situation may occur when a city-state becomes an empire or, less often, when the rank and file of a conquering people settles down in the cities of the land they have conquered. The mob is entreated and bribed, and its privilege is at best a condition of favored enjoyment, backed by a threat of riot or a memory of shared power.

Second, there are instances when the policy of agrarian dualism achieves a temporary balance. One way or another, the village community manages to keep a measure of independence from the magnates and to deal in its own right with the central government. The village, divided internally along hierarchical and communal lines, may have to put up a common front against the outside. Forced often to accept a collective military or fiscal responsibility, it redistributes tax and war burdens periodically in order to hold together under the weight it is made to carry. The greater the pressure on it, the more likely it is to unify and equalize itself; whenever this pressure is relaxed, the village tends to break apart into factions and ranks. (Both the eleventh-century Byzantine and the nineteenth-century Russian village communities illustrate a measure of redistributive equalization and cohesion in response to external force. The role of village officers in the Chinese Southern Sung (1127–1279), of the headmen of peasant-held *raiyati* villages in Mughal India, and of leading village families under the Japanese Tokugawa *bakufu* provide counterexamples of hierarchy when the burden imposed by an external landlord or ruler was less severe or when the outside authority strengthened the hand of already privileged insiders. Ongoing communal strife might then break out as well, whenever there was a basis for it, as in the multicaste Indian village.)

Third, there are the occasions when despair launches the peasants into rebellion. Peasant rebellion is a normal incident of the tailspin that characteristically follows the failure of governmental policies and the disasters of foreign war. When the autocracy is forced to increase its demands on the population and when the peasantry is made to pay the price, the collapse of independent peasant proprietorship and the disintegration of village community create an atmosphere that favors insurrection. But, although the rebellious peasantry may play a decisive role for a brief moment and even establish a state for itself, it is more likely to serve as a tool in the brutal factional fighting that breaks out as the imperial order falls apart. For the peasantry to have a chance, the conditions for a regrouping of the elite power blocs must be shattered.

Why did the antireversion policies repeatedly come to grief? Why in particular did even an outsider like Romanus Lecapenus, a man of humble origins, with a clear appreciation of the issues and a real commitment to the goal, fail to carry through the program of agrarian dualism, the effort to protect a class of state-supporting smallholders? The simple answer is that such a ruler and his regime could not execute his program without allying himself with the smallholders in an all-out struggle against the landowning magnates and officials – the *dunatoi*, the powerful people to whom the Byzantine documents so often refer. This unprecedented social war would have to include a radical expansion and transformation of the governmental bureaucracy. Only such a step could prevent governmental officials from remaining pliant – or identical – to the people they were supposed to control. The regime would also need to encourage authentic self-organization and antiaristocratic agitation and propaganda within the smallholding class. In other words, the ruler would be compelled to adopt the techniques of controlled mobilization and populist despotism that have become widespread in the era of mass politics and modern communication technologies. If he could rehearse such a calculation, he might well conclude that he was unlikely to get very far in the career of a revolutionary despot. Even if he were not crushed by his adversaries, he might soon be cast aside by his newfound allies.

THE EUROPEAN ESCAPE FROM THE CYCLE OF REVERSION

The prime instance in which to study the avoidance of reversion to natural economy is European history. It was in Western Europe and in the colonies of European settlement that the industrial breakthrough first took place. This breakthrough was preceded, in the Western European heartland, by a series of events that effectively foreclosed the return to natural economy. At least, they foreclosed it long enough to make possible the later development of an industrial economy. By an astonishing paradox, this avoidance of reversion was in turn preceded by a particularly thoroughgoing example of the economic and governmental collapse that I have described as reversion. The very severity of this collapse and the particular way the people involved responded to it were crucial to the way later cases of reversion were avoided.

For a long period in the history of Western Europe, in the centuries following the downfall of the Roman Empire in the West – a period extended by the Arab conquest of the Mediterranean – all the defining elements of a reversion episode occurred.

When we consider a later period of Western European history, however – the whole era from the twelfth century to the beginnings of industrialization – we discover an anomaly in the opposite direction. There were often developments that seemed to move toward reversion. This was especially true of those European countries in which aristocratic government and "absolutism" ended up meaning more or less the same thing: a condominium exercised by landholding, bureaucratic, and commercial elites, with the predominance of territorial magnates and the erosion of peasant rights. Yet the characteristic economic and governmental signs of naturalization failed to take place. The commercial economy held up. Central governments were often strengthened rather than undermined in their fiscal and military base. A decisive transformation kept the resurgent power of territorial magnates, and the reunification of elites, from producing the full-scale consequences of economic naturalization. What appeared on the surface to be a movement toward reversion had now become something different.

By understanding this paradoxical sequence – the escape from reversion after and through the very severity of a reversion episode – you can grasp the true political basis and implications of the later European approach to economic success. This understanding can in turn shed light on fundamental aspects of the relation between material progress and social conflict.

The key to my argument is that a particular style of grassroots collective conflict was decisive to this result. The terms of this conflict were an *invented* response to the predicament created by the harshness of the reversion situation in which workers and their immediate masters found themselves. Through the accumulation of comparisons within and outside the European setting, the argument must be made both more particular and more general than it can hope to be in its initial statement. It must provide us with the means to assess the relative importance of different aspects of the avoidance of reversion. It must enable us to see the more familiar lines of the European developments as only a special case of a more ample class of possibilities, some of which were realized within Europe, others in the non-European world, and still others never realized at all.

The starting point of this inquiry into the European experience with the avoidance of reversion lies in the combination of two facts about Europe in the centuries following the disintegration of the Roman Empire in the West. The analysis of these two circumstances, of their relations to each other, and of their larger implications illustrates a more general feature of the relation between opportunities for institutional invention and episodes of protracted group conflict.

The first fact was the nature of the relationship between the working population and their immediate overlords in the long period of reversion to natural economy, with its two high points in the splintering of the Western empire and the Arab mastery over the Mediterranean. All the characteristic aspects of reversion appeared in an increasingly relentless form. The special vulnerability of the urban oligarchies (the municipal curial class) and the smallholders, during the later history of the Western empire, had already fueled the growth of large domains under ecclesiastical or magnate control. The urban monetary economy had already begun its characteristic decline until it embraced little more than the long-distance luxury trade. The apparatus of government had already been shaken as it lost direct access to manpower and production and became more and more beholden to magnates and warlords. The state ceased to be actively engaged in grassroots disputes about control over peasant land and labor. The territorial breakup of the empire in the West was so drastic that it confirmed and aggravated all these aspects of reversion. The economic and governmental collapse was magnified by the actual destruction of state institutions, by the dissolving encounter of entire civilizations, and by the movement of large numbers of people. Before the monetary economy, town life, and structure of government had time to recover or to assume new forms, they were further undermined by the eighth-century isolation of the Western European heartland from the Mediterranean world. (Nothing important in my argument turns on the relative weight of these two waves of economic naturalization.) The single most important result of this protracted collapse was the social situation to which it gave rise. Wherever the large estates prevailed, the people who worked the land faced their immediate master without the presence of a higher government to tilt the scales of conflict in favor of either peasant or lord, without flourishing towns to which they might flee, and without a widespread monetary economy to offer alternative employment and to encourage large differences of wealth and station within the working mass.

The other circumstance that lay at the root of the unique European developments was a form of collective organization brought by the European and specifically the barbarian peoples into their new countries: the village community. The single most important point about the social organization of the European medieval economy was the coexistence of coercive control from above with independent communal organization from below. Although this coexistence was typified most clearly by the manorial system, it extended, in variant forms, well beyond the core areas of feudalism.

Before analyzing the interaction between the pervasive presence of this style of collective organization and the uniquely protracted and extensive European reversion to natural economy, we must rid ourselves of mystical preconceptions about village communities. The village community must not be associated with any one well-defined stage of economic development, like a supposed tribal mode of production before the rise of slave-based economies. We find the peasant households gathered into some kind of collective organization in a very broad range of historical settings, with sharply different forms of economic activity. Nor was the village community inherently expressive of any particular brand of individualism or collectivism, of individual property or collective ownership. If the classic debates about this topic in English, German, Slavic, Byzantine, and Indian historiography can be justified at all, they need to be disaggregated into controversies about the nature of particular approaches to collective organization in particular historical situations.[2]

In fact, some kind of village community has existed in history wherever two very loose conditions were simultaneously satisfied.

[2] For an analysis of the ideological element in the historical debates about the role of peasant communities, see Clive Dewey, "Images of the Village Community: A Study in Anglo-Indian Ideology," *Modern Asian Studies*, vol. 6 (1972), pp. 291–328; J. W. Burrow, " 'The Village Community' and the Uses of History in Late Nineteenth-Century England," in *Historical Perspectives: Studies in English Thought and Society*, ed. Neil McKendrick, Europa, London, 1974, pp. 255–284.

The first condition is that a major part of the population live in the countryside in a society that has not yet been transformed by industrialization. The other condition is that no attempt be made to regulate production closely from above, as it is when, for example, slaves live in barracks and work under taskmasters.

The type of village community most important to an understanding of the European feudal economy is the one that coexists with a structure of domination from above. The collective organization of the workers keeps a measure of independence from the hierarchical order imposed by lords and officials. The relative independence of the household is reinforced by the partial autonomy of the larger collective unit to which it belongs.

In this situation, a struggle goes on between the peasant collective and the overlords who seek to break it to their will. These overlords may be the officials of a government. They may also be territorial oligarchs, often sustained by the state. The bosses usually try to control the village community by an exchange of benefits and threats with a headman or dominant family within the village. By working through this intermediary, the masters avoid the risks and burdens of the attempt to organize production directly.

If the oppression from above is too severe and too successful, the village community will become little more than a device for controlling peasant land and labor. It might degenerate into slavery, were it not that slave labor, especially when destructive of the slave family, tends to pay off only under special conditions. At the limit, this oppression destroys the family and every other trait of independent collective organization. This is the economy of the slave gang. Under such a regime relatively high levels of commercialization and capitalization must be combined with the physical and institutional means to keep the enslaved labor force under control.

Conversely, if the pressure from above is very weak, the village community tends to dissolve into independent households with little shared organization. In the absence of a special circumstance of economic jeopardy or religious coercion, the villagers suffer no counterweight to their impulse to withdraw from risk and subjugation into a large quasi-familial group. This collectivity may have a pronounced internal hierarchy, but it lacks a surplus-extraction order imposed from outside or above the group.

Between these two extreme situations stands the instance of a surplus-extraction apparatus that operates over and apart from a collective of households. Under this regime, the joint household retains a measure of independence and identity, which it strengthens through its resistance to the overlord. (Among the many examples of this form are the medieval European feudal, manorial, and village system and the village community of Tokugawa Japan.)

The differences among these three social bases of economic organization are only relative. For each of them represents a particular way of merging, in different proportions, community, coercion, and exchange. Each therefore draws upon a small stock of recurrent personal relationships. None of these forms of organization treats productive work as a field for the experimental development of personal dealings that may deviate sharply from relations prevailing in the society at large. None of these styles of economic organization can move very far toward the ideal of a relentless interaction between abstract projects and concrete practices. None of them can develop the organizational ideals that sustain such an interaction: standardized operating procedures and the supple combination of hierarchical supervision and discretionary initiative. To be sure, even the most revolutionary form of economic order can depart only fitfully and partly from the pattern of personal dealings already familiar in a given time and place. Yet every major advance in material life has incited such departures.

Each of the three social bases I have described also imposes more particular constraints upon economic advance. In the extreme situations of work-gang slavery and state-imposed, coercive surplus extraction, every opportunity for productive innovation must be sacrificed to the overriding need to keep the sullen slaves in hand and to lash them on in each reluctant step of their work. The size and composition of the labor force cannot be easily adjusted to accord with market changes. The slave family falls apart and, with it, the demographic vitality of the labor fund.

In the situation of the inclusive, quasi-familial, feudal collectivity, the significant constraint is the difficulty of any innovation that threatens the established forms of hierarchy and solidarity within the group. Because these forms are so inclusive and detailed in their requirements, their paralyzing effect may be formidable.

When communal organization from below coexists conflictually with a coercive surplus-extraction system, the constraint on material progress is more subtle than in either of the previous two situations. The actual organization of production remains largely in the hands of peasant households and village communities. But the broader structure of control over tax–rents and special labor services belongs to the overlord. The boss is constantly tempted to extract as much as he can until he has pushed the labor collective into ruin, passive resistance, or active rebellion. The collective, for its part, gives priority to its own self-defense. There is nobody in the situation who can easily define and advance longer-range interests of accumulation and innovation. Hence the characteristic failure to invest in depth and the unexpected quality of the material breakthroughs that do take place. Hence, also, the way in which the struggle between the village community below and the extractors above overshadows all other movements in the economy.

These forces lie behind the talk about the tension under feudalism between small-scale production and large-scale ownership. The mistake is to describe the formative conflict narrowly or to reify a feudal mode of production or to attribute immanent laws to it. The ultimate basis of the human impulses that move such an economy forward are straightforward facts about collective identities, opportunities, and ambitions. These facts become clear only when we have discovered the social basis of economies in a small circle of personal and collective possibilities. The circle is only gradually enlarged, and it is never entirely broken.

These preliminaries help explain the connection between the two facts I took as starting points for an argument about the European avoidance of reversion: the uniquely severe instance of reversion which post-Roman Western Europe experienced and the emergence of the manorial and village complex at the center of the new European economy.

During the long period of deep economic and governmental collapse, the agrarian populations of Europe were left to fight it out with their immediate overlords. Typically, the warlord–landholder lived on his estate rather than in a city that could serve as a place of residence for a parasitic class of magnates and officials. His holdings were concentrated in a single territory. He faced his peasants without the help of a strong state and without the safeguard of diversified investments. His one hope of steeling himself for conflict with rival warlord–landholders and with his own work force was to find allies, protectors, and followers among the great and petty estate holders of the surrounding area.

The working population, for its part, was concentrated in agriculture and relatively undifferentiated by comparison to situations where a high degree of urban and rural commercialism prevailed. The peasants had to stand their ground in the countryside, and they had to stand their ground collectively. There was little chance for purely individual success by escaping to a city or becoming a small-scale agrarian entrepreneur.

In this unavoidable collective test of strength, the peasants could count on two advantages whose simultaneous occurrence was a historical rarity. First, they did not confront an organized central government that might intervene in support of the landowners and tilt the scales of conflict against the peasantry. Second, the relative independence of the village from the manor provided the peasants with an instrument of collective resistance.

Thus, the contest between peasants and landowners over entitlements and income shares could take the route of escalating collective organization on both sides: networks of villages against alliances of landholders. Every time one side expanded the scope of its collective effort, the other side had reason to respond in kind. The customary rights of each side, often written down in charters, represented more or less temporary truce lines in a long-term battle. The entire process amounted to a simplified version of the way social worlds are built, demolished, and reconstructed.

Despite the harsh realities of feudalism, the structure of production, power, and conflict was, by comparative standards, unusually favorable to the people who actually did the work. This production system took advantage of the household unit. It set this unit within the larger cooperative framework of the village. It allowed the village to defend its members against the overlords' predatory, shortsighted, and self-destructive exactions. It provided a protected economic space in the form of the manor. But it avoided the precocious enlargement of this area into a territorial state at a time when the government – like all governments before the advent of mass politics – might have ended up making common cause with the local landholders against the peasant population.

The social consequences of demographic decline and economic crisis depended on the same factors. The decline and crisis might come in the wake of epidemic and military disasters, resulting perhaps from growing pressure against institutionally restricted stocks of land, in conditions of technological stagnation and low-level investment. In some places, especially in Eastern Europe, peasants were then forced into serfdom. In other places, they managed to keep their personal independence but not their landholdings. In still other places, they used the occasions of demographic and economic crisis to maintain and even enlarge their lands and entitlements. This development prevailed throughout Western Europe during the crisis period following the mid-thirteenth century.

In preindustrial Western Europe, as in all agrarian societies, agrarian disorganization and depression were aggravated by their own commercial repercussions. The long-distance luxury trade and the manufacture of basic necessities suffered with the agrarian troubles. But they did not suffer in the measure or way characteristic of periods of reversion to natural economy. The tenacity of commercialization in the agrarian sector; the extent of autonomous corporate organization by manufacturers, merchants, and whole cities; and government's need to find allies and funders – all these enlarged the alternatives of commerce under pressure. Although some commercial regions declined during the "crisis of feudalism," others prospered. In some areas, small-scale industry seems actually to have relocated to the countryside.

During this same crisis period, the conflicts among nobles for

larger pieces of governmental power were intensified by the limits
to agrarian exploitation. In this setting, the economic setbacks had
broader political and military effects. But the consequence of agrarian
decline was to strengthen central government as well as to weaken
it. A more inclusive apparatus of power was needed to keep the
peasantry under control, to impose order on the chaos of aristocratic
strife, and to provide supplements to rent.

This incipient governmental machinery did press down on the
peasant economy with military and fiscal demands. But, contrary to
the usual pattern of agrarian crisis (magnate resurgence and total
capture of the weakened state by landholders and warlords), the
conflicts of the time encouraged state making. It was less a matter
of taking over government by paralyzing its sources of taxes and
troops than of building the state – or allowing it to build itself – as
a providential counterweight to peasant resistance and internecine
warfare.

Initially, central governments, partly called into existence by the
crisis of the agrarian economy, prolonged and deepened that crisis.
They did so in the short run by stepping up its exactions on all sectors
of the population. They did so in the long run by allying themselves
occasionally with organized merchant and peasant groups or with
enterprising factions among the landowning magnates. But the unexpected result of these pragmatic governmental policies was to
transgress the usual limits of politics in preindustrial agrarian countries. The relative dearth of administrative progress in the fourteenth
century turned out to be a temporary slowdown rather than a pre-
nunciation of collapse.

So, the crisis of feudalism, whichever way you look at it, resulted
in a multiplication of strategic responses by different social groups
rather than in the naturalization of the economy and the subversion
of the state. The vitality of the noncommercial parts of the feudal
and prefeudal order – the peasant plot, the household economy, the
village collective, and, indeed, the entire manor–village complex –
paradoxically helped prevent an outright reversion episode.

The continued immunity to reversion and the social facts that made
for this immunity are largely responsible for the relatively high degree of peasant prosperity and demographic growth in long periods
of medieval European history. It was "nonreversion" that made possible the progressive enlargement of the agrarian surplus even in the
absence of any technological revolution. The expanding surplus in
turn provided the material basis for the economic development of
the high Middle Ages. It supplied the wherewithal for the new urban
economy. The urban centers, all but destroyed in their earlier role
as residential centers of a unified parasitic class of absentee land-

owners, governmental officials, and great merchants, could now be reborn with a historically unprecedented identity. They could become places where men of different origins and stations engaged in a broad range of commercial and manufacturing activities, financed at the outset by the commercialization of the agrarian surplus itself. These urban and trading activities, and the agricultural commercialism on which they were based, encouraged in turn the differentiation of the peasantry.

Finally, the agrarian surplus, with its repercussions on manufacturing and trade, laid a basis for direct state taxation. During the long drawn-out process of European state building, emergent governments found themselves confronted with an intense degree of territorial fragmentation and social diversity. All this postponed the appearance or reconsolidation of a more or less unified elite of large landowners, officials, and merchants until economic activity and the relation between town and country had already been irreversibly transformed.

The more successful the peasants were in their collective and individual resistance to the manor, and the larger the range of commercial activity in the surrounding society, the more reason the landholders had to expand the area of their demesnes and to rid themselves of peasants who gave relatively little in exchange for the land they occupied. But this process of engrossment and expulsion was never uniform. Its course depended on the relative collective force of landowners and peasants and on the position taken by nascent governmental authorities.

The initial European experience of collective conflict allowed for a broad range of lines of development. To understand the most important differences among these lines, it is useful to focus on three aspects of change: the structure of control over land and labor, the relation of the countryside and the agrarian surplus to trade and manufacture, and the way government intervened in the dealings between territorial magnates and the peasant mass. In each of these areas – control, surplus, and state building – the earlier forms of collective organization and struggle made possible, although they did not guarantee, later developments that deepened the commercialization of agriculture, revolutionized the relation of town to country, and postponed indefinitely the perils of reversion.

Consider first the countries where collective popular organization in country and town was strongest and most enduring. In these areas the structure of control over land and peasant labor gave a preeminent place to the small family holding within the setting of a loose village structure. This type of land structure became prominent in the Bordelais, the Sologne, and Catalonia after the relative depopulation of the fourteenth and fifteenth centuries. It played a decisive role in the entire economic history of the Netherlands. In the form of the yeomanry and the lower gentry, it was important in England during the sixteenth and the seventeenth centuries before the consolidation of the large entrepreneurial estates. The smallholding might take the legal form of free property (copyhold, absolute dominion) or simply that of fixed rents combined with heritability.

If you now expand the idea of strong popular organization to include the organized power of petty traders and manufacturers as well as family farmers, you can say that any lasting popular organization also favored a particular connection between the agrarian surplus and trade or manufacturing. The peasantry would be highly diverse in occupation and wealth, with ready access to markets and nonagrarian occupations. The handicraft guild would hold its own against the large merchants' guild. Manufacturing would take place through enterprises of widely varying dimensions and it would be based in the countryside as well as the towns.

Finally, the areas and periods where popular organization in the most ample sense was strongest would also be the ones where central government was either largely absent from the contest between large and small landholders, great and petty manufacturers and traders, or, at least, where it successfully refused to support the great against the small. The preexisting level of popular militancy in town and country helped determine the outcome. So did the nature of the state itself: the degree of effective governmental independence from landowning or mercantile magnates. Once governmental power was enlisted in support of the larger landowners and traders, the structure of popular organization and small-scale property in town and country might be quickly disrupted. In sixteenth- and seventeenth-century France, for example, the state allowed its exactions to fall most heavily on the independent peasantry. Thus it halted the fifteenth-century tendency toward the proliferation of small- and middle-sized holdings. It was only later, when central government managed to assert a greater measure of independence in the local control of its power, that small-scale enterprise staged a comeback. In every instance and at every time, the relation between the level of popular organization and the uses of state power remained decisive.

Now consider a second series of developments, in settings where popular organization remained relatively weak and the power of the state was more actively used against it. In the system of control and land use, this meant large-scale entrepreneurial farms, with the engrossment of leaseholds and the dispossession of small-scale tenants and proprietors. In England, this pattern was definitively established only in the second half of the seventeenth century, though the struggles that gave rise to it had become acute in the first half of the sixteenth century. We find the same pattern in Normandy in the sixteenth century, and in Picardy in the seventeenth and eighteenth centuries, often in the form of entrepreneurial tenants strengthening themselves against *both* peasants and rentier landlords.[3] It is certainly not a necessary and universal stage in the avoidance of reversion and the preparation of economic revolution. Even within Europe, instances of successful transition in land systems dominated by family-size independent farms were almost as common as the stereotypical process of land concentrations. The most spectacular example was Dutch agriculture, whose extraordinary and underrated success sustained much of the Republic's economic ascent.[4] Many of the apparent instances of large-scale entrepreneurial tenancy in fact occurred in settings where peasant-dominated small-scale production continued to flourish because peasant collective organization found an ally in central government.[5]

Wherever a concentrationist land-tenure system triumphed, its success depended on the course of fighting among the peasants, the territorial magnates, and the masters of the government. Protector Somerset's attempt to enforce antienclosure policy in the late 1540s, the rapidity with which peasant rebellion got out of hand, and the magnate party's successful reaction and seizure of the state in the late summer of 1549 exemplify such a conflict.

The counterpart to this development of land tenure in the relation of the agrarian surplus to manufacturing and trade was the victory of the big merchants' guilds and of city-based manufacturing and the control of agricultural markets by the greater landowners and merchants. Again, the concrete outcome was always the result of a particular course of struggle, influenced by the preexisting level of popular organization in town and country and by the intentions and ideas of the people who held the central government. Thus, the English crown, acting under pressure from the London mercantile guilds, played a decisive role in crushing the tentative forms of small-scale, country-based manufacture.

Both in the development of land tenure and in the regulation of trade and manufacturing, the situations I have just described stemmed from an active alliance of the state with landholding magnates and elite merchants and manufacturers. Local state power had to be more

[3] See Guy Bois, *Crise du Féodalisme: Economie Rurale et Démographie en Normandie Orientale du Début du 14e Siècle au Milieu du 16e Siècle*, Presses de la Fondation Nationale des Sciences Politiques, Paris, 1976, especially pp. 346–347.

[4] See Jan de Vries, *The Dutch Rural Economy in the Golden Age, 1500–1700*, Yale, New Haven, 1978, especially pp. 119–121.

[5] See Robert Brenner, "Agrarian Class Structure and Economic Development in Pre-Industrial Europe: The Agrarian Roots of European Capitalism," *Past and Present*, no. 97 (1982), pp. 100–104.

or less manipulated by these oligarchic interests. In England, for example, the manor court ceased to be an effective instrument of control over the labor force as the manor–village complex disintegrated. But, by the end of the fifteenth century, the prime weapon of oligarchic control over land and labor had become a local governmental agency, the sessions of the peace.

Then comes the third case, that of Eastern Europe. So far I have alluded to historical situations in France, Britain, and the Netherlands, where popular organization was strong enough, and the use of state power various enough to keep the peasantry from losing its independence altogether and a unified class of magnates, officials, and merchants from achieving undisputed control over land and labor. Only by staying within these limits would reversion to natural economy be avoided. But in Eastern Europe and Russia these limits were broken. Collective popular organization, weak from the start, was effectively destroyed.

At most times, in these societies, a shaky and pliant state lacked the capacity to serve as a counterweight to consolidated oligarchic dominion over land, trade, and manufacturing. At other times, such as at the high points of Russian autocracy, a strong state reduced every element of collective popular organization to a mere adjunct of governmental power. The difference between these two Eastern European lines of development is less sharp than at first appears. Once the peasantry and the petty manufacturers and merchants lost their independence and their capacity for independent joint organization, the autocracy lived in constant danger of succumbing to a unified class of magnates, officials, and great merchants. The force of this tendency is borne out in Russian history by the way in which landholdings conditional on state service repeatedly turned into unconditional and heritable property.

In all these situations of weakened popular organization, crushed under oligarchic or autocratic rule, the peasantry was pushed down into enserfment and into other forms of absolute dependence on the magnates or the state. Merchants and manufacturers became direct servants of the autocracy or of the landholding noble households.

Table I summarizes the results of my analysis of the essential forms of European transition. There are several points to make about the general significance of the scheme presented in Table I.

First, the vitality of collective popular organization and the force with which governmental power is put to antipopular uses are partly, but only partly, independent of each other. A vital, well-entrenched system of village communities made it harder for a class of landowning magnates, bureaucrats, and merchants to seize joint control of the state and, through the state, to master the agrarian economy. The existence of a relatively independent governmental apparatus, anxious to keep its autonomy from a unified elite, increased the likelihood that the village, the handicraft guild, and the family proprietor could flourish as the commercialization of the economy deepened.

An indefinite number of circumstances favored or discouraged the strength of popular organization and the independence of emergent state power from a consolidated elite. But none of these circumstances separately, nor all of them together, determined the outcome of the conflict. The actual result depended in each case upon the blow-by-blow achievements of the contestants.

Thus, the west German and east German territories started with similar types and levels of village organization and state power but developed along very different lines. England saw the early emergence of a strong class of independent small-scale farmers, despite the comparative weakness of its village and state structure. Only later did it fall under the dominant pattern of large-scale entrepreneurial holdings. Wide areas of France underwent precisely the opposite sequence.

The second general point about the sequence is that our entire understanding of the European transition has been distorted by allowing the development summarized in column II of Table I to serve as our stereotype for what happened on the way to economic success. Thus, effective transition to "capitalism" came to be identified with a background of large-scale entrepreneurial farms, of the domination of trade and early manufacturing by large investors, and of the rigid division between town and country. In fact, this stereotype is a tissue of confusions that conceals what the European experience can teach us about the social basis of material progress. First, there is the implied confusion of the breakthrough into industrialism with a protracted commercialization. This commercialization may have been necessary to the later breakthrough but it certainly did not guarantee its occurrence. We must not identify one of many European paths to the avoidance of reversion with an illusory logic of necessary economic development.

Because England was the pioneering industrial power, because its economic history achieved a canonical status, and because the category of capitalism is so equivocal, the English experience has obscured the degree of variation within Europe. In fact, even in England, the domination of large-scale entrepreneurial farming and trade was preceded by a period in which smaller family farms and country-based manufacture and trade played a larger role. When you compare the later economic history of England with that of France, you discover that the French pattern of family farms and a proportionately larger rural population had advantages as well as costs, making for a somewhat higher growth rate in industrial productivity compared to lower agricultural productivity. And it saved France

Table 1. *The European experience of reversion, and of the avoidance of reversion, to natural economy. An aspect of the social prehistory of industrial economies in the West*

	I	II	III Destroyed popular organizations	
	Relatively strong popular organization, favored or tolerated by the state (unfamiliar varieties of Western European transition).	Relatively weak popular organization, disfavored by the state (the stereotypical, i.e. English, transition).	Magnate leadership (Eastern Europe)	Governmental leadership (Russia)
Agrarian structure	Vitality of the smallholder, who characteristically belonged to a loose village community and participated actively in a commercialized agriculture.	Large-scale, entrepreneurial tenants and proprietors dominated land, labor, and markets.	Enserfment of the peasantry. Magnates gained control over peasant land and labor.	Enserfment of large part of the peasantry. State and magnate sectors separated. Periodic governmental attempts to make landholding conditional on state service failed, confirming magnate dominion.
Relation of agriculture and the peasant economy to manufacturing and trade	Importance of the handicraft guild, differentiation within the peasantry in wealth and occupation, manufacturing of varying scale, based on countryside as well as towns.	Government promoted, city-based manufacture and the large merchant guild. Officials, large landowners, and big-time merchants and manufacturers–relatively diverse in interests and identities–effectively ma-	Magnates dominated internal trade, successfully controlling the market-oriented part of the economy, and teamed up with international merchants.	Relative governmental containment of territorial oligarchs fostered diversity in manufacturing and trade. But these entrepreneurial activities grew rapidly only when, much later, government sponsored industrializa-

	nipulated the agrarian surplus.		tion in response to international pressures.
Relationship of central government to local authorities	Government either withdrew from the confrontation between landholders and peasants of different ranks, or else it actively encouraged the independence of smallholders.	Government helped the magnates engross land and labor, but not to the point of forcing the peasantry back into enserfment or suppressing the market in land and labor.	In the state sector the peasant collective was reduced to a control device. In the magnate sector government surrendered power to territorial oligarchies.
		The state, weak or absent, devolved all local power to territorial oligarchies.	

Note the paradoxical quality of these developments. The stereotypical European route to avoidance of reversion (II) appears in many respects closer to reversion path (III) than to the alternative, deviant line of European history (I).

from some aspects of the massive dislocation and suffering inherent in the English growth route. Yet, even in the late twentieth century, the stereotype continued to exercise authority in faraway countries. Leftist ideologues and reactionary technocrats often agreed that entrepreneurial land concentration was a necessary and beneficial, though painful, step on the road to and beyond "agrarian capitalism."

If you consider the entire European scheme, you see immediately that the important thing about the stereotypical development outlined in Table I, column II, is what it had in common with the developments in column I rather than with those in column III. The stereotypical path portrays the quickest route a society could take toward consolidation of a unified elite of landholders, officials, and merchants and the destruction of peasant (or petty merchant and manufacturer) autonomy and organization without becoming vulnerable, once again, to a reversion episode. Thus in late medieval England, forced labor played an unusually important role in the manorial economy, and throughout the early modern period the central government exercised little independent authority over local elites. This was almost Asia in Europe, even when Asian predilections remained concealed by whig pieties. It was like going up to the edge of the cliff without actually falling over.

The developments in column II really were crucially different from those in column III. You can tell the difference because the stereotypical transition path often led to a process that looked superficially like reversion to natural economy but really was not. The difference becomes clear from the effects. Consider the points of resemblance. In some of the countries that underwent the developments in column II, a relatively unified elite of landholders, officials, and merchants later emerged. Much of the village community was later destroyed and large segments of the small-scale proprietors in town and countries were ruined. But such events failed to undermine the monetary economy or the structure of government. On the contrary, all these developments gave new impulse to "state absolutism," to the commercialization of the economy, and to an economically motivated policy of colonial expansion and foreign struggle. The earlier course of development had already blocked the way to an easy collapse back into natural economy. Consider why.

The protracted conflict among landholders, governments, and peasants over portions of the agrarian output meant that none of these groups could afford to dispense with access to markets and money. For this access provided the means for each group to build the wealth and the strength with which to resist or buy off the others. Different categories of workers, tenants, owners, and officials found it hard to make definitive settlements of competing claims to land

and income because such solutions were hard to impose by the application of unified and overwhelming force. Unresolved rivalry provided the impetus to experimentation in estate management, land use, land tenure, and agricultural technology. The resilient forms of marketing and moneymaking then supplied the capital base for investment.

Moreover, both the emergent state structures and the new oligarchies had built their strategies around different ways of profiting from the commercialized economy in town and country. It would have required a much more rapid and more drastic movement toward the triumph of a unified magnate class and the suppression of the masses – the style of development that took place in Eastern Europe – to make reversion possible.

The difference between true and false reversion in European history suggests a third general point about the scheme in Table 1. The escape from the recurrent naturalization of the economy depended on the much longer history of collective conflict and organization evoked earlier in the analysis. Thanks to that longer history, a different kind of city, a different kind of state, and a different kind of oligarchy had been established. Just as the earlier crisis of feudalism in the fifteenth century had not precipitated another episode of reversion, so the triumph in the sixteenth and seventeenth centuries of a new magnate class in some Eastern European countries did not restart the ancient cycle of collapse and regeneration.

Thus, any historical understanding of the events by which reversion to natural economy was avoided in Europe already shows a much deeper range of variation than the stereotypical accounts allow or the isolated national historiographies make clear. The significance of the variation is to turn us away from the idea of a simple evolutionary sequence of forms of landholding, trade, and manufacture to a deeper insight into the decisive link between the uses of state power and the experience of collective popular organization. In this way, our detailed understanding of a crucial turn in material history exemplifies a general, antinecessitarian view of the making and unmaking of social worlds.

But might there not have been a still broader range of possible escapes from reversion? At one extreme, the popular struggles of early medieval Europe might have gone further. They might perhaps have established economic and governmental institutions that would have kept any elite of landholders, officials, and merchants from gaining control of the commercialized economy and the newly established state. Alternatively, strong and independent central governments might have forged successful alliances with an independent peasantry and with the class of petty traders and manufacturers. (The experience of the early Vasas in Sweden, who came closest to such an alliance, showed just how hard such a partnership might be to achieve.)

To assess these counterfactual possibilities and make the argument both more universal and more precise, the scope of comparison must now broaden.

THE JAPANESE ALTERNATIVE TO THE EUROPEAN ESCAPE ROUTE

Japan came closer than any other society in world history to matching the European avoidance of reversion to natural economy. The Japanese case is therefore of extraordinary comparative interest. It helps us disentangle the more contingent and localized aspects of the circumstances that favored this breakthrough from the deeper and more universal features. In some respects, everything that really mattered in the European experience with the avoidance of reversion found a counterpart in Japanese history. But the Japanese trajectory often differed sharply from its European equivalent. This difference enables us to deepen our insight.

Students of Japanese history who want to explain Japan's precocity and success in standing up to the West and in incorporating the technical and organizational means of economic power and military strength readily focus on two periods.

The most obvious period for study is the great movement of renewal: the events that immediately preceded and followed the Meiji Restoration (1868) and the particular nature of the confrontation with the Western powers. Those who analyze these episodes will be inclined to emphasize the decisive importance of national autonomy. The effort to overthrow the shogunate and to adopt the immediate instruments of Western wealth and power might have failed for any number of reasons. The violence of the threat from abroad might easily have been greater. The foreign powers would then have overwhelmed Japan before its renovating elites had had a chance to carry out the program of minimal reform that enabled them to adopt imported technological and organizational devices and to mobilize, from the top, wealth and manpower.

The other era that might be singled out for special analysis is the high point of early Japanese commercial vitality during the Kamakura period (1185–1333). For here was a society that, even more than Sung dynasty China, had anticipated Western Europe in developing a thoroughly commercialized economy, with a broad range of forms of contractual labor and with towns whose relation to the countryside was far more than parasitic. Those who study this phase will tend to emphasize the relatively early achievement in Japanese history of conditions that favored the maintenance of a commercial economy and the advance toward industrialization.

In the next few pages, however, the emphasis will fall on a third period, intervening between these two candidates for analysis. In the time of troubles that led up to the establishment of the Tokugawa shogunate and in the early part of the shogunate itself, a unique association was established among the peasantry, the central rulers, and the large landholding magnates outside the shogunal domain. This relationship is crucial to understanding why the elements of an earlier monetary economy did not fall victim, during this period of violent conflict, to a process of outright naturalization. The mechanism of reversion was irreversibly dismantled. This dismantling had permanent effects on the country's later capabilities. It must be the central topic of an analysis that wants to compare the European and Japanese routes to the avoidance of naturalization rather than to provide some simple explanation for Japan's economic success.

For the purposes of such a comparison the key event was the way in which the newly established shogunal regime of the late sixteenth century dealt with the the peasantry and with the lower rungs of the landholding and military elites. For this stratagem was repeated in broad outline outside the exclusive shogunal lands by the great overlords (*daimyo*) in their own subordinate domains. The formative elements of the strategy were the following.

First, the armed, intermediate levels of landholders – a military retinue endowed with rural benefices – was withdrawn from the countryside into the castle towns. Thus, whereas the shogunate only partly dissociated the *daimyos* from their local bases, through the system of compulsory periodic residence at the capital and of family hostages, the samurai throughout the country were treated to a far more drastic separation from immediate control of peasant land and labor.[6] The exceptions to this rule, like the effort of the Tsugaru clan to settle samurai in the countryside, were few and far apart. These exceptional efforts responded to particular fiscal and military needs in relatively poor or vulnerable regions. They were largely unsuccessful.

The second element of the strategy was the relentless disarming of the peasantry.[7] Successive "sword hunts" liquidated the peasant

---

[6] For a description of the basic structure of the *bakufu*, see Conrad D. Totman, *Politics in the Tokugawa Bakufu 1600–1813*, Harvard, Cambridge, 1983, especially pp. 25–31. For a discussion of the significance of the withdrawal of the samurai class from the countryside, see Toyama Shigeki, "Historical Preconditions for the Meiji Restoration" (1958), summarized in *An Outline of Japanese Economic History*, ed. Mikio Sumiya and Koji Tara, Univ. of Tokyo Press, 1979, pp. 25–26.

[7] See E. Herbert Norman, *Soldier and Peasant in Japan: The Origin of Conscription*, Univ. of British Columbia, Vancouver, 1965, pp. 6–8.

militias. These militias had been active in the generations preceding the founding of the shogunate both as instruments of warfare among oligarchies and, occasionally, as independent armies in the service of peasant rebellion. The decision, much later, to establish an army, on the basis of universal conscription, for the sake of national power and domestic security, would require a state with a still greater capacity than the shogunate ever achieved to override all intermediate powers and tap peasant manpower directly.

A third element was the way in which the overlords, within and outside the shogunal domain, got their tax-rents and ensured their ultimate control over peasant land and labor. The official administrative structure of the shoguns and the *daimyos* was astonishingly thin in the countryside. Shoguns and *daimyos* asserted their claims chiefly through the village headman system. The headman was usually the nucleus of a dominant lineage. This lineage was in turn the beneficiary of a variety of economic, governmental, and religious privileges. It served as the base of the village community. The headman was mediator between local society and the overlord. It was in his immediate interest to keep the tension between the two from exploding. He could be expected to side with his fellow villagers when the level of exactions from above jeopardized his authority among his fellow villagers or threatened the subsistence of the village community. But he could also be counted on to maintain law and order and to arrange local affairs so that the higher-ups would get their due. Alongside the headman, in this mediating role, stood the residual category of rustic samurai (*joshi*), often the remnants of defeated clans.

The fourth element in the situation – and the one least an artifact of overlord policy – was the vitality of the village community itself. The village could serve as the real though fragile basis of cooperative labor and of joint responsibility for the payment of the tax–rent burden. As in many parts of Europe, legal personality sealed the autonomy of the village. This independence also allowed for a significant degree of internal differentiation in hierarchies of advantage and authority.[8]

The single most striking financial consequence of the system comprising these four elements was the ability to combine a permanently high level of land tax–rent with an effective tax–rent yield that remained high over a period of several centuries. The peasants, despite the enormity of their burden, enjoyed the modest but real protection afforded by the village community. This relative independence limited many of the extreme and self-destructive forms of exploitation.

[8] See Thomas C. Smith, *The Agrarian Origins of Modern Japan*, Stanford, Stanford, 1967, pp. 1–11, 36–49.

It permitted an increasing amount of diversity and inequality within the village community as contractual tenancy arrangements and "parasitic landlordism" transformed the structure of dependence and co-operation organized around the headman and the dominant lineage. It encouraged the growth of an agrarian surplus that made possible, and was in turn multiplied by, technical innovations in farming. It was this surplus that eventually allowed the post-Meiji governments to finance the first wave of industrialization with the revenues of the land tax rather than resorting to the dangerous alternative of foreign borrowing and foreign venture capital.

The comparison with Europe illuminates the larger significance of these developments. It also refines our understanding of collective organization from below as an element in the avoidance of reversion. In Western Europe, a crucial factor in the breakthrough had been the ability of the village community to stand on its own feet and to struggle, face-to-face, with the immediate lord over the terms of obligation. It mattered that, for a long season, no central government tilted the scales in the lords' favor. The European peasant had a fighting chance.

In early Tokugawa Japan, this situation was, in a sense, reversed. The immediate lord withdrew from the scene. The overlord dealt with the village community through headmen and officials. He was strong enough to keep a direct line of access to peasant production and manpower but not strong enough to crush the village community altogether and transform the whole peasantry into a vast slave gang. (In this respect, the Tokugawa village community remained a great deal more independent from the overlord or the state than, say, the nineteenth-century Russian redistributive commune which, from the start, was a creature of the government's fiscal needs.) Thus, like their European counterparts, the Japanese peasants enjoyed an opportunity for successful resistance to complete subordination.

The withdrawal in Japan of the immediate overlord, like the withdrawal of the central state in Europe, meant that the peasantry never faced the combined force of local landlords and high officialdom. In both the Japanese and the European instances the practical effect depended for its force on the relative insulation of the village community against control and oppression by local landlords.[9] In both histories, the outcome had a favorable impact on the overall relative prosperity of the peasant mass and the growth of surplus over sub-

---

[9] On the relative independence of the Tokugawa village community from local landowner control and on its direct dealings with the shogunal government, see Harumi Befu, "Village Autonomy and Articulation with the State" (1965), in *Studies in the Institutional History of Early Modern Japan*, ed. John W. Hall and Morris B. Jansen, Princeton, Princeton, 1968, pp. 301–314.

sistence. In both situations, the result laid the ground for the continuing involvement of the peasantry in money-based markets.

The opportunities of commercialized agriculture in turn differentiated the peasant mass. In these circumstances, the large-scale local landholder was kept from asserting his absolute dominion over peasant land and labor. At least, he was prevented from asserting it until the avoidance of economic naturalization had been prolonged and finally rendered irreversible by later industrialization. In earlier periods of its history, before the institutional innovations of the Tokugawa *bakufu*, Japan had repeatedly undergone the familiar ordeal of the reversion crises. The tailspin of agrarian concentration, market shrinkage, and governmental breakdown had been marked by the "commendation" of small landholdings to large estate holders.[10] But once the burden of direct landlord control and oppression was partly lifted from the backs of the peasant mass and the relations between town and country were transformed, the state secured a permanent fiscal base of its own. The elites and the masses alike were more thoroughly fragmented. The rise of country-based landholding magnates could no longer easily unleash the repeated process of reversion that had marked all the great agrarian empires.

The way in which the characteristic European and Japanese situations produced similar results through opposite means helps explain the different course of agrarian development in these two parts of the world. In Western Europe different forms of large- and small-scale property and tenancy combined according to the relative power of the peasantry, the large landholding magnates, and the emergent state apparatus, as well as the local pattern of economic opportunity and demographic pressure. The collective reality of the village might be broken up by the internal differentiation of the peasantry within a larger climate of commercialized agriculture.

Often, this shattered village collective did give way in Europe to large-scale tenants and landowners. These agrarian entrepreneurs counted on the help of a central state, actively present in the countryside and actively allied with the landholding interests through the structure of local administration and justice. The reversion to natural economy might be delayed or avoided but the small-scale proprietor or tenant would still be doomed.

The axis of Japanese agrarian history ran in a direction strikingly divergent from this particular strand within European agricultural

[10] See, for example, Kan'ichi Asakawa, "The Origin of the Feudal Land Tenure in Japan" (1914), in *Land and Society in Medieval Japan*, Kanda, Tokyo, 1965, pp. 1–23, especially pp. 21–22; Elizabeth Sato, "The Early Development of the Shōen," in *Medieval Japan: Essays in Institutional History*, ed. John W. Hall and Jeffrey P. Mass, Yale, New Haven, 1974, pp. 91–108, especially at pp. 94–95.

development. At the start of the Tokugawa, the dominant form of agricultural organization in much of the country was based on a single collectivity whose internal relations emphasized noncontractual and nonmonetary dependence. A larger lineage was organized around a nuclear family and surrounded by a penumbra of quasi-familial dependents. This extended network provided the social foundation of cooperative labor within the village. But already the richer parts of the country showed a different pattern: the replacement of dependent labor by contractual tenancy arrangements. Thanks to these money-based arrangements, wide disparities in the size of ownership units might combine with a tendency to standardize the size of farming units. The outcome undermined the basis of cooperative labor. In its place emerged what remained the characteristic form of Japanese agrarian life up to World War II: the combination of varieties of petty proprietorship or tenancy with "parasitic landlordism."

At first, the axis of Japanese agrarian development seems only to confirm what even the most shallow analysis of European agricultural experience already shows: the variety of legal and social ways of avoiding reversion. The trajectories of agricultural development, like the later and more universal experience of industrialization, were bafflingly varied. It is precisely by understanding the multiplicity of these forms that we gain insight into the deeper links between institutional arrangements and economic breakthroughs.

The Japanese line of agrarian development makes another more focused contribution to our understanding. It shows something important about the connection between social forms and technical opportunities. It does so by throwing light on the significance of the village community, and of the very special collective solidarity this community represented, as an element in permanent economic revolution. You can discover in this experience a distinctive pattern of opportunity and constraint.

The relative vitality of the village community and the limits to direct samurai domination of the countryside favored a long-term growth in commercialized agriculture and continuous progress in the techniques of agrarian production. The technical advances included leveling of fields, use of fertilizers, weeding and selection, and more effective forms of planting. Some of these developments may even have drawn, at the start, on the structure of cooperative labor made possible by the dominant village collective of the early Tokugawa.

Certainly, the revolutionary introduction of the heavier moldboard plow in medieval Europe had also required a pooling of human and animal labor, creating an opportunity for cooperative work within the village community. Nevertheless, the cumulative effect of the technical advances in Japanese agriculture was drastically to increase the complexity and delicacy of agricultural production. This change overtaxed the capacities of the large, cumbersome mass of kin and quasi-familial dependents. The rise in the remuneration that agrarian labor might gain in artisanal or agricultural work outside the village collective combined with the technical challenge to undermine the village community.

In its internal life, the dominant type of Tokugawa village exemplified a style of social organization that superimposes community, hierarchy, and contract. It was far from being a social context in which rationalized collective labor, as described in the preceding section of this book, could flourish. The Japanese union of hierarchy, community, and contract not only failed to secure the open space within which revolutionary organizational ideals can assert themselves; it also restrained the search for standardized operating procedures beyond rigid rules or ad hoc decisions and the quest for a continuous hierarchy combining supervision and discretion at each hierarchical level.

The rigid form of rationalized collective labor that emerged in Europe and was carried from there to the rest of the world drew a sharp and constraining contrast between task-defining and task-executing activities and between the classes of people charged with each of these two kinds of work. This contrast acted as a brake on the full development of the emergent organizational ideals. But the fusion of contract, community, and hierarchy represented by the dominant *tezukuri* style of agricultural organization in early Tokugawa Japan imposed a far more preclusive constraint. This older type of village community was just not up to the demands of a more technically sophisticated mode of agricultural production. It lacked either the coercive power or the collective flexibility and commitment required by the newer agriculture.

These requirements might have been met, in principle, by a variety of social forms: slave labor, family farming, or the internal transformation of the village collective. In the event, the second of these three options proved to be the line of least resistance. Within the shrunken family, cooperation and commitment could be established on a more solid although also a more limited base. Tenancy arrangements could reconcile parasitic landlordism with the rise of the smaller, more independent, and more flexible farming unit. This unit might eventually prove incapable of providing the level of cooperative finance and labor that could sustain another round of technical breakthroughs.

The argument about the transformation of Japanese agriculture can now be cast in a more general form connecting it with many other themes in this book and extending the analysis of reversion and of its avoidance. Collective organization and solidarity at the grass roots may provide a structure for cooperative labor. This structure, sustained against unlimited and self-destructive rapacity from above, may foster technical experiments, capital accumulation (although not necessarily to the benefit of the collective), and demographic growth. But the particular character of the internal relations within the group always imposes a loose ceiling on further advance. The force of the constraint lies in some limit on the perfect revisability of social relations. More specifically, it has to do with a failure to reproduce, in the character of these relations, the free interplay between project and execution, the abstract task and the concrete act. The organizational ideals of supervision and discretion, or of standardized operating procedures, are just partial and provisional approaches to such a way of organizing and liberating work.

In most historical civilizations, the major obstacle to the development of collective labor along such lines has been the fusion of contract, community, and domination in groups like the village community. In the history of industrialized economies, this obstacle has been partly displaced and partly reestablished by the rigid hierarchy of task definers and task executors. To perpetuate permanent technological and organizational revolution, for the sake of wealth and power, the actual forms of collective effort must become experimental and plastic. They must reflect in practice and in microcosm the indeterminacy of social life.

So far my analysis has concentrated on the Japanese counterparts to the European forms of grass-roots collective organization. It has disregarded the other aspects in the European avoidance of reversion: the splintering or postponement of any unified ruling elite of officials, landholders, and magnates, and the partial disengagement of governmental power from oligarchic privilege. The Japanese counterparts to these European developments make sense against the background laid by the earlier stage of the comparison. A distinct way of overcoming the fate of the agrarian–bureaucratic societies emerges.

The thoroughgoing commercialization of agriculture and of the tax-rent taken by shoguns and overlords created an opportunity for rapid economic and occupational diversification within the peasantry throughout the Tokugawa period. It helped the towns become more than parasites on the countryside. It drew the interest of every segment of the upper elites into the manipulation of the agrarian surplus. The tendency toward consolidation of a single oligarchic condominium of officials, landholding magnates, and wealthy merchants was repeatedly checked – by the power interests of the highest authorities in preventing unrestrained landlord domination of the countryside, by the peasantry's own powers of collective self-defense, and by the destabilizing and diversifying effect of commercialism itself.

These facts converged with additional independent aspects of the Japanese situation. One such fact was continued division between shogun and *daimyos* or among the *daimyo* overlords. In Japan as in much of Europe, the absence or fragility of a single overarching governmental order worked against the forging of a single elite.

A second fact was the strength of the distinction between power or prestige, on one side, and wealth, on the other. Precisely because even the richest merchants were not perceived as an alternative power elite, they could be allowed to prosper and to manipulate; they could be courted and cajoled, all without being incorporated into a unified aristocratic, bureaucratic, and mercantile oligarchy. The shogunate certainly tried to "feudalize" the mercantile economy by treating the wealthiest merchants to a full array of honors and threats. But the regulation of mercantile activity never got as far as it did in the Chinese Ming–Ch'ing Empire (1368–1911). Given the thoroughness and endurance of commercialization, and the emergence of trade and manufacture at all levels of society, an inclusive regulatory activity would have required a massive presence of central government and its officialdom in every aspect of national life. The creation of the institutional instruments of this presence would have burst the constitutional structure of the Tokugawa state.

The third fact was the characteristically Japanese tendency to separate accepted authority from effective power: the former moves up the hierarchical ladder while the latter goes down. The sources of unity and the objects of ultimate allegiance stand at the highest rungs of hierarchy, beginning with the emperor. But the dirty work and coercive force of power gets pushed further and further down into the hands of underlings. This pervasive dynamic, rooted in deep forms of imagination and compulsive strategies of personal relations, created an additional difficulty for a policy of oligarchic consolidation. The worth of any ruling condominium would be perpetually undermined from below, through the separation of power from authority.

ESCAPE THROUGH STATECRAFT: THE CHINESE EXPERIENCE

Now comes the third stage of my argument about the reversion to natural economy: the analysis of two experiences, Chinese and Russian, of partial or equivocal success in the attempt to escape the reversion cycles. Rather than just confirming the initial argument, each of these cases adds something important to it – something that links the understanding of particular episodes of material progress to more general insights into the link between the real human conflicts of politics and the seemingly inhuman surface of material constraint and opportunity.

Consider first imperial China. The problem of the reversion crises is posed obliquely by a standard dispute of Chinese historiography: the "buds of capitalism" controversy. One question usually brings this debate into focus. Why did the astonishing commercialism of Sung Dynasty China not lead quickly into a chain reaction of economic revolutions that would have anticipated the material achievements of industrializing Europe? This chain reaction would have brought about much earlier a transformative breakthrough in output and productivity, wealth and force. After all, here was a society that had all the apparent makings of unlimited material success: a flourishing and varied commerce in basic foodstuffs and textiles, as well as luxury goods, enormous cities that were more than parasitic conglomerations of officials, and a level of technological sophistication in advance of anything Western Europe would achieve for several centuries. We are now able to understand more fully two other features of this society that add to the impression that it should have been safe from the perils of reversion.

For one thing, notwithstanding those who imagine the Sung as an age of gigantic manorial estates, it allowed for a large range of forms of small-scale property and semidependent work or tenancy. This variety went all the way from wage labor and relatively free tenancy (the *tien*) to indentured field labor (the *p'u*), serfdom (the *di-k'o*), and slavery.[11] The money-based tax system and the market networks sustained, although they could not guarantee, a significant measure of household independence.

For another thing, the relationships, at the grass-roots level, among governmental officials, big property owners, and village society seemed to favor the proliferation of forms of household autonomy and collective organization within a thoroughly money-based economy. The imperial government had largely abandoned the policy of agrarian dualism to which it returned at its high reformist moments: the maintenance of a separate area of small-scale agriculture and military colonies that would furnish it with resources and soldiers. But local control over land and labor did not fall safely into the hands of any consolidated gentry–official class. Village headmen could maneuver between the competing pressures of their responsibilities for governmental exactions and their

---

[11] See Joseph McDermott, *Land Tenure and Rural Control in the Liangache Region during the Southern Sung*, doctoral dissertation on file at Cambridge University, 1978, giving new force and detail to some of the characteristic tenets of the "Kyoto school" of Sung historiography.

own local commitments and opportunities. The underlings of the officials and large property holders oppressed the peasantry easily enough. But often they also held their own masters hostage. They diminished their masters' hold over what actually went on in the countryside.

But reversion did take place. This critical retreat cannot be understood in the immediate context of the thirteenth century. The puzzling dead-end quality of the Sung remains too narrow a perspective from which to understand the bearing of Chinese history on the problem of reversion to natural economy. This perspective sacrifices the immediate riddle – How could so thoroughly commercialized an economy nevertheless revert? – to the contentious question – Why did things not turn out as in Europe? It also fails to acknowledge that, despite far-reaching advance, reversion did take place. Such an acknowledgment makes the event more baffling and instructive. A reversion episode occurred during the late Sung. It continued to happen in later dynasties as it had in earlier ones. In the late Sung, as so often before and after, it took place in standard form, with almost all the characteristic features invoked by my initial description of the process.

To make out the larger perspective that suggests the strangeness of this experience consider the following facts. First, there is no other great agrarian society, with the possible exception of the Byzantine Empire, in which leading statesmen and practical reformers understood so clearly the nature and danger of reversion crises and were so stubbornly and so often preoccupied with the need to avoid unrestrained magnate domination over peasant land and labor. These concerns were particularly incisive in expression and ingenious in application during the long period of disunity that fell between the Han and the T'ang dynasties (from the third to the early seventh centuries), especially the Ts'ao Wei (220–264), the Toba Wei (386–535), and the early part of the T'ang. It was a time of widespread experimentation with military colonies, small-scale landholding conditional on military service and on tax–rent burdens, and multiple tactics for the defense of the money-based peasant sector of the agrarian economy.[12]

By the time of the Sung, such trials and experiments had become a staple of political debate. In fact, these earlier and more drastic forms of governmental intervention on behalf of direct access by the state to agrarian output and peasant manpower remained at the center of controversy long after they had ceased to be realistic or relevant.

---

[12] See the writings on the policy of agrarian dualism in China listed in the note on sources for the comparative study of the antireversion policies that appears as Appendix I to this chapter.

Their practicality was undermined by the diversity and vitality of the Sung economy and the very modest degree of control that government could exercise over local life in the countryside. Nevertheless, Sung statesmen continued to speculate about their relevance.

The second surprising fact about this instance of reversion in China is that by the time of the late T'ang and during the period of strife and disunity between the T'ang and the Sung, the power of the great aristocratic clans had been definitively broken. The social position of any family, and its chances of local prosperity and privilege, now came to depend increasingly on the ability to be represented by one of its members, a successful examination taker, in state office. In this way, China became the only great preindustrial agrarian empire in which the antimagnate policies required for the avoidance of periodic economic and political collapse had a basis in the decisive defeat imposed on independent magnate power. The aristocratic clans that were so visible as late as the mid-T'ang never did regroup.

After the mid-T'ang rebellion of An Lu-shan (755–762), the change in the nature of the metropolitan elites became unmistakable. They no longer had guaranteed access to office and privilege. While some members of each family ran for the examinations, others merged into the landholding provincial elites. Having adopted the same strategy as their affinal kin among the local gentry, the old magnate families eventually disappeared as a distinct group.[13]

This destruction of the independent basis of a landowning aristocracy should have strengthened the reformers' hands. It should have helped the statesmen who periodically wanted to prevent the engrossment of peasant land and labor by grasping oligarchy. It should have aided these reformers even when they abandoned bolder hopes of redistributing land or of anchoring a free peasantry in a direct relationship of dependence and protection to the imperial household. Nevertheless, in these campaigns the reforming politicians continued to fail, over and over, both in the declining years of the Sung or at earlier or later moments of disintegration. In fact, the traditional conception of the dynastic cycle may be viewed as an aspect of this recurrent disaster, with its familiar impact on village life: the occasional closure of the village to participation in a larger world of markets, governmental authority, and cultural influence.

It is not enough to explain the recurrence of reversion episodes in Chinese history by reference to military threat and disruption from within or abroad. After all, the suppression of the uprising of An Lu-shan – a mixture of civil war and foreign invasion – in the middle

[13] See David G. Johnson, The *Medieval Chinese Oligarchy*, Westview, Boulder, Colorado, 1977, especially pp. 19–20, 149–152; Patricia Ebbrey, *Aristocratic Families of Early Imperial China*, Cambridge, Cambridge, 1978.

years of the T'ang had served as the backdrop for a final stage in the attack on the privileges of the aristocratic clans.[14] To take another example, in the late nineteenth century, the Japanese capacity to meet foreign jeopardy by domestic reform had rapidly magnified what were at the outset only subtle advantages in the marshaling of human and material resources.

A military threat, like any challenge, has double meaning. It can galvanize into reform as well as frighten into inaction. Besides, frequent military defeat, of the kind the Chinese Empire repeatedly suffered at the hands of the warlike peoples on its borders, is no blind fate; it results from prolonged failure in the statecraft of reform.

Again, we cannot explain the results simply by an appeal to the authority officialdom had over the fortunes and tastes of enterprising farmers and merchants. For our attention is now focused less on the abortive quality of urban trade and manufacturing than on the repeated downward swings in the agrarian economy itself. Suppose it is argued that these agrarian setbacks could have been avoided had bureaucracy not stifled the possibilities of further revolutions in the town-based commercial and manufacturing economy. This argument fails to identify persuasively just where this stifling occurred. Political subordination and cultural contempt were sometimes turned by Japanese merchants to their own advantage. Many varieties of governmental penetration of mercantile enterprise and of aping of aristocracies or bureaucracies by merchants are compatible with continuous economic revolution. Modern European history would be enough to show it. The people who lived in the Chinese Empire were no different from the ordinary run of humanity in their ability to go through life in a daze miraculously combining an empty-headed deference to ruling prejudice with a level-headed eye for the main chance.

To understand these events we must distinguish two issues: the undercutting of economic opportunity by the complex process described in this section as reversion to natural economy; and the effect of the accommodations between governmental power and economic enterprise studied in the next section. The essential reason that the reformist impulse was always overrun is that the Chinese reformers never managed to keep the different aspirant factions of the oligarchy, within and outside the state, from coming together. The oligarchies joined to ensure that governmental power at the local level would not be used, if it was used at all, to support the weak against the strong. The degree of any one family's participation in the privileges of state office might vary quite dramatically from one generation to

[14] See Edward Pulleybank, *The Background of the Rebellion of An Lu-Shan*, Oxford, Oxford, 1955, especially pp. 29–30.

the next. But the differential distribution of opportunities to study, the frequent chance to supplement by corruption what "merit" had not won, officialdom's fear of policies that might drum up resistance by the most entrenched members of local society, and the need to reward important supporters with large estates at moments of dynastic foundation or imperial crisis – all these considerations hindered the formulation of antimagnate policies or, when such policies were formulated, undermined their application. In effect, the experience of the would-be reformers was not so different from that of bolder Byzantine emperors, who saw their legal prohibitions of alienation of peasant land and their efforts to secure the return of illegally transferred property effectively undone in the magnate-controlled courts.[15]

Moreover, the constant tendency for the costs of imperial rule to go up (a tendency discussed in the next chapter), combined with harvest failures or sudden crises in military affairs, often pushed up the government's demand for taxes and soldiers. At such moments of crisis, the more prosperous elements of Chinese local society, like their Roman and Byzantine counterparts, would be in the best position to defend themselves against the additional burden and to force the onus upon smallholders and upon the landless. This transfer threw the agrarian economy further into trouble. It aggravated the government's helpless dependence on national or local oligarchies.

Despite the destabilizing impact of the examination system and the distinctive power interests of the high state administration, imperial China witnessed a perennial regrouping of elites. Early modern Europe saw a degree and type of elite fragmentation that lacked any real Chinese counterpart. Different waves of European businessmen, for example, showed themselves able to outdo their rivals and precursors in seizing new opportunities for state-protected trade: say, the East Levant merchants against the merchant adventurers or the pioneers of the Virginia trade against their East Levant forerunners.

To compare this Chinese story with the Western European and Japanese experiences is to understand both the paradoxical futility of so much reforming busywork and the fateful importance of collective organization from below. Chinese history shows the surprising way in which these two facts often connect.

In neither Western Europe nor Japan were the intentions of farsighted reformers enough to secure a breakthrough from reversion. In both cases, the mocking logic of unintended consequences had its

---

[15] See George Ostrogorsky, "The Peasant's Preemption Right: An Abortive Reform of the Macedonian Empire," *Journal of Ramon Studies*, vol. 37 (1947), pp. 117–126.

day. In Europe radical innovation came through the way in which a special destruction of the commercial economy – superficially similar to the typical reversion pattern discussed here – facilitated a decisive rebound at the next stage. The European version of economic crisis gave the peasant community a fighting chance against local landowners. For it dispensed peasants from the need to wage war against a well-organized state at the same time they were struggling against their immediate lords. In the Japanese situation, the favoring background was the unexpectedly favorable effect of the withdrawal of local samurai on opportunities for peasant organization. The outcomes in both Europe and Japan had to be unforeseen to have occurred at all; their production by design would presuppose a revolutionary experimentation with mass activity that would be too much to ask from even the boldest reformers in societies that had not yet undergone the relative breaking open represented by mass politics. Too much to expect from the people on top, all too mindful of their own interests: experimentation would have required unleashing a guided mass movement unlikely to be controlled and very likely to produce relentless reaction by the various oligarchies from which governmental personnel were ordinarily drawn. And too much to expect as a matter of insight into the political transformability of society: in the absence of the experiences of world history, mass politics, and emancipated economic rationality there were too few available and inspiring counterimages of what society might be like.

In China, the destruction of the independent base of the great aristocratic lineages created a potential for disentangling the exercise of governmental power from the support of locally entrenched oligarchies. The diversity of commercial life in town and country and the course of political factionalism constantly recreated occasions for the fragmentation of elites at all levels. But these opportunities would not be realized or even kept open unless they were transformed by a measure of successful, independent organization among ordinary working people. Without such organization, nothing prevented occasional crises from magnifying relatively small social disparities into large inequalities. Nothing saved central governments from having to capitulate to resurgent oligarchies. Nothing stopped the occasionally estranged factions of a ruling elite from joining hands over a tamed peasantry and a subdued state.

In Europe, an element of authentic popular self-organization emerged as the unintended by-product of a protracted disablement of central government. In Tokugawa Japan, the intentional though relative disablement of local landowners by the shogunate produced a lesser but nevertheless significant measure of communal autonomy.

Independent collective resistance and organization, as distinguished from controlled mobilization imposed from the top down, was unlikely to rank as a deliberate goal of governmental policy. A government that willed such a goal ran the daunting risks of populist, revolutionary despotism.

As the Russian contrast will soon show, there was all the difference in the world between a village community created for the express purpose of sustaining the state, like the military colonies of the Toba and the early T'ang or the *ktemata stratiotikoi* of the Macedonian dynasty in the Byzantine Empire, and the self-defensive, though internally exploitative, peasant cooperative group. The village headmen and "double-service" systems in the Southern Sung turned out to be less starting points for self-generating movement from below than dispensable links between local and national power. These links were pushed aside as soon as a reconstituted oligarchy had found its new identity and learned to flourish in the climate of a corrupt and preposterous pedantocracy.

The earlier discussion of the Chinese experience has addressed the recurrence of long reversion crises in Chinese history. But it is not enough to account for the persistence of these breakdowns through so much of Chinese history and for the failure of the reform policies designed to prevent them. It is also necessary to explain why in the final period of its history – the period of the Ming–Ch'ing Empire, which stretched from 1368 to 1911 – Chinese society acquired a measure of the immunity its reformers had vainly sought. The Ming–Ch'ing Empire continued to witness periods of economic contraction, administrative weakness, and political–military jeopardy. But never again did these troubles precipitate the radical decommercialization of the economy and the breakdown of the state apparatus that distinguished a full-fledged reversion crisis. At times of governmental weakness and economic decline – most notably during the two long downward swings of the seventeenth and the nineteenth centuries – peasants and farmers continued to suffer bankruptcy and landlessness. But never again did landowning magnates destroy and engross the smallholding sector of the agrarian economy.[16] The Ming–Ch'ing Empire represented a China that had become relatively safe for the smallholder. The continuing variety of form and scale in its patterns of land tenure bore witness to this safety. China's eventual, gradual

---

[16] For an analysis of the complex and thoroughly commercialized though technologically stagnant agriculture of the late nineteenth and early twentieth centuries, see Ramon H. Meyers, *The Chinese Peasant Economy: Agricultural Development in Hopei and Shantung, 1890–1949*, Harvard, Cambridge, 1970, especially pp. 288–291.

escape from the reiteration of the reform cycles is hardly less puzzling than its prolonged subjection to them. The solution to each of these puzzles must prove compatible with the solution to the other.

Consider first two inadequate explanations of this gradual buildup of immunity to the reversion crises. One hypothesis would invoke an idea of drift and balance. In this hypothesis, few of the periodic breakdowns destroyed all that had flourished during the periods of administrative strength and market vitality. The countermovements to reversion cumulated. They found support in the tenacity of the peasant household and in the imperatives of supporting a growing population without the benefit of a technological revolution. The trouble with this hypothesis is that it simply fails to do justice to the severity of the reversion crises during the long period in which they recurred.

Another inadequate explanation would identify China's forced entry into a commercialized world economy as the leading cause of its diminished susceptibility to breakdown. In this view, participation in a world trade network pushed Chinese agriculture toward a market less likely to close or to shrink, precisely because it was worldwide. The institutional reforms sponsored by an elite anxious to see its country catch up to the leading Western powers confirmed what China's new position in the world economy had brought about. The flaw in this explanation, however, is that it disregards chronology. The change we are trying to explain was well defined long before foreign trade had become a major factor in China's economy. In fact, late imperial China's ability to sustain through thick and thin its elaborate, well-balanced market network and its administrative unity helped insulate it against the disruptive effects of foreign commercial penetration.[17]

For a more compelling explanation we must look to the social facts most intimately linked with the earlier perpetuation of reversion crises: the relation of central governmental power to landowning elites with local roots. The Chinese state, it seems, simply got better at the task its reformers had always understood to be paramount: the partial freeing of central governmental authority from control or immobilization by the landowning elites. This disengagement occurred through two long waves of institutional reform. The reforms that succeeded the rebellion of An Lu-shan during the mid-T'ang, such as the strengthening of the career bureaucracy and of the examination system, represented the first wave. These reforms were sufficiently effective to work a major change in the character and composition of the Chinese elites. They doomed the aristocratic

[17] See Rhoads Murphy, *The Outsiders: The Western Experience in India and China,* Univ. of Michigan, Ann Arbor, 1977, pp. 98–130.

clans. They permitted the more extensive deployment of all the standard antireversion policies. They helped give life to the great commercial efflorescence of the Sung. But they were not enough. Even when the landowners could no longer automatically become bureaucrats, the bureaucrats kept becoming landowners. A hostile bureaucracy kept undermining reform policies. And the traditional breakdowns kept happening.

A second great wave of changes in the organization of the Chinese state and of its relation to the landowning elites took place in the period from the Mongol Conquest (and the Yüan dynasty [1260–1368] established by the Mongols) to the early years of the Ch'ing (Manchu) dynasty (1644–1911). China's nomadic conquerors introduced institutions, practices, and attitudes that strengthened the autonomy of the central government. The Mongols' experience in the steppe and the borderlands and the problems they had to face as a conquest elite prepared them – I later argue – for the role of teachers of statecraft. They taught the lesson of continued mobilization, of hostility to vested rights and local prerogatives, and of insistence on insulating at least parts of governmental power from the influence of local landowners and notables. They taught this lesson through institutional arrangements like the Yüan provisions for secret or sudden inspection of the lower rungs of the bureaucracy, which the indigenous Ming Dynasty further developed, or the Ch'ing banner system, which kept the conquest elite ready for service and prevented it from sinking into a class of landowners anxious about their local interests, or the Ch'ing memorial system by which independent officials gave the emperor confidential reports about the activities of officialdom.[18] The nomadic conquerors also taught their lesson of statecraft through beliefs and attitudes that emphasized the importance of maintaining central government free to mobilize resources and manpower.

Over the final period of Chinese history the development of the new statecraft proceeded in several steps. The early Yüan methods of control over the bureaucracy were soon neutralized, for the Mongols failed to achieve an intimate association between conquerors and

[18] See Jonathan D. Spence, *Ts'ao Yin and the K'ang-hsi Emperor, Bondservant and Master*, Yale, New Haven, 1966, pp. 2–18; Lawrence D. Kessler, *Kang-hsi and the Consolidation of Ch'ing Rule, 1661–1684*, Chicago, Chicago, 1976, pp. 117–136; Franz Michael, *The Origin of Manchu Rule in China: Frontier and Bureaucracy as Interacting Forces in the Chinese Empire*, Johns Hopkins, Baltimore, 1942, p. 118; Robert B. Oxnam, *Ruling From Horseback: Manchu Politics in the Oboi Regency, 1661–1669*, Chicago, Chicago, 1975, pp. 9, 20–23, 121–124; Silas H.L. Wu, *Communication and Control in Imperial China: Evolution of the Palace Memorial System, 1693–1735*, Harvard, Cambridge, 1970, pp. 5–8, 34–51.

conquered.[19] After promising beginnings, they remained more a garrison ruling over an unreconstructed government than the architects of a reformed agrarian–bureaucratic state. During the indigenous Ming Dynasty, pre-Yüan habits of administration and of entente between officials and local elites revived. The eunuch establishment nevertheless performed a role in linking emperor, nobles, and military officers together as a counterweight to the civilian bureaucracy.[20] The Ch'ing regime, established by a border people with a long apprenticeship in mutual assimilation and institutional invention, achieved a more lasting reinforcement of the decisional autonomy and mobilizational capacity of central government.

The Chinese learned what their conquerors had to teach. The lessons had in any case begun long before, during the successive transactions between the Chinese Empire and the peoples of the steppe, especially during the conflict-ridden interval between the Han and the T'ang. Admittedly, the old tendencies that connected state office with private privilege, to the benefit of local elites, never disappeared completely.[21] Nevertheless, the Ming–Ch'ing state was more independent and therefore stronger than the states it succeeded. It can, to its advantage, be compared to the Ottoman Empire – a state founded by the steppe peoples, on principles similar to those introduced during the second great wave of Chinese reforms, and one that never had to face a full-fledged reversion crisis.

Thus, the later Chinese Empire presents the remarkable example of a gradualistic, relatively nonconflictual escape from the pattern of the periodic breakdown. By stratagems of statecraft it accomplished something of what Europe to a greater extent and Japan to a lesser extent had achieved through unplanned and even uncontrolled group conflict between organized peasants and grasping landlords. In this way the Chinese statesmen at last found what they had been half-consciously looking for: a via media between the evils of prostration to local elites and the risks of all-out antilandlord campaigns.

From its very nature, in China as in other agrarian–bureaucratic empires of Eurasia, this gradualistic escape path was not unequivocally successful. It left in power a state primarily concerned with security, stability, and harmony. It allowed a continuous realignment of the ruling and possessing elites. And it limited opportunities for

---

[19] See John W. Dardess, *Conquerors and Confucians: Aspects of Political Change in Late Yüan China*, Columbia, New York, 1973, pp. 75–94.
[20] See Edward L. Dreyer, *Early Ming China: A Political History, 1355–1435*, Stanford, Stanford, 1982, pp. 244–245.
[21] See Jerry Dennerline, "Fiscal Reform and Local Control: The Gentry–Bureaucratic Alliance Survives the Conquest," in *Conflict and Control in Late Imperial China*, eds. Frederic Wakeman, Jr., and Carolyn Grant, Univ. of California, Berkeley, 1975, pp. 86–120.

the institutional experiments that can take place when widening group conflict shakes up social roles and hierarchies and diminishes their power to predefine the practical forms of production and exchange. All these effects help explain why the gradualistic escape route was associated with relative technological stagnation, especially of agricultural technology. This stagnation created the single most formidable obstacle to China's economic progress.

Note that this argument is compatible with many traditional explanations of comparative technological backwardness in China and in other agrarian-bureaucratic empires. At a minimum, it gives each of these explanations a needed institutional vision. Historians have argued, for example, that the Chinese imperial state was committed to a particular conception of welfare and stability that rendered it antagonistic to unchecked and unnecessary innovation in work relations, styles of production, or other forms of association among rulers, traders, and producers. But the state that could uphold such a commitment resulted from the particular sequences of institutional breakthroughs and compromises discussed earlier in this section. The point is not that institutions have primacy over ideas. It is, rather, that people's conceptions of their interests and ideals depend largely on the range of alternative practical forms of social life among which they feel they are forced to choose. They rarely enlarge their sense of the possible terms of cooperation except by fighting about them.

A final section of this essay discusses the transactions between the agrarian–bureaucratic empires and their occasional nomadic conquerors. It does so both to refine the analysis of the gradualistic escape method and to probe further the relation between failures of institutional invention and constraints on group conflict. But before going on to this final step of the argument, consider one more variant of partial escape from the reversion cycles.

FRUSTRATED ESCAPE: THE RUSSIAN EXPERIENCE

In Russian history, state and society combine elements of both the Japanese and the Ming–Ch'ing ways of gaining immunity against periodic breakdowns of agrarian-bureaucratic societies. Like Tokugawa Japan, imperial Russia saw at many points in its history the relative disablement of oppressive landlord practices by a central government. As in the Tokugawa *bakufu* village community, peasant collective self-organization – represented by the redistributive land commune – achieved a measure of vitality. In other respects, the Russian state resembled the later Chinese Empire. Like the Ming–Ch'ing government, it managed to safeguard against landholding magnates a considerable ability to command resources and manpower and to make and implement policy. Moreover, it did so without nomadic tutelage; the impact of the Mongols on Russian history lay elsewhere. The results formed part of the institutional background that enabled late nineteenth century Russia to plunge into industrialization. Yet these results were all achieved in truncated forms and with frustrating consequences.

Chinese society should have been able to avoid periodic reversion but it did not. Russian history presents the still more subtle picture of an apparent, but in fact deeply flawed, success. In Russia the avoidance of periodic collapse was achieved only in a particular and costly way that robbed the postponement of reversion of much of its potential for economic revolution.

The social and economic history of imperial Russia presents a pair of half-illusions. By identifying the nature of these illusions, their sources, and their consequences, you can discover still another facet of the relation between collective conflict and economic transformation in preindustrial societies. There is the illusion of a definitive curbing of magnate ambition, from the time of the struggle between Ivan IV and the great princely families. This curb, however, was weakened, although never entirely lifted, in the course of later adjustments between autocracy and aristocracy, adjustments that foreclosed the possibility of the full-scale periodic collapse represented by the Chinese dynastic cycle. There is also the illusion of a large degree of collective peasant organization from below, culminating in the spread of the redistributional peasant commune during the nineteenth century. But the Russian peasant commune rarely liberated itself from the role of a more or less passive instrument of governmental tax and military policy. The half-hearted restraint on the grandees and the relative vitality of grassroots communal organization seem, at first, to explain each other in just the way suggested by the initial picture of periodic collapse. But though these two forces are not entirely illusory, the manner and the conditions of their occurrence changed their real social meaning and vastly reduced the transformative impact of the apparent achievement.

The only straightforward moment of reversion in Russian history happened very early, during the period leading up to the era of the Mongol invasions. The princely families of the Kievan Rus' had in fact amassed large estates worked by dependent nonwage labor: indentured workers and slaves. The weakness of a realm in which no central government could count on direct access to peasant land and labor was partly to blame for weakness in the face of Tartar power.

Although widespread alodial possession in land seems to have flourished under Mongol dominance, the ordinary counterpart of widely shared access to land and labor – commercial and artisanal activity – was stifled by the predatory practices of the foreign tribute takers. From the time of Mongol withdrawal, there were periods of economic decline but never of outright resurgence of natural economy in the enlarged social sense I have given the term here. These periods of decline – from the thirteenth to the fifteenth centuries and then toward the end of the sixteenth century – were connected to the disruptive impact of the struggles between aristocracy and autocracy and between landlords and autocrats, on one side, and the peasantry, on the other. The uniquely stunted although varied forms of commercial economy in agriculture and manufacture that did emerge were in turn shaped by the way these conflicts got resolved.

For the purpose of understanding the Russian avenue of escape from periodic economic collapse, two series of developments were crucial. One had to do with the ties of the tsars to greater and lesser nobles; the other, with the nature of peasant autonomy and organization.

The structure of relations between autocrat and magnates had its source in the uniquely ruthless and effective campaign of Ivan IV against the serving princes. This campaign resulted in the temporary establishment of the tsar's realm within a realm (the *oprichnina*) on territories effectively confiscated from the most powerful grandees, the use of this confiscated area as a basis of the conditional and initially noninheritable land tenure represented by the *pomestye* grants to the lower gentry in contrast to the fuller proprietary entitlement of *votchina* land, and the imposition of direct military and fiscal obligations on all landholders, whatever the category of tenure. The partnership between autocracy and a dependent lower gentry against both the peasant masses and the high aristocracy describes the gist of the settlement.

Votchina tenure declined until it became a residual category. A state peasantry – the collectively organized "black peasants," as well as the single-family homesteaders – coexisted with the emphasis on the conditional character of landholding – conditional upon the performance of official administrative, military, and fiscal responsibilities – in the nonstate sector. But the long-term movement, from Ivan the Terrible to Peter the Great, brought about a partial reversal of this resolution: *pomestye* tenure increasingly gained the trappings of full alodial ownership within the autocratic structure of the service state.[22] The autocracy joined hands with the larger landholders in the effort to hold the peasantry to the land in dependent status. Although the outright aristocratic reaction of Prince Shuisky failed, the ultimate relationship of the autocracy to the greater and lesser landholders alike became a complex of interpenetration, partnership, and occasionally resurgent dominion. It is important to understand both that

[22] See Jerome Blum, *Lord and Peasant in Russia*, Princeton, Princeton, 1961, pp. 170–188, 252–255.

this undoing of the initial autocratic triumph was only partial and that it was real.

To grasp the genesis and nature of these shifts, you must take into account another reappearing pattern in Russian social history: the pattern of response to the peasantry. The initial restraint on the grandees, although avoiding the disintegration exemplified by full-scale reversion to natural economy, was of no immediate benefit to the peasantry in the very regions of the empire where it was most effective. In fact, the level of exactions on *pomestye* landholders was so formidable that landholders rushed to transfer the onus to the peasantry. This rising burden – combined with the sudden instabilities of crisis in harvests or in the snapping of international trade links – provoked the massive peasant flights that were one of the distinctive traits of Russian history between the Time of Troubles and the rigidification of serfdom.

The autocracy was threatened by this relatively unorganized mass response. It had good reason to refuse the unknown and dangerous path of a revolutionary despotism that would require it to deal directly with the peasantry and to abolish or terrorize intermediate ranks (including its own servants). Once it turned away from the path, however, it had to ally itself with the great landowners and even help them assert control over peasant land and labor. This was the option that the autocracy preferred and that, on the whole, it managed to carry out. All the while, tsardom kept something of its independence from, and ascendancy over, a landowning aristocracy, a superiority won in an earlier round of the contest.

The defeat of the peasantry meant that the elements of collective peasant organization represented by the different forms of *volost*-type village community became effectively powerless in most areas of the empire. When the actively redistributive village commune appeared much later, it arose as response to the government's fiscal demands in both the state and the nonstate sectors of the agrarian economy rather than as a conquest of peasant organization and resistance.

The causes and consequences of the double illusion in Russian social history – the apparent curbing of magnate ambition and the seeming vitality of the peasant commune – now become clear. The staying of the magnate's hand did indeed avoid the continual kind of full-fledged, periodic collapse that recurred in many other societies. At times, and particularly during the Time of Troubles, the savage contest between tsar and autocrats disrupted the economic life of the country. But the successful containment of grandee ambition, a containment never entirely undone in the later drift toward the consolidation of inheritable and unconditional rights over land and labor, made possible the variety of forms of trade and manufacture we find in Russian history. Members of all social ranks – from the peasantry to the nobility – actively engaged in commercial and manufacturing ventures. (Think of the remarkable peasant industrialists.) Manufacturing located in the countryside as well as in the towns. There was an uninterrupted monetary economy. Population quadrupled from 1750 to 1860 in the absence of any technological revolution.

But this apparent vitality hid weakness. The fragility was directly traceable to the particular way in which reversion was held back. There were no commercially and industrially oriented groups between the fancy *gosti* court merchants and the low-level traders. The town lacked real autonomy from the government. Nothing prevented the state from adopting the peace-maintaining but economically stifling attitudes of autarkic imperial order described in the next section. There was no acute and ongoing contest for mastery of the kind that brought the English and the French nobilities of the late sixteenth and early seventeenth centuries to the edge of downfall and forced some of them to master new stratagems of survival.

The outcome of the struggle between the peasantry and its governmental and landlord masters remained a yet more basic source of limitation. The terms of this outcome operated as part of the settlement between autocracy and aristocracy. They were also an economic constraint in their own right.

The nineteenth-century redistributive commune which represented the end result of the peasants' fights with officials and landholders, was a sham example of autonomous collective organization.[23] It could arise, in response to governmental demands, only after earlier, more independent communal organizations had been crushed. The redistributive commune effectively suppressed independent collective struggle by the peasantry. Had such struggle escalated, it would in turn have restricted the ability of government to avoid the emergence of social groups capable of carrying conflict and innovation beyond the low thresholds at which they were considered safe. The redistributive commune stifled innovation both within the peasantry and among the peasantry's masters. It assured the master a relatively tranquil situation. It drove a large part of the peasants to despair of any improvement beyond what was necessary to sustain their households: what government failed to take, the commune redistributed.

The identification of the idea of peasant and smallholder organization with the reality of the redistributive commune favored the fatal illusion among succeeding generations of Russian statesmen,

[23] See Geroid Robinson, *Rural Russia under the Old Régime*, Univ. of California, Berkeley, 1972, pp. 117–128; Francis W. Watters, "The Peasant and the Village Commune," in *The Peasant in Nineteenth-Century Russia*, ed. Wayne S. Vucinich, Stanford, Stanford, 1968, pp. 133–157.

intellectuals, and publicists that there was a necessary choice between two clearly defined roads to agrarian development. One road was the communal principle supposedly embodied in the *mir* or in its collectivist Soviet successors. The other path could only be, it was assumed, the large- or small-scale independent agricultural enterprise associated with the more recent agrarian history of Western Europe. This illusory choice played a decisive part in the debate between Stolypin and his critics at the beginning of the twentieth century. It reemerged, with recognizable but unrecognized continuity, in the conflict between Bukharin and Preobrazhensky over agrarian policy during the late 1920s. It is still not dead today. The alleged dilemma presented by these two agrarian options disregarded the many different ways in which small-scale but technologically progressive and commercialized agriculture might be drawn into cooperative networks. Yet these possibilities had resonances in Russian history all the way from the nineteenth-century voluntary *artels* to the earlier forms of the *volost*.

The Russian argument extends the theme of the Chinese example by confirming the importance of genuine collective organization from below as an encouragement to escape from the reversion crises. The analysis of the Russian experience adds a novel element to this theme. It underscores the importance of sequence in the relation between grassroots collective organization and other incidents in a social transformation of revolutionary economic significance. In Russia, independent collective organization from below was shattered before it could join other factors to produce a decisive widening of possibilities of social and economic conflict and recombination. In most Western European countries of the early modern period, the suppression of the peasant or urban mass and of its forms of organization took place only after a long history of popular collective struggle. This history in turn served as the favoring background to the fragmentation of elites and the partial disentanglement of governmental power from the stranglehold of a unified oligarchy.

The decisive character of the Western European sequence is directly related by its effect on elites to the distinctive and fluid features of mass politics and world history. A twentieth-century state might adopt a strategy of controlled mobilization – the setting up of forms of mass organization at the initiative and under the supervision of the central government. But, in the characteristic conditions of mass politics and world history, the attempt to enlist and channel the working people goes far beyond the realization of particular fiscal or military demands. Its larger motives are reflected in the more broadly defined aims and varieties of the organizations themselves. Modern controlled mobilization takes place in a setting of appeal to the virtual, if not the actual, consent of the people. In this contemporary setting it is acknowledged that the people might get out of hand and that populist demagogues might ride to power on their support. What is controlled today, in the controlled mobilization of mass politics, can easily become uncontrollable tomorrow. The tactic of modern mobilization might at first appear similar to the strategies illustrated by the nineteenth-century Russian redistributive commune. But in the conditions of nineteenth-century Russia, such an escalation was almost entirely unimaginable and only barely possible. It certainly was *not* part of the train of events that led to February 1917.

A final lesson of the Russian experience points to the relation between the independence of grassroots popular organizations and their internal equality. The equality of the redistributive commune was the product of weakness. Frequent redistribution was needed to ensure that the common fiscal burden could be carried. The earlier, more authentic forms of communal association were also more hierarchical internally. But, under the impact of practical and visionary conflict, such a hierarchy might produce a more lasting equality. The path to equality passes through conflict. Otherwise, it is likely to lead to a mirage.

THE REVERSION CYCLE RECONSIDERED: THE SOCIAL CONDITIONS OF GOVERNMENTAL AUTONOMY

Reversion to natural economy represents only one aspect of a more general set of problems in the record of wealth and worldly power. There are two sides to such a more inclusive understanding of the social conditions of economic prosperity and governmental stability in the agrarian empires that existed before the day of mass politics and world history.

One side I have analyzed through my discussion of reversion. Will the landholding magnates take over peasant land and labor or will they continue to coexist with smallholders and tenants of different kinds? Will the high officials, landholders, and merchants or manufacturers coalesce into a single omnipotent elite or will they remain divided among themselves? Will the central government retain direct access to taxes and military manpower from a large part of the population or will it have to content itself with whatever funds and soldiers it can get from the magnates? Will a large part of the populace continue to participate in the monetary economy, or will markets shrink until they have become little more than a clearinghouse for transactions between the magnates and their domestic or foreign trading partners? The answers given to each of these questions determined much of what a society's material life and material prospects would be like.

This is the aspect of governmental and economic affairs that will be uppermost in our minds if we look at things from the perspective of the ordinary working masses or of the more farsighted and independent rulers. The peasants and the sovereigns had a common interest in evading or postponing the disaster, at least so long as the sovereigns were more than frontmen for a consolidated elite of large landholders, officials, and merchants. It is also the perspective that will intrigue us most if we are trying to discover the conditions that might have favored or foreclosed economic revolution at earlier moments in history. For the one clear case of a historical situation that gave rise to worldwide economic revolution was the one in which the repeated collapse was postponed long enough to make possible the irreversible commercialization and industrialization of the economy.

There was, however, another, more obvious side to the problems of prosperity and power in these societies. How could the state in populous countries with a sedentary way of life be kept vital and safe from internal rebellion or foreign threat? Wealth depended largely on the maintenance, growth, and investment of the agrarian surplus. A vast peasantry might always rebel. A foreign foe might always conquer. How could the central government be set up in a way that would allow it to draw effectively on the material and manpower resources of the society and to foster their growth in sectors or areas key to the security of the state? How could the higher reaches of government be organized so that the people on top could act swiftly and decisively when decisive and swift action was needed to keep the show on the road? Power always tended to vanish as through a sieve. It degenerated into an instrument of factional advantage. The state, taken over by new rulers, would then rebound and try to lay low the structure of entrenched privilege. But it would rarely manage to create a lasting improvement in the governmental capacity to mobilize resources and manpower.

To bring these issues into focus it helps to treat the rulers and the grandees as members of a single oligarchic partnership (a dangerous but useful simplification) and to consider the problems of statecraft from their point of view. For the mass of the working population, such anxieties might be largely out of place. The collapse of the state did matter a great deal when it was tied in with the shocks of recurrent market shrinkage, land concentrations, and administrative disorder. But it might or might not matter that, in the wake of a foreign conquest, the central and local rulers were shoved aside and replaced. The strengthening of the state through the growth of local administration would be advantageous to working people only so long as local officialdom was kept from becoming a mere instrument of local landholders.

The two aspects of the history of wealth and power – the prosperity of an independent peasantry and the security of the state – were so closely connected that at first it seems hard to distinguish them at all. The chain reaction of events in the episodes of reversion invariably weakened or destroyed the state, laying it open to foreign conquest. One of two things might happen. A slight addition in military pressure from abroad often served as the immediate occasion for a step-up in the fiscal and manpower demands of the government. In other circumstances, the landholding magnates would manage to transfer the burden to the peasantry; the ruined or frightened peasants might seek refuge with the magnates; and the state would find itself worse off than before and less able to hold back internal disorder and foreign conquest.

Success at avoiding reversion crises required and produced a measure of governmental strength and widened the area of maneuver open to rulers and reformers. Nevertheless, a reversion-avoiding central government might still not prove a match for domestic rebellion or foreign conquest. The weakness of the Ming–Ch'ing, the Ottoman, and the pre-Columbian empires in the face of European intrusion cannot be explained solely by reference to a logic of reversion. None of these states was in the midst of such a collapse at the time of their fatal confrontation with the West. Each of them, in a different way, seems to have advanced far toward a situation in which it would become permanently less susceptible to this disaster.

There is another, more revealing sign of the difference between avoidance of reversion and state building. The process of reversion itself is intelligible only if we assume that central government remained relatively fragile even at the high points of commercial and administrative vitality. This fragility showed up in many different ways: the thinness of local administration, the difficulty of guaranteeing the continued presence of a strong hand at the center, the relative ineffectiveness of the links between the central heights and the local roots of power. The dilemma presented by the choice between revolutionary despotism (the alliance of the sovereign with the peasantry) and aristocratic condominium (capitulation to the magnates) goes some distance in explaining the difficulty. But it does not explain it away. The proof is – as I soon argue – that in many of the agrarian empires the mobilizing and decisional capacity of the state did advance. It took a series of violent confrontations with a different kind of society to achieve this improvement.

The dilemmas of this ancient statecraft repay study despite their dependence on the standpoint of the rulers. The reward is not only a larger understanding of the practical conditions of wealth and power but a renewal of basic assumptions. From the start, one of the aims of the analysis of reversion has been to find a way to think generally about the history of production and power without having to rely on concepts like "capitalism" or the "mode of production." For such

concepts drastically underestimate the opportunities for recombination and reinvention in even those aspects of social life that seem
most subject to an independent logic of material constraint. All such
ideas, drawn as they are from the tradition of necessitarian social
theory, assume that a certain number of elements – of a productive
system, for example – fit together naturally and necessarily. The
prize for pursuing the defunct problems of ancient imperial statecraft
will be to begin making more explicit the alternative mode of understanding tacitly contained in the earlier discussion.

THE CONFRONTATION BETWEEN
AGRARIAN–BUREAUCRATIC EMPIRES
AND THEIR NOMADIC ADVERSARIES:
LESSONS IN THE ANTIDOTE TO REVERSION

These tasks of statecraft were presented most clearly in a particular
geographic theater and a particular conflict of peoples and ways of
life. The theater was the steppe heartland of the great Eurasian land
mass from Mongolia to the Pontic and Danubian steppe. The conflict
pitted sedentary and agrarian empires against mobile and warlike
peoples who combined pastoralism, agriculture, and the protection
or plunder of overland commerce in varying degrees. Let me call
these peoples nomads even though their actual nomadism was often
very limited and the fact of their nomadic life or of their pastoral
activity does little, by itself, to explain what was most significant
about their dealings with the agrarian societies of Eurasia.[24]

The transactions between the agrarian–bureaucratic societies and
the nomadic peoples who occasionally conquered them also have a
more focused interest. For it was in part by assimilating institutions
and assumptions developed by these conquest elites that some of the
agrarian societies escaped their destructive cycles of land concentration, market shrinkage, and administrative collapse.

The nomadic and the agrarian societies of the Eurasian land mass
had common origins. The development of a more intensive agriculture, the domestication of animals, and the establishment of larger
imperial orders resulted in a differentiation of peoples and activities.
Some of the people who had formerly lived together and shared a
common society pushed out into the steppe and adopted a distinctive
way of life. Yet they remained bound to the agrarian populations by
the exchange of tools and animals, by the practical forms of arrangements for the protection of continental trade, by all the possible forms

[24] See Appendix II to this study.

of clientage and tribute through which the agrarian countries attempted to gain safety or advantage, and by the seductive influence exercised upon the steppe peoples of Eurasia by the denser centers of civilization.

Geographical particularities of each region influenced the confrontation between the pastoral and the agrarian peoples. In the Far East, the division between steppe and heartland populations was most clearly marked. In West Central Asia, the contrast was shaded by the overlap of lands with different measures of fertility. In the Danubian and Pontic steppe, the distinction was confused even more thoroughly by the more abundant rainfall, the great riverine systems, and the proximity of forest land ready to be used for slash-and-burn agriculture with even the most primitive tools. Thus, the Eurasian steppe offered the full range of geographic contexts for the mixture and separation of these pastoral and agrarian ways of life. This separation and mixture, driven forward by an astonishing history of conflict and discovery, amounted to a running lesson about some basic possibilities in the relationship between state and society.

The agrarian empires proved repeatedly unable to resist the incursions of their far less populous nomadic neighbors. In much of the Eurasian land mass, the nomads showed, again and again, that they could rule as well as conquer. Their stubborn advantage in warfare and statecraft resulted from deep characteristics of their social existence and social imagination. At their most successful, they exercised a cumulative and transforming influence on the organization of the state and its relationship to society in the agrarian societies. But success required the conquerors to undergo a transformation even more radical than the one they achieved in the countries they governed. The following pages discuss each of these points at greater length and in a way that connects each with the theoretical aims of the analysis.

Consider first the nature of the difficulties faced by the agrarian state in mobilizing manpower and resources and standing up to internal disorder or foreign conquest. Different elements of fragility need to be distinguished. The first element in the vulnerability of the agrarian societies was the whole range of problems I have described as reversion to natural economy. There was also the dangerous balance between a still primitive agrarian technology and a relentless demographic pressure. The repeated internal disruptions of that balance might be aggravated by the effects of domestic or foreign fighting. Mass recruitment and widespread devastation might, at any moment, ruin the country and the state.

But these straightforward material explanations are not enough. The agrarian populations of the cleared forest land in Moldavia, Walachia, and Transylvania worked with more rudimentary agricultural implements and were subject to more constant harassment than any of the major agrarian centers of the East. Yet in Danubian and Pontic Europe, where fragmented nomadic societies were encircled by the Ottoman, Russian, and Austrian empires, the agrarian triumph came earliest and most unequivocally, though at the initiative of imperial centers from outside the region itself. At a minimum, we need an independent explanation for governmental weakness in order to complete our understanding of the reversion process.

In the great agrarian empires, power repeatedly fell into the hands of oligarchies that dominated local administration as well as peasant land and labor. Each segment of this relatively unified oligarchy used its position in the state to entrench its privileges in society. When new and more vigorous rulers took over, they tried to destroy this structure of prerogative. But they rarely managed to bring about a lasting improvement in the central government's capacity to mobilize resources and manpower.

Thus, the history of power in these societies presented, on a vast scale, the characteristic oscillation between moments when power declines into a paralyzing medley of vested rights and moments when the central power holders lash out in an effort to destroy settled privilege and reassert their directive will. This oscillation resembled the rhythms found repeatedly throughout history on the smaller scale of organizations and on the larger scale of whole societies. The organization moves constantly between the paralyzing buildup of local privileges and disruptive bouts of centralization. It frees itself from this swing only through its approach to organizational ideals and practices that in turn reflect a striking change in the character and conception of social life. Whole societies move between their moments of routine politics and transformative politics, between the narcolepsy of closed options and the daze of ill-defined choices.

The practical success of the organizational ideal that could escape the destructive alternation always depended on the ability to use and enlarge an open space of social life where people's collaborative or supervisory relations to one another would not be shaped entirely by the structure of the surrounding society and by its available forms of relationship. The relativization of the difference between living in a closed social world and experiencing the indefinition of society requires a still more radical loosening of the hold of rigid systems of hierarchy and division and rigid schemes of ideal and possible association.

The lesser organizational advance and the greater social breakthrough are linked by their common tie with the problem of emancipation from a determinate ordering of social life. They also connect in a more precise manner. Further experiment with the possibilities of organization is limited by the sharp contrast between the task definers and the task executors. But to revise and abolish that contrast, it would be necessary to revise the formative contexts of power and production. These considerations give clues to the basic nature of governmental weakness in the agrarian states.

Every constraint on the capacity of the agrarian state to mobilize resources and manpower, in moments of danger, bore some relation to the strength of social hierarchies and communal divisions. The imperial government could not go on the warpath and expect internal distinctions of rank and corporate membership to fall away, superseded by the relative and transitory but real and powerful unity of a huge cohort. It could not expect the vast working population, in the fields and in the cities, to feel common cause with the elite of great officials, estate holders, and merchants. It could not treat the divisions that defined the society as something revisable, as subject to the perils and opportunities of the moment. The society's order of advantage and antagonism was its fate – a fate that influenced every aspect of production and attachment. The reality and significance of this influence become clear only when you understand the source of the nomadic advantage.

In both the Far East and West Central Asia, nomadic peoples repeatedly proved able to conquer and to rule. Their tactical advantages, beginning with the elementary fact of their mobility, were only the most obvious aspects of their military capability. This capability resulted from a whole way of life. The rule of the nomads over the agrarian peoples was sometimes only a predatory extension of dominion over animal flocks to the mastery of human subjects. Or it involved a limited partnership between conquerors with well-defined economic aims and international merchants in need of protection. At its most successful, however, nomadic rule amounted to a great deal more. The conquerors, at their most inventive, were able to carry over to the task of imperial government some of the formative devices and conceptions that inspired their initial triumphs. The carry-over changed the character of the conquered state and required a revolution in the life and thought of the conquerors.

The roots of the capacity to conquer and to govern must be sought in the most general characteristics of the nomadic societies. Consider the nature of Mongol societies in the generations right before the Yüan Conquest (though much the same might be said of other steppe peoples at other times). Here was the geographical setting that most clearly separated the nomads from their sedentary neighbors and that therefore presents us with the most distinct picture of life in the steppe. There were two recurrent moments in the history of Mongol society: a moment of quiescence and a moment of activity.

In the moment of quiescence, the chief organizing principle of the society was the division of people into clans united by kinship and by ties of personal loyalty. Certain family lines held primacy within each clan and over the people as a whole. But the fixity of the hierarchical order and even the generic distinction between aristocrats and commoners were softened by the personal and quasi-familial nature of the common bonds, by the relative modesty of differences in the living standards of rich and poor, and by the importance of horizontal clan divisions. These divisions were themselves qualified by circulation through marriage, by joint activities of pasturage, plunder, and trade, and by a loose structure of common rule. Each clan lived on the move, although usually within a limited territorial domain.

The moment of activity began when conflict among the nomadic peoples or with their agrarian neighbors escalated. Usually, this conversion depended on a chain reaction of events that included the collapse of other nomadic client states, worsening conflict in the neighboring agrarian countries, with the process of reversion to natural economy in full swing, and the influence of fugitives, ideas, and techniques drawn from the sedentary peoples. It also required the coming of a leader who could muster an expanding retinue, weld together the clans, and turn his people from the satisfactions of plunder and the politics of preemptive security to the fabulous dream of empire.

In the course of these events, the horizontal divisions among clans weakened and the internal hierarchical order of each clan was undermined. The crucial determinant of each person's life chances became his proximity to the war leader and his position within the war machine. Disparities of power and advantage may have become steeper. But this was a new hierarchy, forged in conflict and for the sake of conflict.

The contrast between the moments of quiescence and activity was less sharp than it looks. In both periods, the structural divisions failed to cut to the bone of felt experience. They were shaken by the material facts of movement and fighting. They were overshadowed by the similarity of people's situation and way of life. They were denied by awareness of membership in one people, exposed to a common predicament. They were, above all, undermined by the personal nature of the bonds among people. For the realm of the explicitly personal is also the circumstance in which society is most likely to appear as indefinite in its range of associative opportunity and transcendent over any limited repertory of social forms.

There are an indefinite number of analogous ways in which a people may be said to be in on the secret of power. Under examination, they prove to be variations on overlapping themes. One such theme is the capacity to create organizations out of promises and wills and to sustain these commitments against the odds, over space and time. This was a characteristic trait of the early Romans and the early Americans. People who want power and who understand it erect temples to promise keeping and to willful association. Another entrance to the inner sanctum of power is the ability to combine a readiness for an engagement in collective enterprises of movement, raiding, conquest, and rule with an assertion of the primacy of allegiances between leaders and followers and of the power of these allegiances to harness kinship types and to override local concerns. The sense of this combination is to devalue and destabilize the rigid order of social life. Here was the negative capability of the steppe peoples.[25]

Once turned into a conquest elite ruling over a conquered sedentary society, the nomadic or border nation could draw on an experience that included alternations between periods of quiescence and agitation, that associated agitation with an aggressive collective enterprise rather than with a condition of collective failure, and that overrode local or factional prerogatives for the sake of shared goals. Moreover, the problems of consolidating rule in an alien society made it all the more important for the conquerors to ensure that their imposed state would prove able to mobilize resources and manpower and that its agents would not betray central policies to the interests of local, native elites. Thus, a long-standing experience converged with a unique administrative challenge. This convergence encouraged the development of governmental institutions that more effectively prevented fragmented, indigenous elites from totally penetrating, subduing, and immobilizing the state apparatus.

Everywhere, landowners kept turning into bureaucrats, or bureaucrats into landowners. Everywhere, the central structure of policymaking, policy implementation, tax gathering, and military recruitment continued to rely on the self-interested cooperation of leading regional families. But wherever the conquerors were most successful, they succeeded by imposing a greater measure of restraint on these entrenched habits.

This characterization of what the sedentary empires had to learn from their nomadic conquerors has a significant though oblique relation to the traditional historiographic debate about "feudalism" among the steppe peoples. The source of all difficulties in applying the category of feudalism to these peoples is their persistent capacity to pass, back and forth, between a loose segmentary form of social organization and a condition of total mobilization. This condition required not only allegiance to a paramount leader but the subor-

---

[25] Many of these ideas first developed in conversations with my friend Professor Joseph Fletcher, Jr., of Harvard University.

dination of more particularistic group loyalties and proprietary concerns.[26]

The conquest of agrarian–bureaucratic societies presented the conquest elite with two fateful and closely linked choices. The conquerors were most successful when they responded in ways that allowed them to import into the government of the agrarian-bureaucratic society an element of the nomadic statecraft of mobilization.

One choice was between a more intimate accommodation with the conquered elite and the maintenance of a distinct and superior position. If the conquerors chose the latter course of action, they would find it easier, in the short run, to retain their customs and their prerogatives. On the other hand, they would remain an alien body grafted onto the conquered people. Two different hierarchies would coexist and crisscross: the hierarchy of the conquerors and the conquered and the hierarchy of throne, aristocracy, and peasantry. Any change in domestic or foreign power relations might then result in the overthrow of the conquerors.

The other crucial decision was whether to mobilize the conquered society's resources and manpower for further conquest on the borderlands or to direct effort inward, to a reconstruction of the relations between state and society and revolutionary reform of the organization of government. The policy of permanent war against neighboring peoples and indigenous oligarchs had advantages. It provided the new rulers the means with which to maintain the right link between land grants and personal loyalty. It gave the rulers and the great landholders together a chance to expand their wealth and power without increasing the burden on the peasantry in destructive proportions. It allowed the conquering people as a whole to use the conquered society in a way that minimized the break with their earlier mode of life. But it also made the conquest regime hostage to the gambles of war, and it postponed the reckoning with the agrarian society.

The harder but ultimately more successful path was to arrive at a settlement with the indigenous elites and to substitute a reform of the state for perpetual external conquest and internal reconquest.

---

[26] This alternation forms a central theme in Khazanov's work, the culmination of the controversy about nomads and nomadic feudalism among Soviet historians. See A. V. Khazanov, *Nomads and the Outside World* (1983), trans. Julia Crookenden, Cambridge, Cambridge, 1984. But the theme of the oscillation is recognized even by the classic expositors of the profeudal thesis as the basis for the distinctive characteristics of what they describe as nomadic feudalism. See Boris Vladimir-stov, *Le Régime Social des Mongols: Le Féodalisme Nomade*, trans. Michel Carsow, Adrien-Maisonneuve, Paris, 1948, pp. 110–123.

Some tangible interests might support this alternative route. Among them were the conquering ruler's desire to lessen his dependence on his own aristocrats, the local oligarchies' effort to share in the privileges of state power, and the readiness of peripheral or oppressed peoples within the empire to get ahead by rising through the lower rungs of state service.

For this alternative strategy of rule to succeed, it was not enough to recognize and marshal such interests. It was also necessary to diminish the susceptibility of the preexisting agrarian state to paralysis. This meant casting aside much of the steppe people's accustomed way of life while adapting their tacit vision of power and statecraft to the problems of governing the agrarian society. The emphasis on personal loyalties could serve as a basis for developing new forms of communication and control to safeguard governmental initiative at the heights of power. The Manchu bond-servant system provides a telling example. The insistence on readiness for service and conflict served to drive forward the effort to join private privilege to effective civilian or military service at every hierarchical level, with the result that the presence of local administration could become more real. The Ottoman system of land grants (*timars*), with its relationship to the development of Ottoman administration, was another instance of a concern for preserving the autonomy of the state.

The hypothesis of nomadic statecraft helps to illuminate the differing fates of the agrarian–bureaucratic societies. A comparative analysis of the influence exercised by the presence or absence of the nomadic element in turn yields a refinement of my initial conjecture about the causes of the reversion crisis.

The history of the Byzantine Empire presents the clearest instance of reversion. Of all the long-lasting sedentary societies of Eurasia, it was also the one least affected by nomadic influence. The dismaying reiteration of reversion crises in Byzantium may explain why it is among modern Byzantinists that we can find the clearest appreciation of the nature and importance of the periodic breakdowns discussed in this essay.

China, before the Mongol Conquest and the Ming–Ch'ing Empire, offers a more equivocal instance of a society capable of steeling itself against the recurrence of these disasters. It is telling that before the Yüan (Mongol) period, the most successful examples in Chinese history of active alliance between the central government and a class of state-supporting, state-regulated smallholders can be found in regimes such as the Toba Wei (386–535) and the Sui (581–618), of the period of disunity between the Han and T'ang dynasties. These governments conformed to governments organized on principles more fully realized in the final period of Chinese history. The new regimes were the direct products of the encounter between the steppe or border peoples and the sedentary society.

At the opposite pole of the spectrum of susceptibility to periodic breakdown stood the Ottoman Empire, a state founded on the axioms of nomadic statecraft. The relative imperviousness of the Ottoman Empire to full-fledged reversion crises demonstrates the beneficial effects of the decision to seek an accommodation with indigenous elites, to resist the enticements of perpetual conquest, and to organize a state that superimposed original techniques of mobilization and control on traditional agrarian–bureaucratic habits of government. In all these respects, the Ottomans had a clear advantage over the Seljuqs, whom they replaced.

But the Ming–Ch'ing and Ottoman examples illustrate the limitations as well as the advantages of an escape from the reversion cycles that relied solely on the cumulative strengthening of a governmental capacity to mobilize manpower and resources and to resist the pressures of local elites. For such a state continued to give priority to social control and social stability. It fell captive to attitudes and policies, like the imperial–autarkic approach to the protection problem,[27] that constrained opportunities for technological and organizational innovation. And it left little room to chance, and therefore to invention, in the push and shove of social groups. Nowhere were the principles of nomadic statecraft sufficient to rescue an agrarian–bureaucratic society from the practices of squeeze and bribe in the dealings of bureaucrats with farmers, merchants, and manufacturers.

The Mughal Empire provides an especially illuminating instance of such a failure. The Mughals differed from the Delhi Sultanate, which they succeeded, in much the same way that the Ottomans differed from the Seljuqs: by going further than their predecessors toward the establishment of an inward-turning state, based on a merger between the indigenous and the conquest elites. But the Mughals, relatively few in number, internally heterogeneous, and burdened with a stark religious separation from their subjects, were less successful at this enterprise than the Ottomans. The failure to extend to the Deccan the assimilationist program begun in the north forced the Mughals back into the position of conquest elite. Such an elite had to be constantly on the march in order to award the prizes that enabled it to stay united and to command allegiance. At the first military setbacks, the Mughal government became vulnerable to heightened factionalism within the conquest elite and opportunistic rebellion by the native nobility.

The failure to merge closely enough with local aristocracies and

---

[27] See Chapter 2 of this book.

to transform quickly enough a conquest regime into a reformed agrarian–bureaucratic empire plunged the Mughals into the familiar downward spiral of the nonassimilated and nonassimilating conqueror. Isolation from the normal allegiances and productive activities of the occupied society revived the imperative of further conquest. Military defeats, against the background of nonassimilation, incited factionalism above and insurrection below. The pressures of foreign threats and internal instability forced the government to step up its tax–rent demands on the peasantry and the native landowners. These more burdensome exactions fell most heavily on the smallholders and encouraged, together with further rebellions, the familiar, connected processes of agrarian concentration, market shrinkage, and administrative breakdown. Thus, an agrarian–bureaucratic reversion crisis reemerged as a consequence of the failure of a conquest regime to change itself.[28]

The history of the Mamluks provides an additional twist on such failures. The Mamluks remained so isolated in Egypt and so committed to the perpetuation of their inherited forms of organization that they could neither take advantage of new technological and organizational opportunities nor mobilize resources and manpower by means more effective than continuous pillage. As a result, they became easy prey to a greater conquest elite – the Ottomans – who had accomplished precisely what the Mamluks failed to achieve.[29]

[28] From the vantage point of this analysis, the available theories of Mughal decline are less rival explanations than fragments of the more adequate account that becomes possible when a comparative understanding of the reversion crises combines with insight into the nomadic–sedentary interaction. Thus, one explanation emphasizes the exploitation of the peasants by the Mughal land-revenue assignment holders (*jagirdars*) and the resulting cycle of *zamindar*-led peasant rebellion, additional taxation, and further rebellion. See Irfan Habib, *The Agrarian System of Mughal India*, Asia Publishing House, Aligarh, 1963, pp. 269–271. Another account claims that the inability of the Mughals to defeat the Marathas in the south left too few land-revenue assignments to go around, and produced an escalation of unkept promises and unsupported bribes within the conquest elite. See M. Athar Ali, *The Mughal Nobility under Aurangzeb*, Bombay, 1966. M. N. Pearson generalizes this second hypothesis into a third conjecture that invokes the failure of the Mughals to escape the compulsion of permanent conquest. See "Shivaji and the Decline of the Mughal Empire," *Journal of Asian Studies*, vol. 35 (1976), pp. 221–235. A fourth approach underlines the incapacity of the Mughals to assimilate the nobility of the Deccan. See J. F. Richards, "The Imperial Crisis in the Deccan," *Journal of Asian Studies*, vol. 35 (1976), pp. 237–256. A fifth view emphasizes runaway factionalism. See Satish Chandra, *Parties and Politics at the Mughal Court*, 2nd ed., People's Publishing, New Delhi, 1972. The sole major consideration the suggested analysis cannot easily incorporate is the disruptive effect of European expansion on Asian trade routes and consequently on the revenues of Asian governments and elites. See M. Athar Ali, "The Passing of Empire: The Mughal Case," *Modern Asian Studies*, vol. 9 (1975) pp. 385–396.

[29] See Chapter 3 of this book.

Thus, an analysis of the successes and failures of nomadic statecraft in Asia suggests several conclusions. First, agrarian–bureaucratic society could escape the ordeal of recurrent breakdown by changing in certain ways the organization of the state and the relation of central government to local elites. Such reforms permanently strengthened the governmental capacity to command resources and manpower and diminished the prostration of bureaucracy to local elites. Second, these reforms were generally sponsored by conquest regimes installed by peoples of the Eurasian steppe who had had a long-standing symbiotic relation with the sedentary societies. As conquerors, these peoples turned to advantage distinctive features of their experience in the steppe. Third, the triumph of nomadic statecraft was far from automatic. It required a long series of compromises and self-transformations that brought conquerors and conquered together and produced a state different from both the conquest regime and the conquered government. Fourth, the failure to carry through these compromises and self-transformations regularly resulted in the disintegration of the conquest empire. There followed a revival of the reversion crisis within the conquered agrarian–bureaucratic empire. Fifth, reformed agrarian–bureaucratic empires did not prove to be institutional settings for worldwide economic revolution. Even where the double transformation of conquerors and conquered went furthest and proved most successful, it failed to substitute for the more radical break and the freer collective self-organization of the European trajectory. The improved agrarian–bureaucratic empires remained social environments unfavorable to permanent organizational and technological innovation or to the independent self-organization of social groups. Unlucky timing aggravated the effects of an inherent fragility: the European powers intervened before the remodeled Asian states had worked out the economic and military uses of the nomadic reforms.

A DIGRESSION ON THE STRENGTH OF STATES AND THE DIVISIONS OF SOCIETIES

The preceding discussion of the nomadic correction to the statecraft of the agrarian–bureaucratic empires implies a view of the statishness of states. By states in this setting I mean central government and the whole complex of local administration as related to central government. The statishness or strength of states designates the ability of governmental officeholders and their supporters to formulate and implement rules and policies that do not merely reproduce current social practices or confirm the present distribution of advantage among groups in society. The implementation of such rules and policies requires government to mobilize and redirect human and economic resources on a large scale.

Defining the view of the conditions of statishness suggested by the arguments of this chapter serves two purposes. First, it makes it possible to reconsider from a comparative vantage point my treatment of the encounter between the pastoral and the sedentary peoples of Eurasia. This comparative perspective illuminates the significance of the limited escape from reversion crises that the reformed Oriental states eventually achieved. The other, more general aim of the discussion of statishness is to develop a theme connecting the distinctive concerns of this chapter to the ideas about social organization and social plasticity that animate this whole book.

The statishness of states depends on two sets of conditions that have a tense relation. A state becomes statish in proportion as the people who staff it can work their will, deploying resources and making plans in ways that disrespect and even destabilize custom and privilege. A statish state can cause surprise because it enjoys freedom of maneuver. The more statish a state becomes, the less successfully can you infer its probable actions from a study of the preexisting distribution of wealth and power in the society it governs.

Statishness also depends on a second set of conditions, less evident in the initial definition of the concept. A strong government needs to rule an organized society. Indeed, it requires a society whose specialized organizations are, to a significant extent, self-constituted rather than utterly dependent on the favor of current officeholders. Governmental efforts will make little headway if they find the bonds among people so fragile or so random that government can count on neither loyalty and consent nor informed criticism and directed resistance. Nor can the state itself be the chief organizer. An all-embracing structure of social organization, imposed coercively and suddenly by central government, will not easily take hold. Its consolidation will demand a veritable war of the state against society. This governmental assault on society threatens to disorganize existing institutions without allowing alternative arrangements to emerge. To the extent that such a war succeeded, it would leave the state bloated and vulnerable to the sullen hostility of an unresigned populace.

The central problem of statishness results from the conflict between these conditions. How may a government count on the interlocutors and partners it needs without being immobilized by them and becoming their passive representative? How can we reconcile the autonomy of states and the self-organization of society?

Answers to these questions may at first seem to concern only the defenders of a strong state. The following pages, however, argue the thesis, already implicit in the discussion of the reversion crises and their resolution, that the fulfillment of the conditions of statishness holds a far more general interest. The satisfaction of these conditions intersects and illuminates key requirements for developing the practical productive capabilities of society. More surprisingly, it also satisfies some of the conditions for either a democratic or a dictatorial breakdown of rigid social division and hierarchy. It opens the way for varieties of freedom and oppression even more extreme than those mankind has known until now.

We have grown justifiably suspicious of theories that pretend to show a natural convergence between the conditions of freedom and prosperity. But we would merely indulge necessitarian prejudice in another guise if we forswore insights into the social circumstances and the social inventions that can reconcile our interest in the development of our practical capabilities with our interest in emancipation from the automatisms of culture and the oppressions of society. I argue here that one way to advance toward this reconciliation involves making contemporary states more statish whereas another way reduces central governments to a nearly residual role.

Consider four situations that show how the twin conditions of statishness may be fulfilled or frustrated. Three of these situations represent simplified approximations to actual styles of dealing between state and society although none of them does justice to the subtle, contradictory relations between any particular state and any particular society. The fourth situation describes the hypothetical extension of tendencies at work in contemporary experience. The four circumstances make up an incomplete, open-ended repertory of directions in the dealings between societies and states. To understand this repertory is to grasp how states become statish and what difference their success or failure at this enterprise makes. It is also to gain a perspective from which to assess the larger meaning of the pastoral improvement on the agrarian–bureaucratic empires.

One situation is *disorganized society*. The second condition of statishness fails. Central government faces a society without stable collective instrumentalities of its own devising. Here central government is weak although it may at first appear strong. It confronts people who seem to acquiesce in the projects of officialdom only because they lack institutional means either to collaborate with government or to resist it. The resources, energies, and anxieties of such a society remain almost entirely absorbed in families and villages. Little is left to be mobilized and everything must be taken by force, in the face of incomprehension as well as resistance.

The circumstance of disorganization is never just natural. It results from something having been done to society, almost always by a state, although sometimes by a state imposed through conquest. Thus, the history of modern European imperialism, especially in

Africa, produced circumstances that occasionally approached the character of disorganized society. In such instances the colonial power smashed the existing structure of social organization, disrupting communities as well as polities. Yet, by its aloofness from indigenous elites, its misunderstanding of local realities, and its persistence in a merely predatory dominion, it also prevented new forms of association from emerging.

A second situation is *divided society*. This situation violates the first condition of statishness, the freedom of governmental maneuver. Divided society obeys a rigid plan of social hierarchy and division. The organized social ranks or communities of the divided society exert a stranglehold over manpower and capital. They deny central government the opportunities, the means, and even the desire to execute plans that change practices, derogate privileges, or shift around people and things. Divided society exists in two main variants according to whether division or hierarchy prevails.

The hierarchical aspect of the divided society predominates when society falls into a number of inclusive, sharply defined social ranks. Normally, birth determines access to these ranks. But merit for service, tested by organized competition, may also play a significant part. Position in each rank affords both a certain measure of access (or lack of access) to governmental power and a certain degree of control (or lack of control) over labor, land, and other forms of wealth. The overriding logic of the hierarchical divided society is that economic advantage sustains political privilege and political privilege entrenches economic advantage.

The upper reaches of government and the poorest mass of propertyless workers may fall outside the corporate institutions of this rank order. But the most powerful ranks are constantly tempted to expand the order upward, turning the state into a tame servant of oligarchy. Thus, in preindustrial societies of the hierarchical divided type, there emerges a relatively unified elite of great bureaucrats, landholders, and merchants who penetrate both central government and local administration. Their influence makes unlikely the formulation of plans to keep the magnates in their place, ensure the prosperity of a large class of smallholders and petty merchants or manufacturers, and draw this class into an alliance with government. When bold reformers nevertheless try to carry such plans out, facing the double risk of aristocratic reaction and runaway popular rebellion, they find themselves bedeviled by less ostentatious forms of subversion. Through their hold on local administration, the magnates undermine the execution of the reforms. The same mechanisms enable the grandees to force upon the smallholders, in times of military strife and crop failure, the burdens of additional taxes or soldiers.

Thus, government may end up even more beholden to the magnates than it was before the crisis or the reform attempt. But this humbling of the state has a cost, which usually also provides its own correction. The complete breakdown of governmental authority, and the simultaneous engrossment of peasant land and labor by the oligarchy, results in impoverishment, internal strife, and vulnerability to foreign attack, endangering the domain owners and warlords who sought to benefit from the disintegration of the state.

The agrarian–bureaucratic empires have been by far the most formidable instances of these hierarchical social orders. The story of the demobilization of government in such societies is the tale of the reversion crises told in this chapter.

At times, social division overtook social hierarchy. Society became a loose confederation of large families, corporate communities, or local domains. Although these groups might have steep internal hierarchies, they did not coalesce into a single societywide order of castes or estates. In such societies the state almost ceased to exist.

Remember, for example, the pastoral societies of Eurasia at their moments of relative rest before setting out on a career of conquest or after returning to their preconquest way of life. These peoples often had dominant lineages from whose chieftains or challengers future conquerors arose. Nevertheless, such lineages rarely managed to impose a single hierarchical system on their countrymen.

Another instance is early medieval Europe, a product of a reversion crisis that got out of hand and destroyed much of the government and the market economy of the Roman Empire in the West. Yet it was precisely the finality of this breakdown that allowed the Western European countries to shatter once and for all the closed logic of the reversion crises and to conquer, materially and spiritually, societies that secured only a more limited freedom from the cycles of the agrarian–bureaucratic empires.

The contemporary North Atlantic democracies present a striking variation on the tribulations of government in divided society although they can just as easily be viewed as incomplete versions of what I later call voluntary society. Elements of social division and hierarchy coexist, and each helps moderate the rigors of the other. The organized interest groups and corporate bodies that proliferate in these countries stand in complex relations of inequality in their control of the society-making resources of economic capital, governmental power, and cultural authority. These relations articulate and sustain the realities of class. But they do not support a hierarchy of social ranks that thoroughly determines the life chances of each individual. Political parties – now the prime agents of dispute over the mastery and uses of governmental power – speak for the perceived interests of particular classes and communities. But they also represent speculative opinions and commitments. The divisions among the supporters of such programs do not neatly track class and communal lines.

The organized interests and corporate bodies lack the power to carve out separate domains of social life in which they can do what they want regardless of government rules and policies. They need governmental support to preserve their cherished practices, privileges, or ways of life. But these groups and associations are strong enough to press their conflicting, insatiable, and unstable demands on governments already weakened by constitutional rules that discourage bold programmatic experiments. The organized interests can paralyze but they cannot rule. Governmental politics become a repeated rehearsal of each party's second-best solutions. This deadlock reveals the distinctive style of restraint on statishness that characterizes the rich industrial democracies of today.

In divided society the scheme of corporate-communal distinctions enforces a particular system of recognized group interests, assumed collective identities, and preconceptions about the possible forms of state and society. The best organized and most powerful groups become the preferred interlocutors and helpers of government but also its enervating and frustrated dependents.

A third situation is *the war of the state against society*, the Tocquevillean nightmare. Government tries to bypass the society organized outside it and to impose coercively a transformative project upon the recalcitrant social body. Such a government exercises a dictatorial power harnessed to radical ends. These plans may include an attempt to weaken the hold of established social roles and ranks upon social life and to strengthen the state as at least the transitional agent of a leveling social program. Whether or not the platform of the state at war with society has this revolutionary aim, it requires the mobilization of resources on a societywide scale. Such a platform presupposes the far-reaching independence of the state from the society it would reform. And it opts for a strategy of violent conflict with the many associations, intermediate between central government and the populace, that detain resources and loyalties the rulers want. A classic instance was the campaign of the Soviet state against the Soviet peasantry, triggered by the grain crisis of the late 1920s and culminating in the forced collectivization drive of the early 1930s.

The war of the state against society cannot last long, although the readiness to wage it may serve as a prop to a dictatorship bent on a revolutionary reordering of social life. No amount of violence or rhetoric can abolish the consensual minimum required by every system of rule. The first condition of statishness – the capacity for transformative action – cannot be satisfied through the suppression of the second condition – partnership with a society organized beyond the state.

A fourth situation, *voluntary society*, exists in alternative versions. One version, *empowered democracy*, satisfies both conditions of statishness. In the other version, *polyarchy*, the devolution of power to local government and specialized representative bodies reduces central governments to residual responsibilities. The development of statishness and the dismantling of states are two roads to a social freedom greater than the freedom we enjoy in contemporary industrial democracies. You can map each alternative in ways either increasing or diminishing its distance from present-day arrangements. What matters is the direction of each trajectory rather than the closer or more remote point at which you choose to describe it.

In voluntary society predefined social roles and ranks speak ever less forcefully and precisely about what people may or may not do with their lives. The routine discursive and practical activities that obey and reproduce basic institutions and preconceptions take on more of the quality of the occasional revolutionary remaking of these arrangements and beliefs. People have more fully available to them the means with which to identify, disassemble, and rebuild such institutional and imaginative presuppositions as they go about their ordinary business.[30] So, too, the practices and rights that ensure the individual of a haven of security against oppression and destitution do not insulate any major area of social life against institutionalized challenge and experimental revision.

A society with such features may seem a fantasy. Yet these traits simply extend advantages contemporary societies already enjoy over the ancien régimes and the mercantilist economies they replaced. Consider, for example, a caste system as a way of establishing a connection between individual safeguards and social rigidity, between the safety of the individual in a core of vital protected interests and the closure of social life against conflict and revision. A system of absolute property rights also provides security against personal dependence and misfortune. But property generates less subjugation and freezes less of surrounding society than caste; it leaves more open to invention and chance. Voluntary society supplies people with guarantees of security standing in the same relation to property that property has to caste.

We may realize voluntary society through polyarchy.[31] Polyarchy

---

[30]   On the connection between the reenactment of social hierarchy and the relative unrevisability of basic institutions, see the companion volume to this book, *False Necessity: Anti-Necessitarian Social Theory in the Service of Radical Democracy*, Cambridge, Cambridge, 1987, chapters 2 and 3.

[31]   The term polyarchy is taken from a certain school of American political theory. In this school, however, it has a more generic and less radical meaning. See Robert A. Dahl, *A Preface to Democratic Theory*, Chicago, Chicago, 1956, chapter

devolves as much central governmental power as possible to local communities of neighbors and co-workers as well as to specialized representative authorities such as elected health and education boards. But governmental devolution proceeds together with social organization. All groups must be organized so that society may effectively and equitably wield these devolved powers, lest devolution become an excuse for surrender to preexisting privilege. The emphasis on the link between the devolution of governmental power and the independent organization of civil society distinguishes the program of radical polyarchy from both right-wing libertarianism and centrist communitarianism.

The ultimate feasibility of this path to voluntary society depends on the resolution of a dilemma. If the rules governing devolution and organization represent a lasting fix, to be revised only occasionally and with difficulty, inequalities of power and advantage may soon accumulate. They will be all the more formidable for not having to reckon with the potential animosity of strong democratic central governments. If, on the other hand, a societywide forum exists for changing the rules of devolution and organization and redistributing powers and resources, that forum will become, under whatever name, the magnet of worldly ambition and the kernel of a renascent state. Democracy will advance only because polyarchy will have withdrawn.

The other road to voluntary society is empowered democracy.[32] Far from dismembering the state, empowered democracy satisfies and reconciles the two conditions of statishness. It tries to give social life a maximum of plasticity. Its key strategy is to combine freedom of enterprise and governance at the local level with the opportunity for political parties in central government to promote decisive social experiments, particularly experiments that change institutions as well as policies.

One development of this intuitive idea proceeds along the following lines. Empowered democracy turns the partisan conflict over the control and uses of governmental power into a chance to question and revise the principal arrangements of social life. It encourages parties to try out clearcut solutions. It therefore prefers constitutional techniques that encourage the rapid resolution of impasse among branches or agencies of government and give wide-ranging revisionary powers to parties in office. At the same time such an empowered democracy makes capital and technology widely available, through rotating capital funds, to workers, technicians, and petty

---

3; Charles E. Lindblom, *Politics and Markets: The World's Political-Economic Systems*, Basic Books, New York, 1977, chap. 10.

[32] I develop a program of empowered democracy in chapter 5 of *False Necessity*.

entrepreneurs while retaining in the core representative bodies of the democracy ultimate decisions about the forms of production and distribution. The rights citizens enjoy under such an empowered democracy mirror this institutional plan. They include absolute individual entitlements to economic and civic security, conditional and temporary group claims to portions of social capital, and individual or group powers to provoke the state-enforced destabilization of organizations and practices marred by routines of subjugation that normal politics have failed to disrupt.

The agent with the greatest responsibilities in such a republic is the movement of opinion, especially when organized as a political party. The arrangements of empowered democracy invite attack on the preconceptions and institutions that enable rigid roles and ranks to subsist. Empowered democracy therefore allows political parties to free themselves from their derivative role as instruments of particular classes and communities and to become ever more fully what they already imperfectly are: combinations of people united by shared opinions and commitments and shared interests as defined by these explicit commitments and opinions. Moreover, empowered democracy requires that political parties act as the bearers, if not the authors, of strongly defined programs. Under this regime parties replace classes as the most influential groups.

The choice between polyarchy and empowered democracy depends in part on judgments of both the practical effects of alternative sets of institutional arrangements and the demands each set makes on conduct and motivation. You may ask, for example, whether the devolution polyarchy requires is in fact compatible with a resolution of the dilemma about decentralization and inequality described earlier.

The choice between polyarchy and empowered democracy also turns on commitments to different ways of life and ideals of personality. You may question, for instance, the threat to the delicacy and persistence of communal arrangements that seems inherent in the frequent and far-reaching social innovations favored by empowered democracy. The alternative constitutions are not just different ways to achieve and sustain voluntary society. They are different versions of voluntary society and of the freedom for which it stands.

Thus, the conditions for the flourishing of statishness through empowered democracy coincide with the requirements for dismantling the state through polyarchy. This thesis sheds surprising light on the idea that the existence of the state is bound up with the perpetuation of social hierarchy and that a truly free society is a society free from a state. There is some truth to the idea. Whatever the original causes for the appearance of paramount governments, the state serves, once established, as an instrument for developing and entrenching social hierarchies. Through the familiar logic of the divided society, access to governmental favor helps consolidate economic privilege, and economic privilege makes it possible to expand influence over government. Moreover, the doctrine of polyarchy suggests how a freer society may indeed begin to rid itself of a central government.

The alternative of empowered democracy nevertheless shows a way to turn on its head the prejudice that states persist only so long as class oppression continues. Not all forms of advance toward voluntary society require statish states. But only a voluntary society can satisfy and reconcile the conditions of statishness. Conversely, an empowered state may serve as the tool of an empowered citizenry.

The argument of this chapter about the agrarian–bureaucratic empires and conquest regimes of Eurasia now gains a broader meaning. The problem of the reversion crises represents the prototypical instance of frustration of transformative state action in hierarchical divided societies. And the failure of rulers and high bureaucrats to establish a lasting alliance with the class of smallholders and small scale merchants and manufacturers played an important role in the history of this frustration. The achievement of the more successful conquest regimes was to loosen the constraints the conquered societies imposed on effective government. The conquerors, however, reorganized the administration of the empire without radically changing the character of the society they ruled. For this relative failure the reformed state was to pay a deadly price.

The secret of nomadic reform was to introduce into the agrarian–bureaucratic empires a truncated style of voluntary association within the conquest elite, inaugurated by a limited war of the state against society. The disruption of the mechanisms that allowed the indigenous magnates to manipulate central and local government almost always stopped in time to allow an accommodation between conquerors and conquered. But the effects of the upheaval survived through arrangements and procedures that carried into the sedentary society something of the spirit of the pastoral people on the move. The bonds of personal allegiance, cemented by a shared stake in pillage and dominion, that we find in institutions like the bannerman system of the Manchu dynasty checked the claims of kinship and locality. Such institutions kept their participants practically and emotionally available for the enterprise of rule.

The style of association imported from the steppe, at once personalistic and inclusive, made possible a measure of vigilance over the conquered landholding elites. It also contained or prevented the diversion of the new governing cadres into the quest for private wealth and local influence. Nomadic statecraft worked because, by means like these, it gave the internal organization of government a crude touch of the flexibility of response that strengthens voluntary society.

THE AVOIDANCE OF REVERSION:
ITS SEQUEL AND SIGNIFICANCE

There were many ways to avoid the disaster of recurrent reversion. The three major routes discussed in this essay – the European, the Japanese, and the Chinese–Ottoman – do not compose a closed list of possible solutions. They suggest many other possibilities that either failed to occur or remained without influence.

Of the three, the European response broke most decisively with the habits, institutions, and social alliances characteristic of the agrarian–bureaucratic empires. For this reason, Europe went furthest toward interrupting the reversion cycles once and for all. The spiraling social conflicts that pitted peasants against overlords, in the absence of governmental intervention, opened society up to a range of experiments previously unfeasible and unthinkable.

Two features of the European escape route from the reversion crises proved crucial to this enlargement of possibility. One characteristic was the relative fragmentation of landholding, commercial, and bureaucratic elites: their failure to cohere into a group capable of perceiving and asserting a shared outlook and interest, especially in conflicts over the mastery and uses of governmental power. The other decisive trait was the continuing vitality of rural and urban enterprises that remained both small and independent from magnate control. The success of such enterprises signaled the persistence of a money-using market economy and laid the basis for complex, shifting alliances between central governments and diverse social groups.

The direction of these European events went into partial reverse during the protracted elite realignment and state building of the early modern period. The emerging central states intervened in support of propertied classes that took up novel activities and absorbed new personnel while strengthening their grip on governmental authority. The partnership of government with the big people prevailed over its alliance with the little people and thereby helped set the path that later organizational and technological innovation would pursue.

This long drawn-out reaction, however, failed to undo the effect of the European rupture. The landholding, commercial, and bureaucratic elites never regained the level of relative cohesion in felt identity, interest, and outlook they usually enjoyed in the agrarian–bureaucratic states. Small-scale business, while ceasing in all but a few European areas to maintain a leading role in the organization of economic life, continued everywhere to absorb a major part of labor and resources. In certain regions it even developed, well into the nineteenth and twentieth centuries, the elements of alternative styles of machine-building, work organization, and economic exchange.

The results guaranteed a definitive triumph over the reversion risk. They also opened the way for the startling economic and political experiments of later periods in Western history. Industrialization could allow many different roles to central governments. But, wherever it occurred, industrialization demanded that innovative groups, whether in partnership or not with central government, be able to defy the settled practices and the perceived interests of any compact landholding–commercial- bureaucratic class. It also required that government abandon the predatory fiscalism and the conflict-averse management of social needs (governmental storing of foodstuffs, selective subsidies, policing of markets and manufacture) that represented the twin poles of economic policy in the agrarian–bureaucratic states.

Similarly, the protodemocratic constitutional innovations of the late eighteenth and the nineteenth centuries presupposed a large populace of active and independent individuals, not a mass of prostrate clients. The new constitutional arrangements and legal systems generalized and simplified the group-specific complexes of rights and privileges that distinguished the aristocratic–estatist polities of early modern Europe. For all their hierarchical characteristics, the legal orders of the *ancien régime* implied societies in which many groups, far from the pinnacles of wealth and power, could make claims against one another and against government. These groups had to rest, with a measure of security, in the enjoyment of certain resources and powers of economic initiative and exchange.

The agrarian–bureaucratic empires that had undergone the correction of nomadic statecraft avoided the reversion crises. They failed, however, to provide an environment congenial to rapid material progress through repeated innovation in the organizational settings of production and exchange. They learned how to keep the magnates at bay. But they hosted no radical change in the composition of the propertied and powerful classes or in the relation of these classes to smallholders, petty merchants and manufacturers, and independent wage earners. Nor did these reformed states repudiate the principles that had inspired the attitudes of their predecessors toward the management of the economy: the damaging alternation between a narrow fiscal perspective (skim off as much as you can) and a conservative thrift (regulate production and exchange to prevent abuse or instability while storing up against dearth to avoid discontent and rebellion).

Had these reconstructed governments and societies benefited from a long series of intelligent responses to crises of manageable proportions, they might have gradually won the flexibility for continued economic and administrative experiments. But they enjoyed no such luck. They found themselves confronted by foreign powers that had passed through structure-smashing changes unknown to their Asian prey.

The contrast between the European and the mainland Asian escapes from reversion suggests a more general idea. A sequence of institutional changes, more or less directed from on top, strikes a balance between accommodation to vested interests for the sake of acceptance and innovation for the sake of survival and success. An institutional reform may meet the crisis at hand even if it merely replaces one hierarchy of protected interests by another. The most successful solutions, however, weaken the hold of such hierarchies on the capacity for further innovation. They make it easier to address not just current problems and opportunities but opportunities and problems yet unforeseen. The trouble is that such solutions require a more decisive break with the ruling influences and interests of the established order. For this reason they have usually been products of group conflicts that got out of hand rather than artifacts of deliberation and compromise. The European escape from the worldwide pattern of the reversion crises provides a spectacular example.

These remarks address the differences among the West European, the Japanese, and the mainland Asian antidotes to the reversion crisis. The argument of this study has shown, however, that all the avoidance paths shared certain characteristics. They all prevented the cadres of great landholders and of their bureaucratic and mercantile allies from gaining untrammeled control over the apparatus of government and over peasant land and labor. In this climate of contained prerogative and checked rapacity, towns and trade could survive the ups and downs of the agrarian economy. Central governments could preserve a modest degree of independence from the propertied elites and keep open a line of direct access to the masses of small-scale property-owners and free wage earners.

The solutions differed in the resoluteness with which they restrained the upper orders and left the little people room. But even in Europe, after the reorderings of the early modern period, the more radical economic experiments based on the cooperation and competition of small-scale enterprises remained exceptions to the prevailing pattern of production. These exceptions were far more numerous, successful, and long-lived than you would infer from the stereotype of country-based manufacture and petty industry as mere stages toward later forms of agrarian and industrial concentration. But they nevertheless came to represent deviant rather than dominant tendencies. Similarly, only at a few times and in a few places did central governments enter into something like an explicit antimagnate alliance with smallholders and petty traders and manufacturers.

Because the modern West broke with the disempowering constraints of the agrarian–bureaucratic societies, it was able not only to overcome the cycles of reversion but also to pioneer the economic and political revolutions that were to change the whole world. But because the bolder petty bourgeois and popular solutions remained confined to special regions and to marginal areas of the Western economies, industrialization followed its familiar course: the leading role fell to large-scale business organizations, committed to sharp distinctions between supervisory and executory roles and under the command of proprietary elites and appointed managers. Small-scale property and organizational forms that effaced the contrast between task-defining and task-following activities occupied the auxiliary rearguard and the technological vanguard of industry. Or they were relegated to agriculture, where the alliance of central governments with small business found the opportunities denied to it by industry.

The successful avoidance paths were surprising and occasional. They do not compose a closed list of possible solutions. Many other combinations of beliefs and institutions might have worked. Many of these untried and unimagined solutions might have cut through the reversion cycles in ways that also encouraged further economic innovation. The makeshift quality of the actual solutions to the reversion problem stands out. What social theory, for example, can successfully assimilate to a higher-order logic of social evolution the peculiar effects of the encounter between pastoral and sedentary societies, marked by the distinctive traits of mainland Asian geography?

Certain themes nevertheless persist. Neither the antinomian social science of our day nor social theories like Marxism that treat certain indivisible institutional systems as indispensable prerequisites of particular levels of productive capability can adequately appreciate these themes.

In preindustrial societies with elaborate administrative structures, sharply defined social hierarchies, and largely agrarian economies, economic prosperity and governmental stability depended on success at keeping the higher landed interest from engrossing peasant land and subjugating peasant labor. Small- and large-scale property had to coexist within a market network that enabled town- or country-based merchants and manufacturers to carry on their activities. Central governments had to maintain fiscal and military access to small-holders and independent urban groups.

Any crisis that struck directly at agriculture or forced the central government to step up its demands for taxes and soldiers threatened the agrarian economy and the administrative machinery with the catastrophe of reversion. The people in high office and the masses of peasants and small-scale proprietors shared an interest in combatting oligarchic power. This shared interest, however, remained insufficient to change the institutions, the alliances, and the habits of mind that presented the danger. Ways out came in mainland Asia through the deus ex machina of reform by conquerors and in early medieval Europe through the extended disintegration of government. Only under the Tokugawa *bakufu* did a central government prove able and willing to contain the magnates. In the event, magnate containment resulted from policies of enforced residence in the castle towns, and one of the conditions that made this unique solution acceptable enough to be effective was the simultaneous disarming of the peasantry during the early years of the Tokugawa regime.

The difficulty faced by reformers anxious to protect the yeomanry is easy to understand. The problem of the reform cycles would never have appeared in the first place if government had enjoyed far-reaching autonomy from grandee influence rather than being more or less penetrated by the very overlords it had to control. Moreover, in the unreconstructed agrarian–bureaucratic society, the reformer determined to stand side by side with the smallholder and the merchant was likely to find himself caught between magnate reaction and runaway peasant rebellion.

The constraints that prompted the recurrence of the reversion crisis represent a special case of a more general phenomenon: the ambivalent role of hierarchy as an obstacle to practical success. At certain levels of territorial size, economic surplus, technological sophistication, and administrative complexity – levels intermediate between the poorest societies and the societies we know today – a rigid, inclusive hierarchy of wealth and power may prove economically useful. It may permit the nearly automatic extraction and reinvestment of a surplus. It can also provide a relatively uncontroversial blueprint for allocating claims to wealth and income among competing social groups.

We need not suppose, in the manner of a narrow functionalism, that these material advantages explain the development of such hierarchies. A more plausible speculative explanation would begin with the consequences of the emergence of central governments and highly developed administrative systems in large populous countries like the societies discussed here. Wherever such governments arose they furnished a basis for the development of hierarchies of advantage: access to governmental power served to entrench social privilege, which in turn helped sustain the power that had created it. If the resulting inequalities had been economically disastrous the societies that bore them could not have survived and flourished as they did. The positive economic consequences of rigid schemes of social ranks weigh more as contributory explanations of the survival of such schemes than as accounts of their origin.

Besides, steep, societywide social hierarchies exact a material as well as a moral price. They give rise to a constraining logic of group interests such as the logic of feasible policy options – feasible because acceptable and imaginable – that beleaguered would-be reformers in agrarian–bureaucratic societies. Constraints like these prevent societies from dealing successfully with their recurrent practical problems and make the most urgent measures seem irresponsible daydreams. They also set up obstacles to the experiments in the renewal and recombination of people, resources, and institutional arrangements that make possible breakthroughs to higher levels of productive capability.

A system of vested group interests operates like an obsession condemning its victims to go through motions whose futility they partly grasp. But these endlessly reenacted collective compulsions are not mere prejudices that better insight can dispel. They draw their force from the unavailability, in ordinary social life, of practices and discourses that enable people to challenge and revise both established institutional arrangements and ruling beliefs about human association. Such arrangements and beliefs keep current strategies and expectations on course.

People have two major ways to break such constraints. One way is to disengage governmental power from oligarchic privilege so that either government itself or nongovernmental enterprises can mobilize manpower and resources on a wider scale and with fewer hindrances. To this end, government need not achieve a position of relative neutrality among the ranks and communities of society. Nor need it enjoy the authority to impose far-reaching plans upon a resistant nation. It must, however, preserve a substantial measure of independence from the upper orders. And it must not allow these orders to serve as its sole intermediary in dealing with the working masses and the lesser powers of society.

The other instrument to break the institutionalized compulsions that impoverish and belittle us is self-defensive mobilization from the bottom up, which enables ordinary people to initiate small-scale institutional experiments foreshadowing alternative forms of economic and social organization. This force can go much further than the carefully laid plans of reformers because it rides roughshod over the fine calculations of probable resistance that reformers dare not disregard. But unplanned uncontrolled mobilization is blind. It can destroy more than it produces, and it lacks built-in direction. Thus, the strange concatenation of events that allowed Western Europe to break so decisively with the conditions of the reversion crisis offers no model for a practice of social invention.

Transformative practice must combine mobilization from above with mobilization from below. It must do so in such a way that the former becomes an instrument of the latter while the latter ceases to be an extrainstitutional accident and turns instead into an institutionalized activity. When people begin to establish institutions that encourage this combination, the collective quest for worldly success through social plasticity joins the history of freedom.

APPENDIX I:
NOTE ON SOURCES FOR THE COMPARATIVE STUDY OF ANTIREVERSION POLICIES

The best introduction to a more textured study of the problems this essay addresses may well be an analysis of the content and the fortunes of the antireversion policies. These policies were the small repertory of reforms through which the agrarian-bureaucratic states of Eurasia tried to avoid or contain the recurrent crises of agrarian concentration, economic decommercialization, and administrative fragmentation. This note lists sources that I found especially helpful. A little curiosity goes a long way: if the list shows nothing else, it demonstrates that materials for broad-ranging yet detailed and disciplined comparison of the experiences discussed here are at hand.[33]

1. The policy of recruiting a bureaucratic staff from groups directly below the landowning aristocracy. On the Chinese experiment in weakening the link between the bureaucratic staff and local landowning elites through the reforms of the late T'ang and the Sung, see James T. C. Liu, *Reform in Sung China: Wang An-shih (1021–1086) and His New Policies*, Harvard, Cambridge, 1959; Denis Twitchett, "The Composition of the T'ang Ruling Class," in *Perspectives on the T'ang*, eds. Arthur F. Wright and Denis Twitchett, Yale, New Haven, 1973, pp. 47–85; Brian E. McKnight, "Fiscal Privileges and the Social Order," in *Crisis and Prosperity in Sung China*, ed. John Winthrop Haeger, Arizona, Tucson, 1975, pp. 79–100; David G. Johnson, *The Medieval Chinese Oligarchy*, Westview, Boulder, Colo., 1977, pp. 19–20, 149–152; Patricia Ebrey, *Aristocratic Families of Early Imperial China*, Cambridge, Cambridge, 1978. To Professor Timothy Brook of the University of Toronto, I am indebted for accounts of writings of Niida Noboru and other Japanese historians of China. On the repeated failure of attempts clearly to sever the connection between bureaucracy and landowning elites and on the consequences for the constraints within which policy had to move, see E. A. Kracke, Jr., "Family vs. Merit in Chinese Civil Service Examinations," *Harvard Journal of Asiatic Studies*, vol. 10 (1947), pp. 103–123; Victor Lippit, "The Development of Underdevelopment in Chinese History,"

---

[33] This note is transcribed from the bibliographical notes to *False Necessity*: *Anti-Necessitarian Social Theory in the Service of Radical Democracy*, Cambridge, Cambridge, 1987.

Modern China, vol. 4 (1978), pp. 251–328. But for a view that emphasizes the role of official status as a source rather than a consequence of landowning status, see Ho Ping-Ti, *The Ladder of Success in Imperial China*, Columbia, New York, 1967.

On the Ottoman palace system as an attempt to achieve through very different measures objectives similar to the aims of the Chinese examination system, see Joseph von Hammer, *Geschichte des Osmanischen Reiches*, Hartleben, Pest, Germany, 1828, vol. 2, pp. 218–249 (at the time of the death of Mohammed II); Norman Itzkowitz, *Ottoman Empire and Islamic Tradition*, Knopf, New York, 1972, pp. 49–60; Stanford J. Shaw, *History of the Ottoman Empire and Modern Turkey*, Cambridge, Cambridge, 1976–1977, vol. 1, pp. 113–139.

For a representative study of the use of this technique by the prerevolutionary absolutist monarchies of Europe, see Otto Hintze, "The Commissary and His Significance in General Administrative History: A Comparative Study," in *The Historical Essays of Otto Hintze*, ed. Felix Gilbert, Oxford, New York, 1975, pp. 267–301. See also Martin Göhring, *Die Amterkäuflichkeit im Ancien Régime*, Ebering, Berlin, 1938; Roland Mousnier, *La Vénalité des Offices sous Henri IV et Louis XIII*, Presses Universitaires, Paris, 1971; Eckart Kehr, "Zur Genesis der Preussischen Bürokratie und des Rechtstaates," in *Moderne Deutsche Sozialgeschichte*, ed. Hans-Ulrich Wehler, Kiepenheuer, Cologne, 1973, pp. 37–54.

2. The policy of making the nobility dependent for land tenure on service to the state. On the system of *pomestye* land in Russia and its assimilation to *votchina* tenure, see Jerome Blum, *Lord and Peasant in Russia*, Princeton, Princeton, 1961, pp. 170–188, 252–255. On the Korean system of Merit Subjects and the comparable development it underwent, see Edward W. Wagner, *The Literati Purges: Political Conflict in Early Yi Korea*, Harvard, Cambridge, 1975, pp. 19–21; Susan S. Shin, *Land Tenure and the Agrarian Economy of Early Yi Korea*, 1973, doctoral dissertation on file at Yenching Library, Harvard University.

Consider as a further example the status of "bannermen" within the Manchu Conquest elite in China. See Jonathan D. Spence, *Ts'ao Yin and the K'ang-hsi Emperor, Bondservant and Master*, Yale, New Haven, 1966, pp. 2–18; Robert B. Oxnam, *Ruling from Horseback: Manchu Politics in the Oboi Regency, 1661–1669*, Chicago, 1975, pp. 38–40, 47–49, 124–126, 170–175. And compare to the Mughal *mansabdars* (rank holders) and *jagirdars* (land-revenue assignment holders). See Stephen P. Blake, "The Patrimonial-Bureaucratic Empire of the Mughals," *Journal of Asian Studies*, vol. 39 (1979), pp. 77–94, and the Mughal studies cited later.

3. The policy of agrarian dualism.

   a. The reliance of central government on landlords who, though not involved in central administration, have special fiscal and military obligations. On the Byzantine *ktemata stratiotika*, see Hélène Antoniadis-Bibicou, *Etudes d'Histoire de Byzance à Propos ou "Théme des Caravisiens"*, Services d'Edition et de Vente des Productions de l'Education Nationale, Paris, 1966, pp. 99–114; Arnold Toynbee, *Constantine Porphyrogenitus and His World*, Oxford, London, 1973, pp. 134–145. On the Ottoman *timariots*, see Stanford J. Shaw, *History of the Ottoman Empire*, vol. 1, pp. 125–127; Gyula Kaldy-Nagy, "The First Centuries of the Ottoman Military Organization," *Acta Orientalia Scientiarum Hungaricae*, vol. 31 (2), (1977), pp. 147–183. On the Mughal *zamindaris*, see Irfan Habib, *The Agrarian System of Mughal India (1556–1707)*, Asia Publishers, London, 1963, pp. 136–189; M. Athar Ali, *The Mughal Nobility under Aurangazeb*, Asia Publishing House, Bombay, 1966; Norman Ahmad Siddiqui, *Land Revenue under the Mughals*, Asia Publishing House, Bombay, 1970, pp. 21–40. On the Aztec military life-tenants, see Nigel Davies, *The Aztecs: A History*, Univ. of Oklahoma, Norman, 1980, pp. 80–81. On the Byzantine *pronoia*, see Georges Ostrogorsky, *Pour l'Histoire de la Féodalité Byzantine*, trans. Henri Gregoire, Institut de Philologie et d'Histoire Orientales et Slaves, Brussels, 1954.

b. The reliance on state-obligated small-holders and peasant communities.

On the exemplary Byzantine developments and debates, see Paul Lemerle, "Esquisse pour une Histoire Agraire de Byzance," *Revue Historique*, vol. 219 (1958), pp. 32–74, vol. 219 (1958), pp. 254–284, vol. 220 (1958), pp. 43–94; George Ostrogorsky, "The Peasant's Preemption Right" (see earlier references), and *History of the Byzantine State*, trans. Joan Hussey, Rutgers, New Brunswick, N.J., 1969, pp. 269–276; Arnold Toynbee, *Constantine Porphyrogenitus and His World*, pp. 122–134. For the aftermath of the failure to uphold the policy of smallholder protection, see Angeliki E. Laiou-Thomadakis, *Peasant Society in the Late Byzantine Empire*, Princeton, Princeton, 1977.

On the policy of agrarian dualism at its most successful and aggressive in Chinese history, see Wolfram Eberhard, *Das Toba-Reich Nordchinas: Eine Soziologische Untersuchung*, Brill, Leiden, 1949, pp. 206–221, which should be considered against the background of Eberhard's "Zur Landwirtschaft der Han-Zeit," *Mitteilungen des Seminars für Orientalische Sprachen zu Berlin, Ostasiatische Studien*, vol. 35 (1932), pp. 74–105; Denis Twitchett, "Lands Under State Cultivation Under the T'ang," *Journal of the Economic and Social History of the Orient*, vol. 2 (1959), pp. 162–336 (on the connection of agrarian dualism with the system of military colonies); Denis Twitchett, *Land Tenure and the Social Order in T'ang and Sung China*, Oxford, Oxford, 1962. For the northern dynasties and Sui versions of the *fu-ping* system (divisional militia based on smallholders with military responsibilities), see Arthur F. Wright, "The Sui Dynasty (518–617)," in *Cambridge History of China*, vol. 3, *Sui and T'ang China, 589–906*, Part I, ed. Denis Twitchett, Cambridge, Cambridge, 1979, pp. 96–103; and for the T'ang version see Howard J. Wechsler, "T'ai-tsung (reign 626–649) the Consolidator" in the same volume, pp. 207–208. See also Philip A. Kuhn, *Rebellion and Its Enemies in Late Imperial China: Militarization and Social Structure*, Harvard, Cambridge, 1970, pp. 15–20. On the effect that the failure of the policy of agrarian dualism had on agrarian structure in the subsequent Sung period, see Mark Elvin, *The Pattern of the Chinese Past*, Stanford, Stanford, 1973, pp. 69–83; and for a somewhat contrasting view, Joseph McDermott, *Land Tenure and Rural Control in the Liangche Region during the Southern Sung* (doctoral dissertation on file at Cambridge University). It is important to distinguish the policy of support for smallholders from the vaguer and looser set of anticoncentrationist agrarian ideals present at all stages in Chinese history. See Hsu Chung-shu, "The Well-Field System in Shang and Chou," in *Chinese Social History*, trans. E'Tu Zen Sun and John de Francis, Octagon, New York, 1972, pp. 3–17; Mark Elvin, *The Pattern of the Chinese Past*, pp. 47–51, 59–63; Denis Twitchett, *Financial Administration under the T'ang Dynasty*, Cambridge, Cambridge, 970, pp. 1–11; Joseph Levenson, *Confucian China and Its Modern Fate: A Trilogy*, Univ. of California, Berkeley, 1968, vol. 3, pp. 16–43.

4. The agency of the common people in a social world that revolves within the limits set by the rehearsal and frustration of the reform options previously discussed.

    a. The privileged urban mob. See Paul Veyne, *Le Pain et le Cirque: Sociologie Historique d'un Pluralisme Politique*, Seuil, Paris, 1976.

    b. The temporary stabilization of the policy of agrarian dualism. On the Byzantine peasant commune, see Georg Ostrogorsky, "Die Ländliche Steuergemeinde des Byzantinischen Reiches im X. Jahrhundert," *Vierteljahrschrift für Sozial- und Wirtschaftsgeschichte*, vol. 20 (1927), pp. 23–108; George Ostrogorsky, "La Commune Rurale Byzantine," *Byzantion*, vol. 32 (1962), pp. 138–166. For a comparative discussion that emphasizes the link between the redistributive and the control aspects of the peasant commune, with the eventual substitution of smallholding by enserfment, see G. I. Bratianu, "Servage de la Glèbe et Régime Fiscal: Essai d'Histoire Comparée, Roumaine, Slave et Byzantine," in *Études Byzantines d'Histoire Économique et Sociale*, Geuthner, Paris, 1938.

On the nineteenth-century redistributive Russian village community, see Geroid Robinson, *Rural Russia under the Old Regime*, Univ. of California, Berkeley, 1972, pp. 117–128; Francis W. Watters, "The Peasant and the Village Commune," in *The Peasant in Nineteenth-Century Russia*, ed. Wayne S. Vucinich, Stanford, Stanford, 1968, pp. 133–157; Jerome Blum, *Lord and Peasant in Russia*, Princeton, Princeton, 1961, pp. 504–535.

On village communities and the role of village officers under the Southern Sung, see Brian E. McKnight, *Village and Bureaucracy in Southern Sung China*, Chicago, Chicago, 1971.

On peasant-held *raiyati* villages in Mughal India, see Irfan Habib, *The Agrarian System of Mughal India*, Asia Publishing, London, 1963, pp. 111–135; Ishtiagi Husain Qureshi, *The Administration of the Mughal Empire*, N. V. Publications, Lohanipur, pp. 281–294.

On the village and the leading village families under the Tokugawa *bakufu*, see Thomas C. Smith, *The Agrarian Origins of Modern Japan*, Stanford, Stanford, 1959, pp. 1–11.

c. On peasant rebellion as a confirmation of the structure it defies, see the discussion of the Japanese experience in Irwin Scheiner, "Benevolent Lords and Honorable Peasants: Rebellion and Peasant Consciousness in Tokugawa Japan," in Tetsuo Najita and Irwin Scheiner, eds., *Japanese Thought in the Tokugawa Period, 1600–1868*, Chicago, Chicago, 1978, pp. 39–62.

APPENDIX II:
THE STANDPOINT OF THE NOMADIC CONQUERORS

A thesis of this chapter is that the encounter between agrarian–bureaucratic societies and the pastoral peoples who occasionally conquered and ruled them played a vital role in the process by which some of those societies eventually escaped or contained the reversion cycles that had beset them. By assimilating governmental institutions and attitudes toward statecraft pioneered by their conquerors, the conquered took an important step in the gradualistic and relatively nonconflictual route of escape from reversion crises. Often this assimilation was the result of episodes spread across many centuries. Thus, in China, not until the Ming–Ch'ing Empire do we find a society seemingly immune to the peculiarly radical combination of economic decommercialization and political fragmentation that had recurred in earlier periods of Chinese history. But the institutional innovations of the Ming had their antecedents in the Yüan (1260–1380) and even in far earlier periods, most notably the long, troubled interval between the Han and the T'ang.

As in almost all the historical literature, this chapter considers the dealings between agrarian–bureaucratic societies and nomadic conquerors from the standpoint of the settled peoples. The following table reverses the perspective. It describes the major ways the pastoral peoples dealt with the agrarian civilizations they conquered, coexisted with, and depended on. All the allusions refer to a single, gigantic theater: the relation of the pastoral peoples of the inner-Asian steppe to the great agrarian states that flourished along the fertile periphery of the steppe. Nothing important in my argument turns on the extent to which problems and alternatives similar to those mentioned here reappeared in other more confined geopolitical settings where pastoral peoples confronted societies of planters: for example, Saharan conquest states like the Songhai Empire in relation to Hausaland, and Hausaland in relation to the West African forest and coastal kingdoms. The point is to identify and explain variable change without appealing to theories that predefine its possible forms and outer limits.

This table, then, has aims that go beyond the attempt to present a fuller view of an important link in the argument of this chapter. It illustrates the conception of branching points and multiple pathways, invoked so many times in this book. It also emphasizes, in a nutshell, a central thesis of *Plasticity into Power*: the homely idea that worldly success requires self-transformation. Moreover, self-transformation must move toward a heightened flexibility of response to circumstances imperfectly foreseen or understood. As a result, it demands not just replacing one particular collective identity with another but also weakening the commitment to any collective identity defined by reference to distinctive practices and institutions. A people that wants to exempt even a small and sacred part of its customs from this self-transformative requirement discovers, sooner or later, that it enjoys no such exemption and that every attempt to secure one proves fatal. However familiar this conception may seem in the abstract, its historical applications go beyond belief. To make the point, there is nothing like the history of these transactions between the peoples of the steppe and the great civilizations of Asia.[34]

---

[34] For a straightforward survey of many of the peoples and events to which this note alludes, see Luc Kwanten, *Imperial Nomads: A History of Central Asia 500–*

The "moments" and options the table describes represent points on an imaginary spectrum. At one pole of this spectrum lies a situation in which the pastoral nation makes only episodic contact with the agrarian civilization along its borderland, and maintains much of its own way of life. At the opposite pole is the circumstance in which the conquerors merge with the conquered elites, changing themselves in the process. The points along this spectrum represent moments in an almost Hegelian sense: possible advances toward more powerful capabilities, through changes of response and changes of self. The goal here, almost never fully grasped or clearly intended, is worldly success – success at rule, production, and war.

The sequence of moments does not delineate a single evolutionary path, nor even a limited set of evolutionary possibilities, open to pastoral peoples embarked on a career of conquest. It plots what actually happened in Eurasia during a particular stretch of time. It suggests why certain responses to a similar predicament turned out easier to come by and why other approaches, more exacting and less probable, allowed some pastoral conquerors to avoid reversion crises and keep the mantle of power.

To the late Professor Joseph Fletcher, Jr., of Harvard University, I owe much help in the study of the materials and the formulation of the ideas summarized in the following table.

_1500_, Univ. of Pennsylvania, 1979. For a more analytic study, see A. M. Khazanov, *Nomads and the Outside World* (1983), trans. Julia Crookenden, Cambridge, Cambridge, 1984.

Table 2. *What happened to the steppe peoples of Eurasia whenever they got involved in "history":*
a study in the open-ended logic of live options and in the imperative of self-transformation

Moment I: The ongoing encounter with an agrarian civilization	
1. Pastoralism as usual, alternating with pillage at the borderland of the agrarian empire	Probable outcomes: (a) long-lasting, low-level stability (increasingly less likely); (b) absorption into the empire (e.g., early Byzantine forced settlement of Slavs; repeated Chinese incorporation of Sinkiang and Turkestan); (c) outright conquest by other pastoral peoples who have mastered some of the organizational economic, or military techniques of the agrarian civilization first (e.g., triumph of the Mongols over the nomadic Merkids and Naimans as well as over the semisedentary and half-sincized Jürchen, the Karts, and the Tartars); (d) conquest of agrarian civilization as in 5.
2. A client kingdom at the frontier of the agrarian empire (e.g., the Arabian Ghassanid kingdom in relation to the Byzantine Empire, the Arabian Lakmid kingdom in relation to the Sassanian Empire, the Samanid Empire in relation to the Abbasid Caliphate; the Crim Tartars in relation to the Ottoman Empire)	Serves the agrarian empire as a buffer against more violent outlanders and as a vehicle for international trade. Receives, in turn, the technological, financial, and spiritual benefits of participation in the world order of the agrarian civilization, together with the opportunity to preserve a relatively independent, though compromised seminomadic existence. Likely outcomes: as in (1), though (a) of (1) becomes even less likely because the stability of the client kingdom comes to depend on the transformations of the agrarian world order, the internal factional strife of the elites, and the struggles of this empire with its agrarian or nomadic enemies.
3. An independent seminomadic community with a center of its own (e.g., the Zaporozhan Cossacks)	A historical tour de force. Hard to stop the community from being wholly incorporated into both the international system and the way of life of the agrarian society. The steppe people may increasingly take on the economic and military techniques, and the social arrangements (pronounced society-wide hierarchy and corporate-communal divisions) of an agrarian imperial civilization or pass into the service of external powers (e.g., the Cossack return first to Polish, then to Russian guidance), or meet one of the other fates described in this analysis of Moment I.

Table 2. *What happened to the steppe peoples of Eurasia whenever they got involved in "history":*
a study in the open-ended logic of live options and in the imperative of self-transformation

4. Creation of a novel form of social life through partnership between an elite of international traders and a military steppe aristocracy, brought together by enterprising leadership and willing to borrow the cultural language of an agrarian civilization (e.g., the Kievan Rus' under Jaroslav).

5. The nomadic invaders put together an empire out of the bits and pieces of previous agrarian or nomadic regimes that they have torn to shreds. They then turn into a landholding warrior aristocracy distinct from the subject peoples.

To the extent that the partnership succeeds, the live options become those of other agrarian empires; nomadism is superseded. The society moves to the characteristic problems of an agrarian–bureaucratic society, as analysed in this chapter, bypassing Moment II. Insofar as the merger comes unstuck, the society is forced back into one of the other options described in Moment I or falls prey to agrarian or nomadic conquest.

Further possibilities of practical empowerment result from this higher measure of self-transformation. (a) The standard case. Examples: Before the rise of the Timurid and Mongol empires: the Safavid, Samanid, Ghaznavid, Qarakhnid, Seljuq, Ghur, and Khwarazmshah empires. The Timurid Empire itself. The Mongol Empire and most of its successor states. After the collapse of the Safavid and Mughal empires: the empires of Nadir Shah and Ahmad Shah Durrani – related to the earlier versions according to the maxim: "first as drama, then as farce." Overlaps with (2). Characteristically encouraged by the transfer of economic, military, and organizational techniques from agrarian empires or from other steppe peoples better aquainted with the agrarian civilization. Important elements of the earlier form of life persist. Minimal central organization; new societywide hierarchies and corporate–communal divisions encrust themselves on preexisting patron–client relations within the steppe aristocracy rather than displacing them; clear-cut division between the ruling and the ruled peoples; impossibility of recruitment of a large-scale peasant army; continuing economic dependence on the international caravan trade; almost entirely parasitic relation to the agricultural and artisanal activities of the conquered populations; oscillation between rearguard effort to uphold customs and perceptions of the nomadic society and fascination with the culture of the vanquished. Crucial vulnerabilities: (1) the largely personalistic and predatory links between capital and outlands;

(2) the failure to develop an internal economic base to replace dependence on the caravan trade and finance continuing large-scale military operations and an enlarged administrative apparatus; (3) the absence of a collective project that can be given both a higher spiritual meaning and a detailed, although changing, institutional form.

(b) A special case. The Yüan and the Manchu (Ch'ing) in China. On the one hand, the conquerors remain largely confined to the political apex of the preexisting agrarian empire. On the other hand, they accept most of that empire's established organizations and the supremacy of its ideals of government and life. The conquerors play a more or less well-recognized role within the conquered society. Their foreignness ceases to prevent them from ruling effectively. The opportunities and risks resemble those in Moment III.

(c) Breakthrough to greater administrative, productive, and military capability, thanks to more radical innovation, further effacing the distinctive, original identity of the conquering people. Examples: Toba Wei Empire in China; the Safavid, Ottoman, and Mughal empires. A marginal case: the Il-Khanate. Aspects of the breakthrough: (1) Strengthening of relatively impersonal links between central government and the conquered regions and between higher and lower levels of the governmental hierarchy. (2) Continuing effort by government to shape or regulate large segments of society and corresponding multiplicity of avenues by which these segments can participate, more or less obliquely, in the contest over central governmental power. (3) Direct participation of the conquerors in landholding and tie-in of land tenure to military obligations. (4) Reliance on conquered peasants or gentry for crucial military support; agrarian policy to protect these sources of military strength. (5) Direct governmental sponsorship of agricultural, artisanal, and mercantile activities. No major dependence on international caravan trade; greater economic autarky. (6) Centrality of labor-intensive food-grain agriculture; dangerous oscillations between predominance of protected medium farms and smallholdings in hands of groups with military obligations and

Table 2. *What happened to the steppe peoples of Eurasia whenever they got involved in "history":*
a study in the open-ended logic of live options and in the imperative of self-transformation

land concentration in favor of magnates; confinement of international commerce to relatively isolated position in economy and polity; linked with the conversion of tax duties to monetary form as well as with elite luxury or limited foreign trade; manufacturing subordinated to military needs and palace splendors. (7) Development of a new vision of imperial order, inspired by beliefs of conquering and conquered peoples, and almost always related, in tense and ambivalent fashion, to a religion. Clearer conflict between imperial and priestly, scholarly, bureaucratic authorities. (8) Softening of the felt conflict between the collective identities of ruling and ruled peoples. (9) Decisive and irreversible abandonment of the practices and ideals of nomadism but carryover of the outlook of a warrior despotism from an earlier historical moment. (10) Strengthening of societywide hierarchies and deepening of the divisions: (a) between the privileged, ruling nation (together with its clients, allies, and favorites) and everyone else; (b) between the privileged ranks of societies, almost always beneficiaries of agrarian–military privileges, and the nonprivileged peasant mass. Special incongruity and instability of the place occupied by the commercial elites, especially when they do not belong to the conquering people. (11) Importance of patron–client ties, both reinforcing and undermining societywide hierarchies and corporate–communal institutions. These developments produce a new set of options, described in Moment II.

Moment II: The dream of empire (especially as arising from the reform of a preexisting agrarian–bureaucratic state by a conquest regime, as in
Moment I-5c)

The impulse to raid and conquer on the borderline of the empire (Examples: the Ch'i-tan, the Seljuqs, the Mughals in relation to the Deccan)

The benefits of uninterrupted conquest.
(1) To the central rulers in relation to the landholders: makes it easier for the imperial government to insist on a close link between land tenure and the satisfaction of military obligations; provides a constant stream of benefices

ing their permanent settling down as hereditary landowners; postpones or moderates conflict between emperors and magnates for control of land and work force; deflects from factional struggle among the magnates and notables for fixed stores of land, power, and honor (an effect similar to that of economic growth on the class rivalries of contemporary industrial democracies); (2) to the rulers and landholders alike in relation to the peasantry: expansion at the borderlands serves as a source of wealth and manpower; makes it less necessary to step up exploitation of the peasantry; by limiting economic parasitism, contributes to the relative stability of agrarian relations in the heartland of the empire; (3) to the conquering people in relation to the foreign and unassimilated masses or notables: postpones the choice between the practices and perceptions of an earlier warrior despotism and the responsibilities of agrarian empire.

The perils of the commitment to conquest:
(1) Mounting likelihood of contact with strong foreign centers of power.
(2) Possibility of reaching unproductive desert areas at the fringes of the empire.
(3) Diminishing returns of size. The larger the dimensions of the empire, the more probable it becomes that increased costs of maintaining the broader administrative and communications network counterbalance the economic advantages of size. Moreover, expansion multiplies the strategic difficulties of defense, attack, and repression of internal sedition.
(4) As the maintenance of the structure of rule becomes more costly and fitful and the strategic burdens greater, several destabilizing forces operate.
(a) Stepped-up competition among the notables for land, power, honor.
(b) Attempts by the emperors to induct part of the native peasantry and notables into the military and administrative structure of separate imperial domains, aggravating the rivalry between the imperial rulers and the magnates.
(c) Increased exploitation of the peasants: by the emperors to meet the burdens of bloated empire; by the landholders, to satisfy fiscal and military obligations. The disturbance of agrarian relations fosters peasant rebellions and encourages the magnates to create large estates through the engrossment of

Premises of thesis of diminishing returns of size.
1. The overwhelming majority of population and economy remains agricultural.
2. No technological revolution has yet diminished the cost of imperial rule to the populace in general and the working classes in particular.

Absence of technological transformation intimately connected with whole character of society. (See discussion of full-scale agrarian empires in the main body of Chapter 1.)
3. Especially great difficulty in eliciting and maintaining loyalties of large number of peasants and soldiers because of superimposition of two hierarchies: (a) the conquering foreign–native conquered hierarchy; (b) the hierarchy of throne, aristocracy, and peasantry.

Table 2. *What happened to the steppe peoples of Eurasia whenever they got involved in "history":*
a study in the open-ended logic of live options and in the imperative of self-transformation

The impulse to turn inward, toward rule of an agrarian empire, with no commitment to perennial conquest	peasant land and labor. (d) If there is a stratum of native landholding nota-bles below the aristocracy of the conquering people (e.g., the Hindu *zamin-dars* in relation to the Mughal *jagirdars*), the central power and magnates must step up the pressure on this autochthonous ruling class while also be-coming increasingly hostage to its economic and military contributions. (5) Conquest as a high-risk venture: defeat or even absence abroad encourages peasant rebellion, aristocratic conspiracy, and insurrection by the native land-holders. (6) Danger of being lost in a larger sea of alien peoples. For all these reasons, the first impulse tends to give way to a second one, less a distinct option than a changed emphasis. The emerging features of this society: (1) The basics of power: control of governmental patronage, military recruitment, and land tenure. (2) The cen-tralizing policies of the ruling cliques must work through some combination of the following strategies: (a) constitution of royal agricultural domains as an independent resource and/or military manpower base; (b) protection of a class of smallholders as a source of recruitment for peasant infantry and a counterweight to the aristocrats; (c) attempt to establish or maintain a close link between large-scale land tenure and military and tax obligations, avoid-ing the transformation of estates into alodial property and turning the aristo-cratic cohorts or lower gentry into a service nobility; (d) setting up of an independent line of dependent, landless, and unarmed bureaucrats to preside over some aspects of administration, tax collection, and recruitment as well as to regulate relations between landholders and peasants. Rarely are these policies carried to their final antiaristocratic conclusions. To the extent they fail, the imperial government falls under unchecked magnate influence, serv-

ing as a device by which the great landowners uphold their common interests against invasion from outside or rebellion from below. (3) Relative diversity and autonomy of the peasant masses persist as long as: (a) an autocracy has failed to exert direct, societywide control over the peasantry through its lower-echelon agents and (b) the relation of the landholders to the peasants has been kept from the extremes of parasitism by the vigilance of the central government, the resistance of the peasants, or the relative military and economic stability of the country. Thus, aristocratic factionalism may coexist with various forms of peasant–village community. (4) The agrarian economy becomes more market-oriented, allowing for part payment of taxes in money, which in turn facilitates the emperor's freedom of maneuver in military recruitment. (5) Development of cash–crop agriculture and urban artisanal activity, connected, on one side, with the partial commercialization of food-grain agriculture and, on the other, with the desire for luxury by more sedentary imperial courts and landholding aristocrats. (6) Commercial groups remain enclaves – either relatively self-ruling cysts in the agrarian society or direct dependents of court and magnates. (7) Multiple opportunities for disintegration once the march of conquest is brought to a halt: (a) the military–administrative aristocracy tends to merge into a class of hereditary landowners, in constant rivalry with the emperor or with one another for control of land and labor; (b) the scribal–bureaucratic cadres increase in number and develop administrative procedures that impose limits on monarchical discretion and information; in the course of their rise, they try to merge with either the landholding aristocracy or the relatively independent religious functionaries; (c) the religious functionaries try to assert their independence as custodians of the sacred law representing the fount of imperial authority.

Table 2. *What happened to the steppe peoples of Eurasia whenever they got involved in "history": a study in the open-ended logic of live options and in the imperative of self-transformation*

Two possibilities of development

The aristocratic condominium.

(1) Abandonment of the peasantry to aristocratic–gentry control. (2) Conduct of imperial ritual and development of imperial–gentry outlook. (3) Near total dependence of the imperial government on aristocrats and/or gentry for military recruitment and taxes. (4) Coordination of conflicting aristocratic claims on governmental patronage. The aristocratic condominium succeeds so long as: (a) the weakness of the monarchy does not encourage aristocratic usurpation, foreign invasion, and peasant rebellion; (b) the level of exploitation of the peasantry does not become so great as to wipe out all elements of peasant community and to disturb all agrarian relations; (c) demographic changes fail to lead either to relative overpopulation and pressure on the land or to underpopulation and struggle among landholders for peasant labor; (d) the aristocrats with access to the spoils of government are hierarchically and spiritually continuous with the landholders who are in effective control of the land and the peasants. (On the significance of failure to satisfy this fourth condition, see the section below labeled the cost of failure.)

The overweening autocrat.

The success of an autocratic centralizing policy requires: (1) playing social classes or estates and corporate bodies off against one another; (2) keeping ultimate control over the appointments of scribes and priests as well as over the content of religious and social doctrine; (3) making sure that large-scale land tenure continues to be impressed with military and service obligations to central government; (4) creating a manpower base for independent recruitment into a peasant army and lower-level administration or government-directed craftsmanship and commerce; (5) building an independent tax base through totally dependent (gentry or bureaucratic) functionaries or through magnates whose tax liabilities are checked by an independent bureaucracy; (6) stable succession rules, preferably combining heredity and free selection by the ruler; (7) building a common front – spiritual, political, and economic – with the notables of the conquered peoples. (On the limits to the pursuit of these policies, to the fundamental alteration of peasant life, and to the technical revolution of the instruments of work and warfare, see the discussion of reversion crises in the main body of Chapter 1.)

A necessary though insufficient precondition to the success of either line of development is the relative dissolution of the barrier between the conquering and conquered. The conquerors must accept an intimate and stable association with the indigenous landholding aristocracy. If the native ruling class cannot be effectively destroyed and replaced, a new, relatively unified ruling class must be created, in direct possession of the land and of peasant manpower. Conversion and compromise must create a lasting spiritual basis on which the conquerors can bind themselves to the notables among the conquered and, if possible, to the native peasantry as well.

Breakthrough: merger with the native elites and reform of the agrarian–bureaucratic state

Examples: Mongols in China, Mughals in India.

The cost of failure

(1) The native landholders remain in direct control of most land and peasant labor. These landlords hold the keys to the expanded economic and military resources the conquerors need. They are able to turn every weakness of the imposed regime to their own benefit and eventually either to overthrow or to manipulate it. The exactions of the conquering rulers and aristocrats increase the exploitation of the peasantry and therefore the instability of agrarian relations. The conquerors suffer from ignorance and lack of control over the countryside. At crucial moments, the native gentry can turn the peasantry against the foreign rulers. (2) The effective ties of communication and commerce among regions owe more to relations among native landholders, merchants, and administrators than to the central government of the empire. Tendency of the country to fall apart into segments only tenuously connected by these local or personalist ties. (3) The conquered gentry justify resistance or insurrection by appeals to outraged collective identities and standards of civilization that the conquerors cannot live up to.

Table 2. *What happened to the steppe peoples of Eurasia whenever they got involved in "history":*
a study in the open-ended logic of live options and in the imperative of self-transformation

The price of success	A major example of breakthrough and partial unification by the conquerors: the Ottomans, especially through the *timar* and *devshirme* systems. Major factors bearing on the feasibility of the task: (1) The numerical strength of the conquerors relative to the overrun landholders. (2) The solidity of preexisting landholder–peasant relations and of joint participation by native landholders and peasants alike in a vision of civilized life that extends down to the governance of relations among individuals and of passions within individuals. (3) The availability to the conquerors of suitable models of government (e.g., Ottoman use of Sassanian statecraft, conveyed by the Seljuqs) and their boldness in going beyond previous practices and beliefs. The earlier scheme of a warrior despotism turns into a more complex program of culture and state-making. A high religious tradition often plays a crucial role in this regeneration. The achievement of relative unification, far from solving the problems of relations among peasants, aristocrats, and emperors, poses these problems with new clarity. The options become those common to all agrarian empires.
Moment III: The reformed agrarian–bureaucratic state (as described in this chapter)	

2

Wealth and Force: An Antinecessitarian Analysis of the Protection Problem

TWO TRADITIONAL SOLUTIONS TO THE PROTECTION PROBLEM

No country has ever been able to buy itself out of war for very long. No wealth has ever been so great that it can defend itself against the outsiders who covet it. The strategy of paying the foreigner to fight for you or not to fight against you proves at best a transitory device. There has never been a single, riskless method for turning the wealth of a country, a faction, or a family into military force. On the contrary, the efforts to secure wealth against violence (or the threat of violence), and to get violence for wealth and wealth for violence, present hard problems. For much of world history two solutions have prevailed.

One solution is the quasi-autarkic empire. Its most tangible feature is the overall coincidence of economic and political boundaries: most trade takes place within the borders of a territory that a single government and its officialdom claim to rule. This government takes charge of protection, safeguarding production and trade from domestic or foreign disruption. The other, more intangible but equally important trait of the autarkic empires is that the government takes more than a parasitic interest in trade and production: it understands, if it understands anything at all, that the breakdown of the economic order will not only starve the empire of taxes and soldiers but also produce dangerous unrest among grandees, petty proprietors, and propertyless laborers alike. The agrarian empires of antiquity were the major and, in fact, the only clean examples of the autarkic–imperial approach to the protection issue. Nevertheless, that approach has recurred in compromised form, not only in some of the naval empires of the ancient Mediterranean (e.g., the Athenian Empire) but at several turning points in modern Western history itself (e.g., the sixteenth-century Spanish and French bids for an imperial organization of the European economies; the European colonial empires; the twentieth-century German and Japanese programs of the *Grossraumwirtschaft* and the Greater East Asia Co-Prosperity Sphere).

The other, historically common solution to the protection issue is the partnership of the overlord and the peddler. It can be defined, initially, as a neat contrast to the autarkic empire. For one thing, in this scheme, trade and even the stages of a production process are carried out in territories that a number of independent authorities make claims to rule and tax. For another thing, the overlord–peddler approach presupposes no long-range commitment of either partner to the other and no thoroughgoing supervision of the peddler by the overlord. In fact, the entire partnership comes down to a simple exchange of protection and taxes: the overlord hopes to skim off as much of the peddler's profits as he can; his parasitic attitude is moderated, if at all, by the fear that the peddler may ply his trade elsewhere or that he may be overcharged into ruin for the benefits of economic protection. Among the classic examples of the peddler–overlord pattern are the dealings between the early European slave-trading companies of Radhaniya and Rus', based in post-Roman Gaul, and the principalities that directly preceded the Kievan Rus; the slave trade with the kingdoms of the Niger Delta; and the resilient accommodations between Iranian merchants and a series of Central Asian nomadic empires.

In the overlord–peddler system, both protection and exploitation are more narrowly focused than in the autarkic empire: protection, because it is pressed on the peddler without any pretense of regulating him thoroughly and without any larger interest in the connections between his activity and the surrounding life of the society; and exploitation, because it results from unequal power in setting the terms of the deal about protection and profit. The predatory practices of the autarkic empire become more or less genuinely mixed up with larger concerns for social stability and respect for established expectations. In the overlord–peddler situation, the predatory intent stands out undiluted and unabashed. This naked racketeering does not shock the peddler although it may ruin him; he takes it as part of the cost of doing business.

The protection policies of the overlord–peddler deal and of the autarkic empire have been juxtaposed often enough. Some autarkic empires of the standard agrarian sort were in fact periodically open to foreign trade but then allowed that trade to be carried out by special corporate groups, often of foreign origin, with which the government had the characteristic overlord–peddler dealings. Other empires were less prone to such arrangements: the overlord who was master of a stable territorial base had a mass of subjects, the conquering or the conquered peoples, whom he was more likely to treat – and who were more likely to treat one another – as members of an autarkic empire than as peddlers, coercively paying off their protection fees.

Modern Europe would find yet another path to protection, but the characteristic early modern European treatment of the protection problem fails to fit neatly either of the two earlier models. From the scheme of overlord and peddler, it took the acceptance of the incongruence between political and economic boundaries; from the autarkic–imperial scheme, it took the more than predatory attitude toward productive and commercial activity within the country. This European remaking of the protection problem – the interplay between force and wealth – was more than a smooth synthesis of elements. It was something genuinely novel, although it might easily slide into those other, more familiar arrangements. To grasp the true nature of this novelty, however, as well as its bearing on the West's great leap to wealth and power, you must first step back and understand the earlier significance of autarkic empires and of overlord–peddler dealings for the business of production and trade.

The chief attraction of the autarkic–imperial approach was its unequivocal solution to the problem of external security: as long as the borders hold, the protected economic space is clearly safeguarded against internal disruption as well as foreign invasion. The crucial flaw in the autarkic empire is the almost irrepressible tendency for the prices, and even the actual costs, of protection to escalate to the point at which they threaten economic growth and, ultimately, economic stability.[1] In the past, this escalation contributed decisively to reversions toward natural economy. The very real perils of the autarkic empire for the making and exchange of wealth have a number of distinct aspects.

First, there is the danger that any wealth on which officialdom finds it easy to lay its hands will be treated, in a crunch, as simply a source of governmental income. Although the autarkic empire is less likely than the overlord–peddler arrangement to treat marketable wealth in a shortsighted, predatory fashion, it may in fact reach this result by the combination of fiscal pressures with de jure or de facto constraints on the kinds of assets that are vulnerable to governmental exactions. The implications of this vulnerability for economic growth and organizational reform in the productive and military realms will then depend on just which groups are more defenseless. In the agrarian empires, the small cultivators were relatively weak. So, often, were merchants and manufacturers who did not themselves belong to the landholding and official elites or who did not manage to join them quickly or to establish clientalistic arrangements with them.

---

[1] See A.H.M. Jones, "Over-Taxation and the Decline of the Roman Empire," *Antiquity*, vol. 33 (1959), pp. 39–43; Charles Henry Wilson, "Taxation and the Decline of Empires, an Unfashionable Theme," in *Economic History and the Historian*, Weidenfeld, London, 1969, pp. 114–127; Carlo M. Cipolla, *The Economic Decline of Empires*, Methuen, London, 1970, pp. 1–15.

Taxes can rise because the rulers of the autarkic empire are able to impose a monopoly price for their protection of economic activity, a price limited only by the differential ability of groups to resist the fiscal demands of the state, by the vitality of the wealthmaking activities themselves, and by widely held ideas about the proper and realistic aims of governmental action.

The second danger of the autarkic empire for the possibility of leaps in production, productivity, and capital accumulation lies in the subordination of economic opportunity to social stability. The autarkic empire is a society in which the monopoly position of the overarching protective organization allows it to keep a close watch on the interplay between technical or organizational innovation, on one side, and the maintenance of stable relationships of hierarchy and exchange, on the other. Such relationships are inconsistent with rapid and far-reaching changes of relative wealth; they are also incompatible with the unrestricted power of well-placed merchants, landlords, and officials to use their offices and privileges as weapons with which to get as much as they can from laborers and provincials. The autarkic empire that strives for domestic peace as well as external security will have to keep its tax farmers, its military officers, its slave traders, and its monopoly merchants on a leash, however long the leash may be. So the history of autarkic empires is full of instances in which central governments came to regulate severely those forms of profit taking that depended directly on the manipulation of governmental offices and governmentally guaranteed privileges. (Consider, for example, the heightened policing of the depredations wrought by equestrian tax gatherers and provincial governors during Augustus's principate.)

The full impact of this urge to repress exorbitant profit taking in order to guarantee minimal peace becomes clear only when it is set in the context of that other feature of the autarkic empires (not unique to them), the importance of arming oneself with governmental privileges and well-placed friends the better to evade the tax collector and share in the booty of power. The prudent must encrust themselves in the state to survive and prosper; the state must in turn moderate the voracity of these parasites to keep the whole country from going to wrack and ruin. The combination of the dependence of wealth making (especially nonagricultural wealth making) on governmental favoritism with the recurrent need of governments to behead or downgrade their own economic creatures has exercised, over and over again, a fatally constrictive role on organizational and technical innovation. It has therefore also restricted economic growth. It has helped check the dynamism of markets, even when thoroughgoing commercialization might already have seemed irreversible. It has contributed to the destructive escalation not only of the prices charged by government but of the actual costs of maintaining a protected economic space. When fortune and even safety lie in achieving some bundle of privileges and immunities but when, at the same time, the range of the business that can be done with those favors is narrowed, speculative profit making and innovations in the technology and organization of production come out the losers.

There is all the difference between the autarkic empires that existed before the modern Western European breakthroughs in production and productivity (i.e., the standard agrarian empires) and the throwbacks to imperial autarky that occurred and may yet occur after these breakthroughs have already been achieved (e.g., the latter-day colonial empire, the *Grossraumwirtschaft*, the Greater East Asia Co-Prosperity Sphere). For these later efforts already appear against a background of machine production, mass politics, and worldwide rivalry among nation-states. Because of the incomparably higher levels of production and productivity, transport and communication, the costs of running a government – even a government that is expected to subsidize a broad range of special interests – goes down relative to the total amount of wealth and the total scope of wealth-producing activities. Because of mass politics – with its direct appeal to large segments of the working population and its characteristic multiplication of aspirant elites – the central government becomes less likely to sacrifice the productive to the parasitic. Because of the immediacy of military and economic threats from abroad, interest in maintaining the integrity of the established order remains nearly indistinguishable, in the short run and most of the time, from the commitment to economic growth.

The autarkic empires predating the European breakthroughs, unlike their European successors, chose between a small number of difficult alternatives in the effort to contain the economically destructive consequences of the attempt to uphold protected economic space. Consider for the purpose, the military strategy of such an order. Once the autarkic empire ceased to expand and started to consolidate its holdings, it had to make do with some combination of two strategic options. One of them was the strategy of in-depth deployment: troops might be deployed at various crucial places within the territory of the empire so that they might move quickly to a place of emergency. The frontiers themselves would be left largely unprotected: the cost of maintaining a permanent defensive army or navy would thereby be limited. But this technique would provide effective security only so long as the autarkic empire retained the influence and the credibility to surround itself with smaller client states or to pacify its potential adversaries. Otherwise, the strategy of in-depth deployment would be at best a bid for survival in the face of the foreign invader; large areas of the population might be at the mercy of foreign

raiders and substantial portions of the economy periodically destroyed. The other strategic option was fixed-line frontier defense.
If this defense were dense enough, it might indeed make the territory
militarily impermeable, but only at the cost of potentially unlimited
expenses in manpower and material. The alternative posed by the
two characteristic military options shows that the effectiveness of a
combination of limited defense expenditures with effective protection, in a preindustrial society, depended either on the intangibles of
authority or on accidents of geopolitical isolation. Only after modern
technology had multiplied the amount of violence a single man might
cause and nineteenth- and twentieth-century mass politics had facilitated national mobilization for production and fighting, could the
relation between defense and economy be decisively altered.

Consider now the administrative and fiscal options of a preindustrial autarkic empire when it tried to combine effective protection
with limits on the deleterious consequences of the protection apparatus. The outright expansion of paid officialdom would increase the
costs of government: there are severe constraints, in a preindustrial
economy, on the availability of taxable wealth sufficient to pay for
this governmental hypertrophy. Moreover, the growth of the bureaucracy, by emphasizing the omnipresence of government, might
aggravate everybody's need to remain well connected with officials
and the commitment of officialdom to drive all profit margins down
without threatening established hierarchies – a combination whose
ominous economic significance has already been made clear.

Neither were the alternatives to enlargement of the bureaucracy
more satisfactory. The problem of financing the governmental apparatus while simultaneously encouraging advances in production
and productivity was insoluble. Reliance on local notables and landholders to exercise jurisdictional, police, and fiscal authority bartered
away state power. This dependence strengthened established interests
against both working masses and potentially innovative elites; it increased opportunities to tax and browbeat the productive and the
unprivileged into bankruptcy. The resort to tax farmers and financiers increased the opportunities for economically destructive depredation and then stifled this state-dependent finance whenever central
governments managed to regulate tax farming and public finance
effectively.

The central point about autarkic empires is that they could offer
a satisfactory solution to the protection problem only after a fundamental breakthrough in the techniques and institutional context of
economic production had already been achieved. Only a leap in output, productivity, and communication might create a situation in
which bureaucracy could pay for itself as it grew. The realities of

mass politics could provide new ways to recruit officialdom and to use it against any number of privileged groups. Yet the characteristic traits of the preindustrial autarkic empire presented a host of obstacles to just such an economic revolution. You can say the same for different reasons, of the other historically common arrangement of force and wealth: the overlord–merchant deal.

The chief attraction of the overlord–peddler approach to the protection problem is its promise to realize a prince's and a businessman's dream at the same time.[2] The prince's dream is to tax without responsibility. The businessman's is to pay off his several protectors, to move among them freely, and then to suffer as little interference from them as possible. At best, wealth will be almost invisible and infinitely mobile, like some high-priced manna. The fundamental weakness is the reverse side of this relative dissociation between force and riches. The protector who does not himself, out of improvidence or need, kill the goose that lays the golden eggs, may still see it fly away. The moneyman can easily be undone by the uncertainties of his position. First, there is the threat that comes from the protector's irresponsibility. If the people with the guns can exact from the merchant a near-monopoly price for not taking away his wealth and for defending him against others and if they treat him as nothing more than a temporarily useful source of tribute, then there is the very real danger that shortsighted financial stringency will generate ruinous tribute taking. The prince's only constraint is his desire to maintain his tax base, and the businessman's, the opportunity to find other protectors and other places to ply his trade. Second, the protected enterprise faces the prospect of violent and unforeseeable oscillations in prices, supply, and demand. The uncontrollable quality of these reversals results from the difficulty of enlisting force directly to ensure the stability of markets as well as from the need to deal with a variety of protectors with disparate aims, provoking the ups and downs of tribute demands. Third, the enterprise that operates in a number of different protected economic areas is very dependent on the ability to turn their diversity to profit: to take advantage of disparities in the prices of produced goods or of factors of production from one economically protected space to another. These crevices may disappear. Political hostilities may make the frontiers between one area and another impassable. Or the protectors may prefer to trade directly with one another or to shift to an imperial–autarkic arrangement.

[2] My conception of the overlord–merchant approach to the protection problem is greatly influenced by Niels Steensgaard, *The Asian Trade Revolution of the Seventeenth Century*, Chicago, Chicago, 1974, pp. 12–113.

For all these reasons, the overlord–enterprise solution to the protection problem usually proved precarious. It interrupted or halted
promising spurts of capital accumulation. It offered a sandy foundation at best to large-scale governments. The doubly heavy constraints on the effective protection of wealth and on the financing of
force made the overlord–enterprise scheme an unlikely setting for
revolutions in production.

The significance of these drawbacks might be greatly lessened,
however, once the capital reserves and technological capabilities of
latter-day industrialism are at hand and business moves within a
world economy less fragmented than a set of mutually closed autarkies, and less dangerous than a collection of predatory overlords
and their clients or victims. The cumulative impact of these conditions would be to moderate the nefarious consequences of market
instabilities and the surprises of tributary extortion. At this limit, the
twentieth-century dealings between national governments and multinational corporations can look like just such a reincarnation of the
protector–peddler arrangement. Another candidate for the role of the
peddler redivivus is the small, high-growth, export-oriented country
that specializes in the international sale of services or in the manufacture of light goods with foreign raw materials. But this renewal
of the tribute taker–merchant option is largely illusory, for it ordinarily presupposes a much closer partnership between business and
protective governmental power than the true prince–peddler system
would allow (Woe to the multinational corporation that lacks a great
power on its side!), and it survives in a world accustomed to even
closer forms of association between governments and producers.

THE EUROPEAN INNOVATION

In early modern European history, as in the history of Asia and the
Middle East, both the autarkic–imperial and the overlord–enterprise
protection strategies made a mark. Yet, in Europe neither of them
turned out to be the winner. To the extent that these strategies
worked in the western tip of Eurasia, their form was drastically
modified. The modifications were not enough.

The attempt to construct semiautarkic economic empires closely
linking government and business was a theme in Hapsburg policy
as well as in the French effort to achieve an alternative hegemony
within continental Europe. Two crucial circumstances worked
against the semiautarkic strategy. They would have worked against
it even if it had been formulated more clearly and pursued more
relentlessly. One of these obstacles was the multiplicity of social and
legal obstacles to the governmental leadership of business enterprise.
In the realm of taxation, these obstacles prevented the Spanish crown

from laying its hands on the wealth of Aragon, while allowing it to do all too much to drive the Castilian economy to ruin. When this exhaustion of the tax base combined in the 1550s with the uncontrolled demands of warfare and war finance, the resulting bankruptcy forced the fighting to a halt (by the treaty of Cateau–Cambrésis in 1559), weakened the Spanish government's ability to defend Spanish economic interests effectively, and worsened the country's economic decline. In the field of foreign economic policy, the same constraint on the partnership of government with business showed up in the ability of crucially placed producers to block the protectionist measures required to give agrarian and manufacturing innovation a chance. Sheep grazing and merchant interests in the wool cartel – the *Mesta* – kept the crown from adopting policies that would have restricted the export of unfinished wool and thereby gave a push to English cloth manufacturing.[3] The other obstacle to the success of economic autarky in early modern Europe lay in the failure of real economic isolation for any of the would-be autarkic units. Thus, the Spanish Empire at its most successful was heavily involved in foreign trade in which the export of bullion and raw materials played a major role. The failure of the condition of autarky meant that the Spanish economy lacked a favorable environment for a widespread internal division of labor; at the same time, the crown continued to follow policies and respect privileges that kept the country from seizing an advantageous position within the emergent international division of labor. Every political and economic initiative on the part of the Spanish government became vulnerable to competition by countries where a different association between business and government had already been established. The very same circumstances that functioned as obstacles to the success of economic empire, under unified political rule, were seized upon in these other European countries as occasions to develop a novel solution to the protection problem. The play of disparate conflicts and the discovery of an unsuspected opportunity could end up magnifying small differences in circumstance into vast disparities of power and wealth among European states over the next several centuries.

The overlord–enterprise option also had its counterparts in late medieval and early modern Europe. Thus, for example, the Portuguese conduct of the East India and Levant commerce (unlike Portuguese actions in Brazil) failed to depart sharply from the traditional overlord approach to the relationship between force and wealth. When the Portuguese opened up the sea route around Africa, they did not suddenly try to displace the caravan trade toward the West

---

[3] See José Larraz, *La Epoca del Mercantilismo en Castilla (1500–1700)*, Atlas, Madrid, 1943, p. 20.

by undercutting it in costs and prices. Instead, they attempted to blockade the Red Sea passage and to achieve absolute naval dominance in the Indian Ocean with the thought of charging high monopoly prices on the sea route. At the same time, they tried to impose heavy protection charges on the merchants who plied the still resilient caravan trade. This strategy required heavy military expenses on the part of the *Estado da Índia*, and the commitment to it kept the Portuguese crown from experimenting with other, more revolutionary ways to ally force with wealth. The policy failed in any case and left the Portuguese open to destructive competition from countries that did so experiment. The fall of the Red Sea fort of Hormuz in 1622 to an Anglo–Persian expedition marked the end of the effort to organize the major part of East-West trade along overlord–enterprise lines.[4] But the sequel would reveal a conflict between two distinct alternatives requiring analysis.

Consider now the peddler side of the prince–peddler deal. One way to understand Venice at its most successful would be to think of it as a syndicate of wholesale merchants who built their wealth less upon territorial gain or military force than in the traditional fashion of the peddler stranded in a world of princes: to pay off the princes for protection and keep from falling too far into the clutches of any one of them. Venice might stand in this respect as a surrogate for aspects of the activities of other merchant towns in European history, were it not that Venetian prosperity depended from the start on the judicious use of force. The single most important example of this dependence in the history of the city was the Venetians' ability to secure trading privileges and tax exemptions from the Byzantine Empire, under threat of military force. These favors, first won in lo82, were repeatedly confirmed and enlarged, most dramatically in 1176, when the Emperor Michael sought Venetian help to defend himself from the danger of a Norman attack. Venice was an armed peddler: the belligerance of its trade, with a European martial tradition on which to draw, and the military capabilities of its ships and fortresses remained crucial to its continued prosperity.[5] Moreover, within their small territory, the Venetians proved able to mount a range of collaboration between the state and business that was all the more spectacular because it often escaped the recurrent imperial–autarkic vices of ruinous fiscal depredation and stultifying fiscal privileges. The main aspects of this interplay of trade and politics were

---

[4] See Niels Steensgaard, *The Asian Trade Revolution of the Seventeenth Century*, pp. 331–343.
[5] See William H. McNeill, *Venice: The Hinge of Europe, 1081–1797*, Chicago, Chicago, 1974, p. 29.

the establishment of the funded public debt, the close governmental supervision of arms manufacture in the Arsenal and of rope trade in the Tana and in the hemp marshes of the surrounding countryside, and, most important of all, the state-sponsored maritime ventures that allowed small investors to participate in big gambles. The social foundation of these collaborative schemes was the deal that emerged from the crisis of the 1170s: the ascendancy of a closed commercial patriciate combined with economic opportunities for much broader sectors of the Venetian population. Finally, the decline of Venice cannot adequately be credited to an economic shift caused by the rise of the Atlantic trade, for, well into the sixteenth century, Venetian commerce underwent startling revivals. A decisive factor was the change in the overall military situation of Europe, when the territorial monarchs gained the ability to build large fighting navies and to win sufficient direct control over grain supplies to feed their land armies and sufficient tax money to pay for them. Venice lost its relative capacity to protect itself or to exact privileges from the intimidated princes with which it was used to dealing; the walls of its own protected economic area caved in. So, both at its zenith and in its dotage, Venice showed that the overlord–enterprise arrangement could work only so long as it counted on a direct coordination of force deployment and wealth making.

To return to our model, even the closest European approximations to autarkic empires and protector–enterprise schemes remained ill defined and unsuccessful efforts. The main line of development in Europe toward a protective state lay in a third and truly different solution to the problem of wealth and force.

The novel European response to the protection problem can be discerned in the general nature of governments' dealings with trade and manufacture, in the conduct of public finance and the specific methods adopted for organizing and funding armies, and in the particular way in which military strength was used to create a protected economic area. The common theme in all these fields of activity was the halting and often unintended and unexpected development of an association between the state and the economy that gave the government a stake in collective prosperity far beyond the predatory interest of the prince in the peddler, while at the same time checking the ruinous aggravation of governmental costs and burdens.

Governments were present at every crucial juncture of the history of early modern European economies. The English government, for example, engaged in the forceful development and protection of foreign markets against rivals (e.g., the Anglo–Dutch trade wars of the seventeenth century). The English state regulated domestic economic conflict among the possessing classes (e.g., decisive governmental action against rural industry and in favor of town-based manufacture and trade). It endeavored to establish a regime of minimal stability for the work force. It searched for rules and institutions that combined a money-based labor market with governmentally backed coercion against employed and unemployed alike and with the assumption by national or local government of minimal welfare duties.

These varied governmental commitments to a particular vision of prosperity and its conditions could join with a wide range of ways of relating governmental power to both production and trade. Many countries witnessed outright governmental production or supervision of production – especially in the strategic area of military preparedness: weapons manufacture and shipbuilding. This concern with arms manufacture might take the form of the state-guided development of raw materials abroad, as in the Dutch efforts to develop Swedish iron ore.[6] One way or another, the often desperate struggle to make more and better weapons repeatedly had a multiplier effect on demand in nonmilitary sectors of the economy and was responsible for many of the formative technological breakthroughs of preindustrial and industrial Europe. Again, the state might act to establish privileged monopolies with differing degrees of financial, managerial, and military independence from the central government. In still other spheres of the economy, the government might withdraw even more from the immediate conduct of production and trade. It would then limit itself to the more or less active and conscious defense of a particular scheme for guaranteeing the docility of the working population and the availability to national entrepreneurs of opportunities to profit abroad.

None of these ties between the government and the economy, nor all of them together, are peculiar to European history. In fact, each and every one has its counterpart, for instance, in Chinese imperial history. The distinctive quality of the European solution to the protection problem becomes evident only when we move beyond the surface forms of collaboration between the prince and the entrepreneur and focus instead on the mechanisms of public finance and of the military defense of prosperity. Taxes and armies – these were and are the law and the prophets for the ambitious ruler. The task was never simply how to get hold of funds and soldiers and how to use each to get more of the other; it was also how to accomplish these objectives in a way that would strengthen rather than weaken the productive capacity of the economy as a whole.

---

[6] See Eli Heckscher, "Un Grand Chapitre de l'Histoire de Fer: Le Monopole Suédois" in *Annales d'Histoire Economique et Sociale*, vol. 4 (1932), pp. 127–139.

THE EXAMPLE OF PUBLIC FINANCE

Consider first the methods of public finance in general and military finance in particular. The generic problem is to mobilize the maximum martial strength with the least possible fiscal strain. The essence of the chosen solution is to carry to the extreme the farming out of responsibilities for tax collection and military recruitment while at the same time placing more or less severe constraints on the predatory abuse of these privileges. The elements of this solution can be sorted out under a number of different headings; however disparate their origins, they easily reinforced one another. Superficially, they seem little more than a hodgepodge of institutional devices drawn from different periods and suited to different interests, and their very co-existence over long stretches of time was as much a demonstration of weakness as a show of strength on the part of central governments. Yet, in the end, it was this improbable blend, together with the special combination of powers and disabilities it manifested, that allowed the more successful European states to cut through the dilemmas presented by the overlord–enterprise and imperial–autarkic responses to the protection problem.

The central governments of early modern Europe varied widely in their choice of fiscal devices and in the degree of success they achieved in marshaling them for the objectives of national power and prosperity. Nevertheless, the arrangements they made reveal the particular pattern of strength and weakness in the state's relation to the economy that made it possible to escape the depressing economic consequences of the overlord–enterprise and the imperial–autarkic approaches to protection.

One such development – perhaps the most fundamental and least precise of all – was the gradual separation of tax from rent.[7] The counterpart to this separation was the development of the modern idea of property. The true economic significance of this event, it must also be said, cannot be found where it is usually looked for: the discovery of a pure property right, with an in-built structure, and the ability to ensure the "predictability" that enterprising private activity allegedly requires. In fact, property is just a conventional name for a conventional set of powers, defined broadly or narrowly, that may be distributed among many right holders or concentrated

---

[7] General discussions of the tax–rent problem have been largely confined to the internal Marxist debate about the "Asiatic mode of production." See Barry Hindess and Paul Q. Hirst, *Pre-Capitalist Modes of Production*, Routledge, London, 1975, pp. 193–200. Nothing in my argument presupposes the polemical contrast between the "Asiatic mode" and a supposed mainstream of development from feudalism to capitalism.

in the hands of one. If a market means simply an economic order where a significant number of units trade on their own initiative and account, then a market can be realized through very different systems of contract and property rights, each with its own consequences for the distribution of power and wealth and for the tenor of life in the society. Which of these systems is more likely to promote effective decentralization in a given situation is an empirical question to which no certain or permanent answers can be given. This legal indeterminacy of the market means that any given market takes a certain assignment of rights for granted; no such assignment could ever be deduced from the abstract idea of a market. Similarly, the ties among legal rights, the predictability of their economic consequences, and the encouragement of economic growth are changeable because they are empirical; whether predictability is good or bad for growth depends on the extent to which the particular groups whose expectations are being made more secure stand a better chance of contributing to some desired growth path than the groups whose expectations become relatively less secure. To have totally or equally safe expectations for all groups is hardly separable from a situation of vested rights that spells the paralysis of both reforming power from above and entrepreneurial innovation and collective mobilization from below.

The real economic significance of the movement to distinguish more clearly between tax and rent did not lie in the discovery of absolute, unified property rights. It lay instead in the combination of three facts.

First, the separation made it easier to vary the impact of the costs of government on different social groups. The more payments to government became separate from payments for the immediate use of the factors of production, the more readily could the burden of governmental expense be lifted from some shoulders and the more brutally could it be imposed on others. The result was to multiply opportunities for certain crucially placed and privileged groups to enter into a more or less explicit economic partnership with government while being relatively safeguarded against runaway fiscal exactions.

Second, the modern idea of property gained a very concrete meaning in context. Property, as a right to command material resources within a rigidly defined sphere of absolute discretion, had a double use. It constrained discretionary fiscal predation. But it also organized the relationship between employers and their dependent, although legally free, employees in a way that dispensed with much of the overt coercive apparatus of slavery and serfdom and with most of the ill-defined and costly mutual obligations of the patron–client relationship.

A third effect of the emergence of absolute property and of the clearer division between tax and rent was to furnish the institutional solution to a political paradox. It showed the general terms under which the central state could become stronger at the same time that particular classes of property owners were made more secure against government. They were protected more easily against fiscal extravagance or desperation as well as against a conception of statecraft that would subordinate economic initiative to the perceived needs of social harmony. The culmination of such a vision lay in the nondemocratic version of liberalism, the idea of the rule of law as security from governmental intervention rather than as a license for participation in affairs of state.

The separation of tax from rent and the disentanglement of property from the claims of larger social responsibility were only the background of the new public finance. Its heart lay in the ability to combine, under the pressure of fiscal necessity, sources of revenue that seemed to belong to different worlds, such as the sale of offices and the funded debt. Together, these new sources minimized the ruinous impact of governmental spending on some kinds of enterprise while laying the foundation for a more intimate, revolutionary partnership between force and wealth. In this modern, eclectic public finance, the most important economic effect of the older elements was to provide money without driving national governments into a remorseless fiscal centralization that would have repeated the characteristic financial and economic woes of the older autarkic empires.

Many of the new monarchies could still draw a significant part of their revenue from the exploitation of royal domains and feudal privileges. These moneys would serve as a financial minimum in whose collection and disposition the sovereign and his ministers were little if at all accountable to larger elite constituencies.

The sale of offices, if prudently managed and counterbalanced by other devices of central control, might enable the government to extend its presence without adding immediately to the costs of running the state.[8] The initial payment for the office might turn out to be less useful than the continuing deal that allowed government to skimp on salaries and the officeholder to use the powers of the office in half-licit ways to earn his living and recoup his initial investment. The success of this tactic depended on the ability to keep corruption within bounds, to find occasions to exact new payments from the same or successive officeholders, and, above all, to preserve an effective chain of command. If, by art or luck, these goals were at-

---

[8] See Martin Göhring, *Die Amterkäuflichkeit im Ancien Régime*, Ebering, Berlin, 1938; Roland Mousnier, *La Vénalité des Offices sous Henri IV et Louis XIII*, Presses Universitaires, Paris, 1971.

tained, the fabrication and sale of offices – capable of creating a tool of power in the very act of providing ready cash – might turn out to be even better than the printing of money.

The sale of offices and the manipulation of proprietary rights were common enough expedients in societies of many different kinds. In early modern Europe, however, they joined with two other fiscal procedures that had no close counterparts in other periods or civilizations. One was the development of the funded debt, pioneered by the Venetians and carried to a larger dimension by the English "financial revolution" of the eighteenth century.[9] William of Orange was said to have landed at Tor Bay with the secret of running a state over its head in debt. Godolphin, Carlisle, Walpole, and Pelham devised a scheme that, by 1720, had crossed the point at which long-term debts were no longer considered self-liquidating. Its development, always closely linked to war finance, reached a measure of perfection by the war of 1739–1748.

The real impact of the funded debt lay in the discovery and refinement of a way of calling on "private" capital that drew a major segment of the property-owning classes into a stable association with the power interests of the state. In the past, such alliances had been part of unstable situations in which governments were at the mercy of short-run demands by small cliques of financiers and in which they escaped from this dictatorship of finance only by ruthless policies of debt cancellation or judicial prosecution that threatened to dry up the sources of finance capital. This new financial situation stood in contrast to an earlier pattern of transactions between princes and their bankers: that previous scheme provided no device for the holding of a long-term debt, except by the progressive mortgaging of revenue sources (e.g., the farming out of customs rights); there was no easy way by which the prosperous but nonspecialized investor could do business with the treasury; and, for these two reasons, governments were under steady pressure to swing between debilitating surrender to their bankers and attempts to bully them into submission.

The funded debt also provided a way to associate private investment with the profits of rule. This association made it possible to circumscribe the private use of public powers without closing off opportunities for private gain. In the finances of the Roman Republic, for example, the economic interests of the provincial administrators and their equestrian partners – interests in rapacious tax farming, outright bribery and extortion, and lucrative supply contracts – conflicted with the attempt to limit public corruption and avoid the

[9] My discussion of the English experience owes much to P.G.M. Dickinson, *The Financial Revolution in England: A Study in the Development of Public Credit, 1688–1756*, Macmillan, London, 1967, especially pp. 3–16, 76–89.

hostility of the subject populations.[10] The effort to vindicate these latter objectives knocked one of the main props out from under Roman finance capital and strengthened all the forces that made the monetary sector of the economy more dependent on the natural sector. By contrast, the "open-market operations" and the consolidated financial obligations of early modern European regimes increased opportunities to check the destabilizing consequences of outright rapacity in the private use of public power. These financial inventions helped insulate governmental policy from private finance.

The eighteenth-century polemicists who attacked the funded debt as a plot to make the activities of government a new occasion for speculative gain by the privileged were not mistaken. They neglected to mention, however, that before the invention of these financial arrangements, finance policy had always had to spin variations on a few elementary options. One strategy was to accept the oscillation between bullying and ingratiation of the financiers. Another method was to weaken and finally overwhelm finance capital altogether by thoroughgoing governmental regulation of its activities and total reliance on officialdom for tax collection and military recruitment. A still more radical solution was to seek alliances with broader segments of the populace – modest farmers or small-time merchants – who would answer to the state for money and recruits.

It is a sign of the incoherence and superficiality of the standard eighteenth-century critics of the new public finance that they attacked the novelty without embracing the commitments and risks of any of the other options. The solutions actually adopted made a formative contribution to the loose alliance of interests and outlooks between the men directly in charge of government and the broader elites that, thanks to devices like the funded debt, gained a larger stake in the financial and power interests of the state – the aristocracy and the larger landed interests as well as the elite financiers. It is easy to forget that such alliances – so compelling in retrospect – were in part artifacts of these institutional inventions rather than their causes.

The system of military entrepreneurship was, alongside the funded debt, the other remarkable novelty in the financial organization of power. Unlike the funded debt, which developed most strikingly in north Italy and England, military entrepreneurship made its strongest showing in Central Europe. It reached its zenith in the course of the Thirty Years' War, long before the eighteenth-century English statesmen had laid out the groundwork for the public finance of the latter-

---

[10] See E. Badian, *Publicans and Sinners: Private Enterprise in the Service of the Roman Republic*, Blackwell, Oxford, 1972, pp. 82–118. On the continuing European counterparts to these Roman problems, see J.F. Bosher, *French Finances, 1770–1795: From Business to Bureaucracy*, Cambridge, Cambridge, 1970, pp. 92–110.

day industrial democracies.[11] Military entrepreneurship amounted to an extension of tax farming into the area of martial recruitment and organization. At its most thoroughgoing, it signified a delegation of power to recruit and to fight.

The military entrepreneur himself might be paid by a combination of initial and ongoing payments and expectations of participation in the booty of war. Yet, more often than not, the seventeenth-century military entrepreneur failed to fit the traditional picture of the mercenary captain: he was part of an ongoing rather than a sporadic arrangement, and he was often bound to the power interests of the state for which he fought by ties that went far beyond the attractions of quick enrichment. He was a successful or aspirant warlord – but a warlord who understood the importance of balancing his books, who was a banker as well as a captain, and who took seriously his entanglements in the state conflicts of the day.

Military entrepreneurship made several contributions to the European restructuring of the protection problem. First, it dealt with recruitment in a way that minimized its disruptive impact on the economy (a very different matter from the unsettling effect of warfare). The standing army put together by the military entrepreneur represented an alternative to the citizen militia of independent farmers whose prolonged absence from their farms would drive agriculture into ruin or make way for radical shifts of wealth and power in the countryside, as the experience of the Roman Republic in the generations following the Second Punic War had shown. Yet the Romans had shied away from private armies, despite the ability of military leaders, like Scipio Aemilianus, to convoke hosts of private retainers, whereas the entrepreneurial armies of seventeenth-century Europe often abandoned all disguise of direct governmental supervision. The military entrepreneur's operation also differed from the foreign mercenary army that could not be counted on to provide a reliable instrument of warfare. For the mercenary option represented unabashedly what military entrepreneurship was always in danger of becoming: a country's attempt to buy itself out of war.

Second, the practice of military entrepreneurship turned the European economies further toward money and markets. As a result it also increased the ability of governments to rely on money taxes and monetary public finance. Cash payments had to go in all directions: from the prince to the warlord, from the warlord to the soldiers,

[11] The fundamental study is Fritz Redlich, *The German Military Entrepreneur and His Work Force: A Study in European Economic History*, Steiner, Wiesbaden, 1964 (published as supplement no. 47 to the *Vierteljahrschrift für Sozial- und Wirtschaftsgeschichte*). See especially vol. 1, pp. 30–34. See also Thomas M. Barker, "Military Entrepreneurship and Absolutism: Habsburg Models," *Journal of European Studies*, vol. 4 (1974), pp. 19–42.

and between the soldiers and the various stripes of merchants with whom they dealt and to whom they sold the pillage of war. Moreover, the funding of such an army was a subtle financial achievement likely to involve the application of risk capital by the entrepreneur and by outside capitalists, as well as advances from the prince. Only such financial amalgamations could stay the danger that the fighting would be forced to stop through sheer insolvency, as had happened to both Hapsburg and Valois combatants at the time of Cateau–Cambrésis (1559).

The third major contribution of military entrepreneurship was the opportunity it offered for organizational experiment. The warlord army, unlike an army closely integrated into the apparatus of government and recruited under its auspices, existed on the fringes of the social order. New forms of association and hierarchy, command and control, might be tried out without presenting an immediate challenge to the interests and prejudices of officialdom and its friends among the privileged sectors of the population. Once these organizational forms had had a chance to consolidate and to prove their effectiveness in their relatively isolated havens, they might then be introduced into other aspects of the society, under the pressure of intensified industrial or military competition among states or of individual greed and ambition. In fact, the internal structure of the warlord armies of the seventeenth century presented a degree of task orientation and collective mobilization that had few rivals in other fields of social life. Not only was there considerable mobility in and through the officer corps, but the developed habits of communication and control moved toward those forms of continuous hierarchy (the combination of supervision with discretion at every point of the job structure) and standardized operating procedures (beyond rigid rules or shared purposes) that were to be carried to such paradoxical refinement by later institutions of production, administration, and warfare.

Together, devices such as the sale of offices, the funded debt, and military entrepreneurship held out the hope of combining a maximum of power in the hands of the state with a minimum of cost. But this hope could be easily disappointed even when it was consciously entertained and actively pursued. The sale of offices could provoke a situation in which government increasingly lost the ability to have its orders carried out, to limit the exploitation of the working classes by officialdom, and to turn existing offices to financial account by finding frequent occasions to exact payments from the officials. The short-term or consolidated debts could quickly get out of hand and be manipulated, to their own advantage, by semiautonomous financial cliques rather than by the government's own ministerial staff. The combination of these two misfortunes might make for the financial dearth that had come to aggravate the reformist paralysis of the French monarchy in the years between the conclusion of the Seven Years' War and the onset of the Revolution, a condition that made a neat contrast to the more successful English manipulation of the public debt and the patronage of office. Finally, the potential advantages of the system of military entrepreneurship might be annulled and reversed if warfare itself were used to pursue dynastic ambition rather than trade aims or, simply, if the course of battle went too unfavorably for too long. Failure to pay off the warlords and their soldiers could lead, at any moment, to sudden military collapse. In the meantime, the protective shell of trade might be broken open by the fighting. The perennial quarrels between soldiers and peasants, anxious to defend their lands, houses, and families, might throw agriculture into chaos.

So, not even under the best of circumstances and with the wisest of leadership, was there ever a guarantee that any of these instruments of public finance, or all of them together, would pave the road to national wealth and power. After all, in many periods of the great agrarian empires of antiquity, there had also prevailed a pattern of simultaneous strength and weakness in the state's relations to the economy. The capacity of this particular European pattern to change the givens of the protection problem was not a foregone conclusion: at a minimum, it also depended on the separation of rent from tax and on the particular way in which military force came to the aid of economic prosperity.

THE LESSONS OF STATE RIVALRY: ABORTIVE AND SUCCESSFUL EUROPEAN SOLUTIONS

Early modern European history witnessed a great range of experiments in the use of force to create or to protect wealth. Remorseless, continuing state competition meant that any country or group of countries that failed to keep abreast of the most successful innovations in the mutual adaptation of wealth and warfare was headed for serious trouble, unless it was favored by special circumstances or extraordinary luck. Consider the long list of failed or abortive solutions – failures and miscarriages that became clear only in hindsight, in the light of some leading power's unprecedented success in drawing wealth from force and force from wealth.

The Dutch decline in the eighteenth century cannot adequately be understood as simply a negative consequence of prosperity and self-contentment, the failure to pass from commercial to industrial innovation. The decisive edge England achieved over the Netherlands did not initially involve any major shift from commerce to industry or from one set of industrial technologies to another; for instance, some of the characteristic English innovations, like the "new draperies," represented little more than English variations on Dutch models. An important element in the Dutch decline was strictly military: a failure to arm fast enough and on a large enough scale. The ingenious arms procurement and weapons manufacture of the early years of the republic were not followed by a consistent program to strengthen the navy and the standing army. The reasons for this failure may perhaps be sought not only in the recurrent illusion of a commercial people who hope to buy themselves out of war but in the characteristic Dutch fear of an overweening state. A people said to have become a nation to avoid having a state could not easily come to terms with the harsh demands of military might.

Moreover, in the early generations of the republic, every additional step toward military strength aggravated the conflict among the major contestants in Dutch society. Either the armed forces would be under the control of the princely factions and their entourage or they would be closely regulated by the united commercial oligarchies of the Dutch towns. The failure clearly to resolve such conflicts created a formidable obstacle to any program of armament.

Whatever the reasons for Dutch underinvestment in armed strength, its consequences were reaped in the Anglo-Dutch trade wars of the mid-seventeenth century.[12] England was able to exact exclusive or favored trading privileges in an increasing number of areas, from Asia to the Baltic, and to gain the naval supremacy, both in armed and unarmed ships, that formed a major part of the protective shell of commercial prosperity. Dutch money, attracted to the London capital market, helped finance English campaigns against France and limit the disruptive effect of English war finance on regional investment within England.

Other instances of failure to come up with a powerful alliance between force and wealth were relatively more straightforward. The French and Spanish monarchies stubbornly pursued dynastic wars often unrelated to any clear plan of national economic warfare. The combination of an intense pressure of war finance with a capricious distribution of the tax burden – aggravated in Spain by the disparity between the pitiless subjection of Castille and the relative immunity of Catalonia and Aragon – brought repeated bankruptcy to the treasury and ruin to some of the most dynamic sectors of the economy. Colbert's efforts at a close partnership between the government and

---

[12] See Charles Henry Wilson, *Profit and Power: A Study of England and the Dutch Wars*, Longmans, London, 1957; J.E. Farrell, "The Navigation Act of 1651, the First Dutch War, and the London Merchant Community," *Economic History Review*, 2nd ser., vol. 16 (1964), pp. 439–454.

the entrepreneurs, efforts that looked beyond shortsighted fiscalism, were, in the long run, dwarfed by the costs of battle. The Italian and German states proved unable to achieve the degree of territorial integration and consolidation that was the indispensable condition for claims to build or to resist political and economic hegemony.

In another, abortive approach to the protection problem, great trading companies, like the English East India Company and the Dutch United East India Companies – and its forerunners, the *voorcompagnieen* – were established under the aegis of government.[13] Whatever the variations in their constitutions and their relations to government, the trading companies represented a departure from the conventional pattern of dealings between the overlord and the enterprise, the peddler and the prince. Just how far this departure reached appears when you contrast the operations of the Dutch and the English East India Companies not only with the structure of the traditional caravan and caravan trade but with the activities of the Portuguese *Estado da Índia*.[14] As has been seen, the Portuguese did little more than put themselves in the place of earlier overlords in trade originating from the Indian Ocean region and use their hold on the Cape route to exact monopoly prices rather than to undercut the caravaks and the caravans.

The new commercial companies went further. By carrying out military operations in their own right or in close association with their sponsoring national governments, they countered the danger of exploitative monopoly prices for the military protection of trade. By setting up a unified military and commercial network that linked the local factor in Asia to distributors and investors back in Europe, the trading companies created a structure for relatively more stable demand and investment flows. By giving primacy to the aims of

---

[13] My understanding of the Dutch *Verenigde Oost-Indische Compagnie* (VOC) leans heavily on Hannah Rabe, "Aktienkapital und Handelsinvestitionen im Ueberseehandel des 17. Jahrhunderts," *Vierteljahrschrift für Sozial- und Wirtschaftsgeschichte*, vol. 49 (1962), pp. 320–368, and George Masselman, "Dutch Colonial Policy in the Seventeenth Century," *Journal of Economic History*, vol. 21 (1961), pp. 455–468. On the actual operations of the VOC, J.C. van Leur, *Indonesian Trade and Society: Essays in Asian Social and Economic History*, van Hoeve, The Hague, 1955, and M.A.P. Meilink-Roelofsz, *Asian Trade and Influence in the Indonesian Archipelago between 1500 and about 1630*, Nijhoff, The Hague, 1962, have proved especially helpful. My discussion of the English East India Company has been greatly influenced by K.N. Chaudhuri, *The Trading World of Asia and the English East India Company, 1660–1760*, Cambridge, Cambridge, 1978, especially pp. 1–18, 57–78, 109–130, 453–462.

[14] See Vitorino Magalhães Godinho, *Les Finances de l'Etat Portugais des Indes Orientales (1517–1635): Materiaux pour une Etude Structurale*, Fontes Documentais Portuguesas, Paris, 1982.

immediate profit rather than territorial integration or social stability and by limiting the size of the administrative apparatus that kept the system operating, they checked the imperial–autarkic tendency for overhead to devour earnings and productive labor or profitable exchange to be crushed under the ever heavier weight of costly rule. Here was a technique that initially gave wealth and force a direct stake in each other and that created the conditions for their stabilizing mutual reinforcement.

The more the trading companies lived up to these ideal characteristics of protection policy (and they never fully did, as the stubborn vitality of the overland trade demonstrates), the greater the dilemma they posed for European national governments. Failure to resolve this dilemma was one powerful reason preventing the companies from becoming models for a solution to the protection problem in Europe.

If the possibilities most clearly manifest in the Dutch United East India Company had been worked out, the result would have been a thoroughgoing "political capitalism," with the lines between government and enterprise frankly and entirely blurred. But, if this merger of public administration and economic management had been perpetuated on a larger scale, the society as a whole would have moved toward a tighter and more inclusive reciprocal dependence between governmental office and private economic privilege. The ensuing stalemate would have resembled the situation in China at the time of the mid-T'ang. This stultifying outcome would have entailed the reversal of the forces that had encouraged both the relative separation of rent from tax and the emergence of the modern idea of property. Such a reversal would have implied as well a successful attack on the whole vision of private rights, privileges, and immunities in which the bourgeois–aristocratic ideal of freedom had expressed itself. Moreover, it might have reproduced in Holland the standard imperial–autarkic threats to prosperity through growth: the sacrifice of profit to harmony, of production to officialdom, and of economically prudent to economically reckless warfare.

The other horn of the dilemma represented by the trading companies was better exemplified by the English East India Company. It was the threat posed by enterprises that combined military capability of their own with a broad margin of autonomy from governmental control. Each firm might therefore become a veritable counterstate. Such a state within a state would be an inherently unstable body, constantly struggling to redefine, in its own favor, its relation to the national government and constantly unsettling the foreign and domestic policies of the state.

The future in the West and in the world beyond belonged initially to a solution in which Venice and its early rivals had pioneered but which England developed more fully. At its first moment, this solution revolved around two elements.

One was the constant threat or exercise of armed force to secure mercantile privileges and favorable terms of trade or to undermine the advantages of commercial rivals. The trade war was the most spectacular example of such a policy, but it was not the only one. The intimidation of local potentates, the defense of the merchant marine (as by the Cruisers and Convoys Act of 1708), and the conquest of far-flung territorial enclaves and bases all contributed to the larger aim. Strategic issues, like those raised by the Spanish succession, were closely bound up with the defense of the Levant and the Mediterranean trade and with access to America, and that is how they were perceived by the English leaders. The same interweaving of commercial and strategic aims marked operations in the Baltic and Indian theaters.

The second element in this winning solution was a relatively loose but stable association between the commercial and the military–political arms of national power. The masters of the polity, and of its armies and navies, recognized a stake in the foreign successes of national merchants. They stood ready to use a whole range of forms of pressure and coercion to assist traders in their gambles. But commerce, rule, and force, although ordinarily committed to the same hands, might momentarily part company. Rule and force might be separated from trade. It was this separation of economic and governmental power that made possible what the system of the belligerent trading companies had not: the marshaling of the full might of the country on behalf of discrete commercial objectives. It also allowed the relative independence of economic elites from direct governmental definition and control, as well as the avoidance of a counterstate whose uncertain claims to power would have provoked new conflicts within the privileged segments of society.

As late as 1857, Cobden had lamented that "the manufacturers of Yorkshire and Lancashire look upon India and China as a field of enterprise which can only be kept open by force." When, in the aftermath of the Seven Years' War, some of the City merchants began to doubt the adequacy of war as an instrument of commerce, their disillusionment had less to do with doctrinal conversion than with disappointment at France's ability to recoup in peace what she had lost in battle.

By the middle of the nineteenth century, this new approach to the quest for wealth through force had been refined into a policy that alternated, according to economic convenience and political opportunity, between protectionism and free trade, between the overt domination of foreign peoples and their covert economic subjection through privileges of access and exchange. Success lay in movement from one of these directions to another; certain failure lay in taking any one of them too seriously. Free trade made sense when the country that espoused it was already in some forward wedge of technological innovation or industrial output and could count on armed support if the trading system degenerated into a military free-for-all. Formal rule rather than informal economic advantage was desirable only if the local powers were too weak and unreliable to provide the local protective shell for profitable trade, or if the area to be governed was a source of crucial raw materials and labor, or if the colony had special strategic importance to the promotion of national power interests. All these policies required the intelligent manipulation of tariffs or finance, and implied the pegging of certain regions at distinct places in the international division of labor.

The stability of the revised political and economic system was vulnerable from the start to at least three hostile forces: the influence of rigid doctrines of free trade or protectionism, imperialism or antiimperialism, among the elites of the expanding countries; the worldwide resistance to the advanced Western powers; and a change in the nature of warfare.

The contending doctrines of free trade and imperialism – typical mixtures of prejudice about facts and seriousness about interests and ideals – kept a disillusioned statecraft from playing freely with the possibilities of protectionism and empire. Even the master players, like Disraeli, who believed themselves beyond faith and illusion, were caught up, if only for the sake of their own careers in office, by the myths and countermyths of imperial rivalry.

Then, the freedom to maneuver between the options of free trade and protection, formal and informal rule, was soon narrowed, first by the sheer resistance of the foreign peoples and then by their selective ability to catch up and to do so by routes that increasingly departed from the stratagems of European wealth and power. Once the world had been put on fire, it would no longer be safe for anybody, least of all for the original incendiaries.

Finally, reliance on trade war as the last resort in bringing force to the help of wealth depended on special conditions, conditions that eroded long before the technology of massive destruction had been invented. The classic trade war, with its heyday in the mid-eighteenth century, belongs on a spectrum of modes of warfare in modern European history. At one pole of this spectrum was the modest dynastic or territorial war, fought for limited power objectives and compatible with the inconclusive comings and goings of mercenary armies and with the habit of feckless plots. At the other pole of this spectrum lay the war of national conquest or liberation. Modern war, because it requires the support of large populations asked to suffer or die for the state, cannot openly be fought to flatter some politician's conspiratorial scheme or to enlarge some rich man's bank account. The economic motive of total wars must be held in the background and quickly overtaken by broader and less well-defined national objectives. In such objectives – the ones for whose sake men go into battle – the economic interests of factions will be confused with those of entire populations, and these latter motives will in turn be mixed up with spiritual aims and collective loyalties that, once evoked, cannot easily be guided.

The trade war leads a precarious life between these two extremes. As part of a sequential strategy, it requires a clarity and a continuity of purpose that transcend the involutions of diplomacy and dynasticism and demand a reliable source of recruits – preferably a well-defined segment of the national population. But the trade war is also incompatible with the more inclusive participation and the more visionary goals of total war. In the age of inclusive conflict, the trade war, along with its corollaries and counterparts, does not suddenly disappear. The greater the change, however, in the character of actual or potential warfare, the more pronounced the shift in the predominant economic significance of war. The establishment of the protective shell may become relatively less important than the experience of comprehensive mobilization itself; for that experience may shatter many of the social obstacles to technological and organizational innovation, as privileges are sacrificed for the sake of national triumph or survival. In such a conflict, defeat may be even better than victory, if the victors are looking for partners rather than subjects and if surrender is the occasion for reform. No change in war, however, except its abolition, could do away with the protection problem: force will still be required to stay the danger of conquest.

In both its early and revised moments, the mutual adaptation of force and riches was most successful when it managed to heed Josiah Child's early advice that "Profit and Power ought jointly to be considered," and yet insisted on cutting the costs of the military apparatus to the minimum compatible with strategic security and commercial advantage. Readiness for war was not just a matter of weapons, ships, and troops; it also depended, according to an 1818 report by the Select Committee of Inquiry on Finance, on the economic prosperity and the financial reserves that cost cutting might foster. In the 1830s and 1840s, before imperialist ideology had become a major independent force and before the English had to confront serious challenges to their hegemony at sea, this attitude made it possible to flaunt naval power while containing the naval budget within modest proportions.

THE ANTINECESSITARIAN IMPLICATIONS OF THE ANALYSIS

Implicit in this account of the novel European accommodation between force and wealth is an apparent paradox whose resolution drives forward the analysis of this book and whose implications extend far beyond the bounds of the protection problem.

The preceding argument strikes one more blow against the idea of a natural and necessary path to industrialized production and warfare and to perpetual technological innovation. It does so by criticizing the assumption that each level of success in production and productivity automatically generates the degree and the type of military force required to ensure its subsistence and progress. On the contrary, an economy may be even more the child than the parent of force, and this reversal or reciprocity of relations is likely to be most acute when a new set of productive organizations is in question. At these moments a breakthrough may require not just a shift in the relative commitment of resources and ingenuity to production or protection but a change in the very quality of the connection between economic and military activity. The outcome will then be the unanticipated effect of a chain reaction of mutually reinforcing inventions in statecraft and moneymaking; a different solution to the military problems might influence the most basic features of the economy, even those that seem to be sequences in a natural history of machines and techniques. So this argument has a close affinity to the observation that there was no compelling link, even in the comparatively similar societies of early modern Europe, between the generic outcome of industrialization and any particular redistribution of property and power, such as the sacrifice of the family farm to the large estate.

The emphasis on the contingency of the ways by which force and wealth multiplied each other seems to stand in tension, in the preceding analysis, with a theme of compelling progression. The argument contrasts failures or false starts in the handling of the protection problem with the uniquely successful combination of elements in the European (or English) solution and in its latter-day variants. The winning European powers seem to stagger from one stratagem to another until finding and opening the hidden gate to success. This impression suggests that, whatever the vicissitudes preceding the emergence of the successful European approach to the protection problem, the ultimate line of advance was somehow foreordained. Here you have the picture of contestants guessing what is under the hat.

Such an interpretation of the argument, however, underempha-

sizes both the subtlety of the link between context and solution and
the formative significance of the particular sequence of failures and
success. The advantages of a way of exploiting the mutual reinforcement of military and economic power are always relative to a particular situation and to the available ability and willingness to change
the givens of that circumstance. The more that is taken for granted,
the narrower the range of potentially successful solutions is likely to
be. For example, suppose there had been in early modern Europe a
triumphant effort to merge elite position almost completely with
governmental office (in the fashion of some periods in the history
of the agrarian empires). But imagine as well that this effort had
been accompanied, as it had generally not been in the imperial autarkies, by persevance in the determination to limit governmental
overhead and to favor innovation in market structures, techniques,
and organizations. Then, the closer merger between enterprises and
protection pioneered by the trading companies might have become
the basic model, on a larger scale, for the dealings between force and
wealth. The uses of such a more intimate alliance became clear at
later periods in the history of worldwide modernization; post-Meiji
Japan supplied the most remarkable example. Moreover, no matter
how much of the established configuration of interests, powers, and
alliances might be taken as given, this configuration would always
retain an important element of ambiguity and openness.

In England, the relationship between new and old elites and government after the Restoration was not just the clearly defined basis
of the winning strategy of wealth and warfare. It was also, in its
increasing clarity of definition, an outcome of the strategy itself.
Only in retrospect does it seem a natural direction. The most that
can plausibly be claimed about late seventeenth-century Britain is
that the chosen tactic followed a path of least resistance and that in
most of the other countries of western Europe similar ploys would
have had to reckon with more formidable opposition. Beyond that,
such comparisons among the opportunities of the Western European
countries make sense only if one assumes that an innovative approach
to the protection issue had been made possible and necessary by a
fundamental situation more or less shared by all these countries. For
seventeenth-century Europe, in any case, this claim would be difficult
to support.

The other underrated point in the necessitarian interpretation of
the argument is the brute, dumb weight of sequence. Once a country,
or a bloc of countries, has managed to push ahead in the mutual
reinforcement of force and wealth, its immediate rivals come quite
literally under the gun. For the losers, it becomes proportionately
more difficult and dangerous to experiment with wholly different
solutions. Until they have managed to catch up and to safeguard

themselves against one brand of subjection or another, they must balance the costs of blind imitation against the perils of time-consuming experiment. In the first flush of jeopardy they are likely (out of lack of imagination) to exaggerate the perils and underemphasize the costs. The rush to repeat in sequence the successes of a path-breaking competitor will give a specious appearance of naturalness and necessity to the favored solutions. This appearance may fade away only gradually as the true extent of freedom in recombination and invention becomes apparent. This familiar story forms a major part of the history of dealings between the Western and the non-Western worlds, from the middle of the eighteenth century to the end of the twentieth.

This clarification of the general sense of the analysis makes it important to identify the European experiences and inventions that made a reordering of the relations between force and wealth both possible and urgent.

THE TECHNOLOGICAL SETTING OF THE SUCCESSFUL EUROPEAN SOLUTIONS

The technological context of the early modern European redefinition of the protection problem was a selective increase in the productivity of labor and in the deadliness of weaponry. This advance gave to some Western European powers a decisive edge over others and to the whole bloc of them a partial but mounting advantage over the rest of the world. The reshuffling of the conventional relationship between force and wealth made it possible for Europeans to exploit breakthroughs in military and productive capability to higher mutual advantage; there would be a more effective counter to the threat that new wealth would be left either relatively unprotected or all too vulnerable to the appetite of government. At the same time, however, the advances in production and warfare entered, from the very start, into the new protection strategy. These gains made it possible to expand the base from which taxes and military power might be drawn so that a proportionately smaller part of the economy might be sacrificed, in times of crisis, to the imperatives of war policy. (Just how fragile this development was can be inferred from the recurrence of fiscal crisis in even the luckiest and best-managed European states.) Greater wealth and power also enabled the leading states to undertake, more readily and more successfully, the risks of confrontation. The prosperity of each of these countries – Great Britain first among them – came to be decisively influenced by the ability of each to achieve military and economic gains, even beyond the boundaries of a consolidated territorial empire. If the technical bases for such renewed gains had not been at hand, the pressure would have been very great for modern European states to fall back, as Philip II's Spain had done, into a variant of the autarkic–imperial program.

These technological advances in production and warfare might be overshadowed, for the moment, by mere shifts in commercial organization or by the more effective employment of already existing instruments of fighting, agriculture, and manufacture. Technological change could depend on a wide spread of heterogeneous causes ranging from the long continuance of a high level of commercialization in the economy to governmental initiative under the spur of state competition and to the geographical traits and challenges of the Mediterranean and North Atlantic worlds. (The nature of the relation between the social conditions for the industrial–military breakthrough in Europe and the world and the actual technological instruments of that advance is a topic of Chapter 3.) Most remarkable, the technological edge might start out by being very slight and nevertheless carry a heavy weight.

At the same time, we should not exaggerate the scope of the material instruments of force. Many of the non-Western powers with which the Europeans entered into contact were able to catch up to the European level of warfare without any drastic revolution in their domestic arrangements. The Aztecs never had a chance, but the sixteenth-century Ottomans, for example, learned to use European firearms to advantage against less adaptable Mamluks and against the Europeans themselves, despite the self-defeating Ottoman preference for unwieldy artillery. In dealing with geographical areas still farther away, the early Western intruders were even less assured of carrying the day. Until the stepped-up technological innovations of the late eighteenth and early nineteenth centuries, and the reforms in military technique, organization and tactics produced by the Napoleonic Wars, the European military advantage was slight in every area except naval supremacy.[15] Naval inventions were decisive in enlarging the shield of force and in restraining the Westerner from precocious territorial ambitions that might have pushed him in the direction of imperial autarkies. Think of the adoption, after 1300, of the square rig on the mainmast and the ensuing turn to three-masted ships; of the use of packing ships with offensive and defensive cannon; of the ingenuity of a naval architecture that learned to combine the sturdiness of the man-of-war with the dexterity of the galley – a com-

---

[15] The point becomes clear by contrast to the sudden advance of the technological instruments of imperialism during the nineteenth century. See Daniel R. Headrick, *The Tools of Empire: Technology and European Imperialism in the Nineteenth Century*, Oxford, New York, 1981. See also Rhoads Murphy, *The Outsiders: The Western Experience in India and China*, Michigan, Ann Arbor, 1977, pp. 14–15.

bination that provided a visible image of the alliance of trade with war; and of the numerous navigational devices that served these improved vessels.

In other respects the European edge in productive or commercial efficiency was even more tenuous, if it existed at all. In the mid-eighteenth century, the Lancashire cotton industry did not stand much of a chance of surviving in a genuine free-trade war with Indian cotton, an example that could be multiplied many times over for every sector of production. In all such instances, no sensible businessman or politician would have taken seriously the votaries of the law of comparative advantage. In fact, a great deal of the profitable exchange that Europe did carry out in Asia up to the start of the nineteenth century depended on two of the consequences of naval primacy and military success: the use of American bullion and the prosecution of the interregional Asian trade.[16]

The uncertain nature of Europe's technological advantage, especially in early modern times, reinforces an emphasis on the decisive role of the new stratagems for associating wealth with force. Again, technical innovations had played a subsidiary role in these achievements. It was agricultural progress, which might or might not be linked to the concentration of landholdings, that ordinarily ensured a threshold of national prosperity. Without such a foundation of agricultural welfare, specialization in other sectors of the economy would have been seriously hindered. Still more important, the state, in moments of fiscal crisis, would have had less flexibility in exacting resources from an economy that kept the working masses closer to the margin of survival. Such demands as the government did make, under the pressure of fiscal crisis, would have been more likely to ruin economically dynamic groups and to precipitate tendencies toward reversion to natural economy.

THE SOCIAL SETTING OF THE SUCCESSFUL EUROPEAN SOLUTIONS

Two themes of social organization seem to have been especially significant in the restructuring of the relation between force and wealth. One of them has to do with the government's ties to various rich and powerful groups; the other with the relationship of state and elites to the working population.

It was important to the success of the new ways of enlisting coer-

---

[16] See the discussion of the country trade in Kristof Glamann, *Dutch–Asiatic Trade, 1620–1740*, Danish Science Press, Copenhagen, 1958; M.A.P. Meilink-Roelofsz, *Asian Trade and European Influence*, pp. 264–268; K.N. Chaudhuri, *The Trading World of Asia and the English East India Company, 1660–1760*, pp. 191–213.

cion in support of prosperity that central governments not be faced with a relatively unified elite of landholders, merchants, and officials. Such an elite would have forced developments in one of two directions. The first part of this book provides examples of each.

One direction was a mounting circumscription of the central government's freedom of action – a starving of fiscal or military resources and reformist capabilities. Such a solution could hardly have permitted the flexibility of transactions with independent financiers and military entrepreneurs that played so large a part in the European developments. Nor could it have allowed the more successful states to get hold of enough soldiers and funds in hours of crisis and opportunity.

Constraint might have occurred in other circumstances as well. The unified elite might so thoroughly invade the state bureaucracy, and be so thoroughly penetrated by it, that private privilege and governmental office converged. This phenomenon, as has been shown, recurred in different periods of Byzantine, Ottoman, and Chinese history to an extent that even the fifteenth-century Kingdom of Naples, sixteenth-century Piedmont, and prerevolutionary France, in their most statist aspects, failed to match. Under such conditions, the differentiation of ground rent from taxation and the consolidation of a system of rights and immunities could hardly have gone far. The concern of each elite group to ensconce itself in certain privileged positions within the government and from there to work in defense of its interests in the society at large would have been the overwhelming constraint on state policy.

A government that is the victim and the beneficiary of such constraints tends to be both strong and weak. Neither its weakness nor its strength, however, equals that of the state that can devise and practice the protection scheme discussed in the preceding pages. Its strength is the force of elite condominium: the lack of surprise that the custodians of an order may hope for when the potentially warring oligarchies merge, infusing the state. Its weakness is the fragility of statism itself. Governmental power becomes a carcass upon which each segment of the largely unified elite feeds. Every reorientation of public policy amounts to a direct reordering of society, or at least of the interests of society's most advantaged members. The more public-spirited officials or ambitious rulers of such a state may well despair of cutting some of the ties between governmental office and private privilege (if they as much as recognize the desirability of such a severance). They may fall back, instead, on the more manageable objectives of ensuring the minimal welfare of the population, the indispensable supply of taxes and troops, and the regulation of both military and economic activities that least threatens to destabilize the larger social order or to provoke the antagonism of the most powerful factions. Historically, it may be added, we can observe a natural affinity between such a rampant statism, under the sponsorship of a unified elite, and the quest for imperial autarky as the model of relations between force and wealth. Even the twentieth-century partial throwbacks to the imperial–autarkic idea – in Nazi Germany and fascist Japan – were closely linked with the ascendancy of counterparts to these familiar varieties of statism.

These two dangers, of a weakened state or a unified elite, would have slowed Western Europe's progress to wealth and power. The pattern of strength and weakness in a state that could launch the new approach to the protection problem was of a different order. Under the successful dispensation, governments would have to find it relatively hard to expropriate directly the resources of prosperous groups and to raise the price of protection. But they would have to find it relatively easy to make deals with some such groups to the detriment of others and to take decisive action that would necessarily have a very different impact on different elites. It was a strength that had as one of its premises the uneven development of elites, in the light of new economic opportunity, and the deep cleavages among them. Another premise – no direct consequence of the first – was the authority of an idea of rights. This idea was economically important not because it satisfied the predictability allegedly required by some abstract conception of the market but because it set precise limits to the potentially predatory fiscalism of the state and made the search for an alternative accommodation between force and wealth all the more pressing.

Turn now from the relation between government and elites to the situation of the populace. It was a condition of the new scheme that large segments of the population be subject to the activities of the tax farmer or the military entrepreneur. More generally, it was important that the central debates about how to support wealth through force and force through wealth not have to reckon with the commitments to mass mobilization and consent. For such commitments generate a whole new world of obstacles and opportunities. When large masses of people are expected to provide the central government, in their own right, with moneys and soldiers, the crucial pattern of strength and weakness in the mutual adaptation of force and wealth shifts once again. As the opportunity increases to appeal from the very centers of government directly to the masses, the possibility of multiplying power and prosperity through various levels and versions of popular involvement coexists with the risks of mass conflict, risks for collective welfare as for factional interests.

All the chief strands in the early modern European treatment of the protection problem presupposed that the working classes would be almost exclusively objects rather than subjects of the compromises struck at the upper reaches of society. In the event, this requirement demanded more than a weakening of active popular organizations. It demanded as well the removal of contention to areas and arenas less responsive to grassroots association and militancy – a shift exemplified by the contrast between haggling over feudal dues and setting centralized tariff policies. It would take a new apprenticeship of organization and conflict to draw these more remote issues into the vortex of popular agitation. Even then, a more complicated set of group alliances would be required, as in the campaign against the British Corn Laws.

The subjection of the working population was implied still more directly by other elements in the winning approaches to the relationship between wealth and warfare. Among these elements were the active aid offered by governments to various types of coercive though contractual employment relationships; the effort to take care, through public charity and supervision, of some segments of the destitute population; and the near abandonment of more ambitious programs of paternalistic reform, like Protector Somerset's half-baked and halfhearted sympathies with the small farmer.

If the two principal elements in the social context of the new protection system are put side by side, they can be summarized in a striking partnership of complementarities and tensions. The comparative fragmentation of elites and the central government's corresponding freedom of maneuver helped unify the rich and the powerful and enable them to join forces against the masses below.

This way of putting the issue immediately suggests the major alternative possibility of development that this one, for the while, excluded. The alternative would have been a more direct, mutually reinforcing association between the elite and the mass, between the factions in control of the central state apparatus and its armies, on one side, and broader sectors of the ordinary population, on the other. The emergence of this possibility would have spelled a more decisive conflict between the state and many old or recently established elites. It would have pushed the whole problem of the relation between national power and wealth into the realm of accelerated popular mobilization. In this realm the chances of both material success and material disaster were heightened.

The alliance between the elites and the masses remained, in one form or another, a latent possibility throughout modern European history. In widely different settings, this possibility was almost realized. Its manifestations ran from Florence in 1494–1498, to the chance that Cromwell's New Model Army might have gotten out of control and succeeded in institutionalizing a regime under the aegis of some of the ideals and alliances it had evoked, and to the more populist impulses in the German armaments politics of the early twentieth century. The triumph of these suppressed impulses – not necessarily more benign but surely very different in effect – would have required a greater reordering of privileged interests and influential beliefs than did the arrangements that prevailed. Undoubtedly, this fact helped ensure the failure of those bids. But to recognize this fact, as one element in a more complex explanation, is not to interpret the European protection devices as the unique "best" solutions to the European protection problem nor the factional victories and defeats that produced them as the indispensable path to worldly success.

THE GEOPOLITICAL SETTING OF THE SUCCESSFUL EUROPEAN SOLUTIONS

Alongside its technological and social conditions, the new protection approach also had a geopolitical context: the permanence and ferocity of state conflict within the European state system. This circumstance excluded the overall territorial integration within Europe itself, if not in far-flung lands, that would have suited imperial–autarkic ambitions.

This geopolitical rivalry put heavy pressure on the need to carry through reforms that would enlist force in the support of wealth without crushing productive wealth under military costs. States like Olivares's Spain that failed to adopt such reforms and to balance economic and military or diplomatic policy soon paid the price in both economic crisis and political decline.

Moreover, the continuing intensity of conflict among European states contributed to one of the social conditions of the new protection strategy. War – even limited war – brings instability as nothing else can. For each successful or failed military adventure, there are some elites in the contending countries that are gaining and others that are losing, in riches, power, and honor. The repetition of war – great wheel of fortune – helped check tendencies toward the unification of landholding, mercantile, and bureaucratic oligarchies.

In another setting of wealth and power, contention among states would never have sufficed to inspire or sustain the European protection innovations. That much can be inferred from some ready comparisons. Think of the state system of the Hellenistic world before the Roman and Sassanian conquests, or of China in the Warring States period before the Chin unification.

Preimperial China, especially, bore many resemblances to early modern Europe: the enduring viciousness of battle among countries; the relative multiplicity of elites, combined with a variety of forms of contractual and coercive dependent labor; and the concern with experiments in statecraft. There is no reason to believe that the margin of surplus over physical subsistence was much greater in seventeenth-century Europe than in the China of the fourth and third centuries B.C. If the times of Han Fei and Chuang Chou lacked the religious and political conceptions of right that influenced the European developments, it is nevertheless true that preimperial religion and social thought had a wealth of tendencies that later orthodoxy and eclecticism easily obscure. So it is not surprising to find in this era of Chinese history – as in certain periods of other civilizations – policies and proposals that moved beyond the imperial–autarkic and the overlord–enterprise approaches to a partnership between force and wealth. These tendencies linked the conventional concerns with military, agrarian, and fiscal reform to an explicit acknowledgment of the mutual translatability of wealth and force. They ordinarily put the emphasis, however, on social stability and geopolitical success, rather than on economic growth at home and commercial advantage abroad, as both engines and artifacts of military ascendancy.

This partial similarity of context, however, did not serve as the basis for similar developments. For one thing, the Chin and their Han successors brought about what the Hapsburgs, the Valois, and the Bourbons did not have but wanted to have and might have had – an early unification. The handiwork of that unification was, moreover, never entirely dismantled in later times of trouble. The legacy of early unity made it that much easier, in an atmosphere of imperial–autarky and political consolidation, to achieve, by the time of the mid-T'ang if not, before, of the Ts'ao Wei (220–264) and Toba Wei (386–535), a much more inclusive overlap between private place and governmental office than was to emerge in any Western European country. Moreover, China lacked at the time of its unification a level of technological dynamism and improvement comparable to the one achieved by early modern Europe. Throughout its history it took but few and halting steps toward the incorporation of technology into an incipient unified practice of analytical reason, machine production, and rationalized collective labor.

The European resolution of the protection problem was inseparable from the accumulations of these circumstances – technological, social, and geopolitical. To aim beyond the imperial–autarkic or the overlord–enterprise schemes, and to do so in a way that could have favored quantum leaps in productivity and production, other societies would have had to formulate different responses, suited to their own conditions.

The general lessons suggested by this discussion of war and wealth are almost entirely negative. The first lesson reminds us that we cannot understand a sequence of institutions of production and exchange apart from the means for protecting them. Nor can we treat these protection devices as passive artifacts, without influence on the economic arrangements that they safeguard. We must recognize the unsettling effect of battle and its fortunes on even those lines of economic and social change that seem most deep-seated and impervious to disturbance or control. And, in distinguishing circumstances that proved favorable to more successful approaches to the protection problem, we must also acknowledge the gap between all such circumstances and the actual event of technical and organizational innovation. The second lesson is the heavy burden that both the prince–peddler and the imperial–autarkic solutions impose on economic growth. They exact this price most directly through predatory fiscalism and runaway costs. They impose it more subtly through the lack of governmental concern for long-run economic growth that both these protection strategies reveal. Both solutions sacrifice material dynamism to collective harmony, oligarchic unity, or imperial ambition. Third, the discussion discredits the idea that, under any conditions, only a few alternatives to the prince–peddler and imperial–autarkic approaches could possibly succeed.

The more successful European solutions to the protection problem made sense only in European circumstances. Even in Europe the emergent protection strategies might have been different and still not barred the way to later industrialization. With different protection strategies, however, industrialization would have followed a different course and produced different social consequences.

The technology of warfare might have given greater emphasis to enormous land armies and their weapons, both in the European theater and in operations outside Europe. After all, England's ability to exact favors through a pretense of naval supremacy was partly a matter of bluff and, by the middle of the nineteenth century, the bluff was called. An earlier and larger reliance on mass armies might in turn have precipitated, well before the Napoleonic Wars, efforts at popular mobilization. The technology of production, from the time of its relatively slow progression in the generations before the industrial revolution, might have been more slanted toward the skills and interests of the small-scale farmer, the domestic worker, and the many cadres of artisans that abounded in the early modern European economy.

A closer partnership between central rulers and small-scale farmers, merchants, and manufacturers might have accompanied the fragmentation of mercantile, official, and landholding elites that occurred in several European countries during the early modern period. Such a partnership might in turn have led in two ultimately, although only ultimately, opposing directions. It could have moved toward experiments in controlled popular mobilization and populist autocracy – a dream that could go anywhere, from the characteristically disappointed aspirations of the most farsighted Chinese, Byzantine, and

Ottoman autocrats to the more tangible achievements of twentieth-century Communist party elites. Or it could have pushed toward a less easily managed experiment in mobilization and in the redistribution of power and wealth, given the ease with which the led overtake the leaders in a situation of expanding conflict.

Territorial unification might have moved further and more quickly in early modern Europe. The result might have either greatly weakened or greatly strengthened government and, in the latter event, either to the benefit or the detriment of the ordinary population's claims on central power and its uses. Although rivalry within the European state system may, at the earliest stages, have been crucial to the actual path on which Europe traveled beyond the imperial–autarkic and overlord–enterprise schemes, the rivalry was not indispensable to any imaginable path. In fact, it seems hardly more than a contributory influence on the route Europe actually took.

Moreover, the effort to bring the protected economic area under a single sovereignty might have succeeded at later moments in Western and world history. When twentieth-century Germany and Japan attempted to build forms of autarky on economies similar to those of the Western powers of their day, they were defeated because they were defeated. No inherent illogic vitiated their plans for semiautarky.

Outside Europe, and therefore outside its superimposed technological, social, and geopolitical circumstances, countries might take other, yet more divergent routes of escape from the overlord–enterprise and peddler–prince cycles. The non-Western or relatively backward world would have to discover this room for maneuver in its own time, slowly and dangerously, as it responded to the leading Western powers. Who knows how much of this potential for variation remains undiscovered?

NOTE ON A PROBLEM IN THE RELATION BETWEEN THE ARGUMENTS OF CHAPTERS 1 AND 2

There is a puzzle in the relation between the terms of the successful European response to the protection problem and the conditions that allowed European societies to escape the recurrent cycles of commercial prosperity and reversion to natural economy, governmental unification and governmental fragmentation, that plagued the traditional agrarian–bureaucratic empires of world history. The key devices of European protection policy took for granted the existence of relatively unorganized and passive working masses. But I have argued that European societies were able to evade the disintegrative cycles of the agrarian–bureaucratic empires, thanks to the comparative empowerment of peasant communities at an earlier phase of European history: the varying ability of these communities to organize collectively and to stand up to local magnates without having to confront central governments capable of tilting the scales of conflict in the magnates' favor. Two complementary ideas resolve the apparent inconsistency. They also help dispel certain ambiguities in the argument of this chapter.

The first point to bear in mind is the importance of sequence. Reformers hit upon the winning solutions to the protection problem long after their societies had set the path-breaking agrarian pattern, after a long series of half-failed experiments, on the very eve of Western industrialization and in the very course of Western world conquest. Suppose that at the earlier time, when town–country relations were taking shape, the working people had been disorganized and crushed under the weight of a unified oligarchy in charge of an active government. They might then never have become, in another era, the passive objects of the tax farmer and the military entrepreneur. There simply would have been no strong, relatively independent government capable of resorting to the expedients of the military entrepreneur and the tax farmer. The emerging European states would have shared in the reversion cycles and the protection strategies of the agrarian–bureaucratic empires. At times of additional economic or military pressure, they would have fallen victim to the disasters of land concentration, market shrinkage, and administrative collapse. In their moments of strength, they would rarely have departed from the overlord–peddler or the imperial–autarkic approaches to wealth-making activities.

There is another way to make the same point. My earlier discussion of the European escape from natural economy emphasized the important difference between two historical situations. There were circumstances in which elites crushed popular peasant or town-based organization only after long-drawn-out conflict had already changed the nature of peasantries, elites, and towns, and shattered the agrarian patterns characteristic of so many other, non-European societies. Then there were situations in which the magnate triumph was precocious or radical enough to impede or undo such a breakthrough. This contrast tracks the difference between the column II and the column III developments of Table 1 (pp. 38–39), between the stereotypical (though in fact exceptional) English experience and the Eastern European or Russian contrasts to it. Even within this stereotypical line of development, both government and the working people had to retain some of the capabilities they characteristically lost in the more common experience of agrarian empire. The state lacked the means to centralize power, expropriate resources, and thoroughly regulate the activities of the landholding and merchant elites. But it could still mobilize power against foreign and domestic enemies. It could still multiply its sources of revenue and recruits. It could still play some elite factions off against others. The peasants might lose their smallholdings, and the petty manufacturers and traders their chances of independent existence. But economically dependent and disciplined labor kept its chances for contractual freedom and alternative employment.

Another line of thinking helps resolve the apparent paradox. Governmental protection of economic activity might well have allowed for a much more intimate partnership between popular groups and central rulers. A slightly different course of group conflict over the mastery and uses of governmental power might have drastically expanded the recourse to a popular soldiery. Such an approach might have anticipated the era of people's wars and of universal conscription and taxation. And it might have done so in a climate that allowed for a significant measure of independent popular organization. The character of the state, and the relation of government to the economy, would then have been changed. The result would probably have deviated even further from the overlord–peddler and imperial–autarkic solutions than did the protection strategies that won out in early modern Europe.

Thus, what seems to be an unjustifiable inconsistency in the argument turns out to be a telling asymmetry. An early and relentless crushing of popular organization would probably have prevented the innovative European solutions to the protection problem. By contrast, the vitality of popular organization would simply have made feasible other, yet more drastic ways to escape the constraints that had held agrarian societies captive.

3

Plasticity into Power:
Social Conditions of Military Success

THE THEME AND ITS SIGNIFICANCE

WHAT social conditions enable societies to initiate and to exploit breakthroughs in military capability? A comparative-historical study that begins to answer this question must anticipate a style of social and historical analysis that gives a prominent role to two theses. Let me call these claims the thesis of institutional indeterminacy and the thesis of plasticity. Both of them implicitly criticize Marxism and modernization theory for embracing the idea of a one-to-one relation between a particular level or mode of practical productive or destructive capability and particular sets of institutional arrangements. (In Marxism, for example, capitalism serves as the indispensable vehicle for a certain level of growth of the productive forces of society.) According to the thesis of institutional indeterminacy underlying the argument of this book, the development of productive or destructive capacities does indeed depend on institutionally articulated social conditions. But we can acknowledge this dependence without subscribing to the belief that only one institutional system, or only a particular set of alternative institutional systems, can sustain a certain measure of advance in the improvement of practical power to produce or to destroy. In place of the idea of unique, determining institutional conditions for practical success we can put the notion of crucial qualities of institutional arrangements. In this alternative view there is no way and no practical or explanatory need to define a closed list of the sets of institutional arrangements or of the trajectories of institutional change that can display these success-favoring qualities.

Prominent among these characteristics is the attribute of plasticity. By plasticity I mean the facility with which work relations among people – in a plant, in a bureau, in an army – can be constantly shifted in order to suit changing circumstances, resources, and intentions. Plasticity is the opportunity to innovate in the immediate organizational settings of production, exchange, administration, or warfare and to do so not just by occasional, large-scale reforms but by an ongoing, cumulative flow of small-scale innovations. According to the thesis of plasticity, the advantages of rigid control or surplus-extraction schemes outweigh the benefits of plasticity only at relatively low levels of resource availability and technological sophistication.

Plasticity does not mean a social *tabula rasa*. Definite institutions and institutional innovations are required to increase the plasticity of work relations. The thesis of institutional indeterminacy merely forbids us to insist that only a predefined list of institutional systems can do the job.

In this chapter, I explore the themes of plasticity and institutional indeterminacy from the limited and distorted but also illuminating perspective of military history. Taking destruction as a mirror of production, I examine, comparatively and historically, circumstances and institutions that have favored or hindered advances in the destructive capabilities of rival states and societies. Admittedly, the productive and military angles cannot be completely separated: industrial capacity has become ever more intimately linked with military power, and the machines of production have always proved at least partly interchangeable with the machines of warfare. There is nevertheless enough of a difference to make a distinct vantage point possible.

The main attraction of the military perspective is relative simplicity. The enabling conditions for the development of practical capabilities stand out more clearly and crudely in the concentrated, specialized arena of warfare than in the complex and ill-defined history of productive techniques and economic institutions. A subsidiary advantage of military history is that less theoretical prejudice has been invested in it. Our ideas about the bases of military empowerment have suffered the direct influence of the reigning traditions of social theory a great deal less than our views of economic progress. People who, through the study of economic and social history, long ago made up their minds about the familiar controversies of social theory may find in the surprises of military history reasons to change their minds.

SOME CATEGORIES OF ANALYSIS

Long-term advances in military capability require improvements in the technology of destruction and extensions of the material resources and the manpower that can be made available for the war effort. Call these elements, respectively, the technological and the mobilizational opportunity.

Manpower and resources may be needed for the actual fighting, or for the financing of battle, or for the production of the technology of combat. As the destructive technology improves and the material and human elements that can be committed to the struggle expand, the war itself becomes potentially more absolute. The conduct and outcome of combat can consume the collective efforts, power, and resources of an entire people. War can shatter the protective structure of the state, lay bare and open the social order, and dissolve fixed hierarchies and divisions in a nightmare of violence drawing society back into a circumstance of relative indefinition.

Of course, many advances in destructive power have involved merely a broadening of the resource and manpower base of warfare, without technological innovation. Conversely, many technological innovations have not been used to widen this base. Some innovations have allowed states to commit fewer people and less capital to war or to production for war. But the strongest pressure for organizational and social transformation has occurred when a state pioneers or emulates developments requiring both the expansion of resources and the improvement of techniques. The existence of these two parallel lines of pressure characterized the military rivalry of the Western powers from the Renaissance to the industrial revolution. It then became a characteristic of world military competition.

Weapons do not fight. Enlarging the recruitment, productive, and financial bases of the war effort does not by itself solve the problem of how to organize and operate a fighting force. At least until the very highest levels of destructive power are reached, every attempt to take advantage of technological and mobilizational opportunities depends heavily on the structure and, conduct of the fighting force. Even under the most extreme conditions, there must be a will determined to escalate the use of these destructive forces. There must be an organization capable of delivering or countering blows. Technological and mobilizational advances prove futile unless the army, thanks to its structure and organization, can exploit them to the hilt. Repeatedly, the history of war shows that the possibilities of a weapon fail to be adequately exploited or even perceived because of constraints imposed by the army's organization (the force at rest); its operational style (the force in movement); or its tactical procedures (the force at the moment of shock).[1]

As advances in weaponry accumulate and interact, they often require ever greater degrees of skill and judgment. Soldiers must be able to bring out the fullest capabilities of the weapon in the midst of the confusion, terror, and exhaustion of violent conflict. They

---

[1] See Edward N. Luttwack, "The Operational Level of War," *International Security*, vol. 5 (1980–1981), pp. 61–79. A central concern of the present essay is to investigate the conditions that enable societies to exploit what Luttwack calls the relational-maneuver style of warfare as opposed to the rigid and costly attrition style, which requires clear superiority of manpower and resources.

must learn to defend themselves against their adversaries' use of these weapons. They must reconstitute the elements of order, resistance, and direction despite the intensified destruction each advance in weaponry is likely to produce.

At times, war leaders have tried to use technical advances as an alternative to delegation of authority. Often, the combatants themselves have hoped to make the more advanced weapon an alternative to the horror of the shock. Their dream has been to deal a deadly blow from a distance while remaining in an invulnerable position. But almost invariably each of these hopes has been disappointed. The futility of one is closely bound up with the futility of the other. The effort to escape from action in violent surroundings, like the attempt to establish a central command that makes all subordinate discretion unnecessary, is a fruitless struggle to wage war while escaping its characteristic traits of untrammeled violence and extreme contingency.

It may seem that instantaneous weapons of mass destruction make this hope of avoidance more realistic. But even this prospect is doubtful so long as these weapons are not monopolized by one power and so long as they fail to annihilate the enemy at a single first strike. In the atmosphere created by such a conflict, the shock of mass destruction must be followed – if anything can follow it at all – by efforts to impose the rudiments of order and to disarm the remnants of resistance, in an atmosphere in which all established bonds have been torn violently apart.

Consider now the organizational, operational, or tactical implications of attempts to respond to a mobilizational opportunity. The effort to expand destructive power by simply increasing the funds and the men available for battle, support, and armaments production may fail because the army is unable to operate in a way that puts these additional resources to the most deadly effective use. There is, in fact, a familiar process by which quantitative extension may bring qualitative degradation. The war leaders try to win by simply piling on soldiers, workers, and weaponry. In their strategic, operational, and tactical procedures, they subordinate the demands of maneuver and surprise, daring and ingenuity, in warfare. They try to concentrate all discretion in headquarters and gain absolute control over their soldiers through centralized commands or threats. By these devices, the generals attempt to rigidify the distinction between the task setters and the task appliers.

When war is waged in such a spirit, victory between equal forces becomes nearly impossible. Battle declines into mindless slugging. The army becomes hostage to the adversary who can imagine a procedure that restores maneuver and intelligence to the contest and that makes tactical flexibility and operational discretion vary directly rather than inversely with the quantitative enlargement of the resources and manpower available for war. The style of command and communication of such an adversary must make it possible to preserve a unified thrust while giving and absorbing surprise in the field. The army must be filled with soldiers who can be given this manner of discretion.

So the attempt to make the most of a technological or mobilizational opportunity is likely to require a series of organizational, operational, and tactical inventions. The overall direction of the demands that successive technological and mobilizational advances place on the nature and action of armies seems to be relatively constant. The effort to make good on technological and mobilizational opportunities accentuates rather than abolishes the most characteristic features of warfare: the capacity to surprise and to survive surprise, the ability to preserve order and momentum in conditions of intense variety and violence, and the successful combination of practical opportunism in the moment and in the field with a continuous structure of guidance, communication, and coordination.

The pressure of technological and mobilizational opportunity on the organizational, operational, and tactical style of the army is the specific military form of a general linkage in social life: the linkage between capacity to produce or to destroy and the organizational conditions of this ability. Organizational, operational, and tactical reforms work only if accompanied by changes in aspects of social life outside the military setting. Power and production must somehow be reordered in a way that changes government's relation to society and shifts the relative positions of elites and classes. This requirement generates, in warfare and production, a second linkage: the linkage between the immediate organizational setting of practical capabilities and the larger ordering of society. Changes in the broader, extramilitary context are relevant, both directly and indirectly, to the state's ability to exploit technological and mobilizational opportunities to the hilt.

The direct relation is straightforward in principle although its actual historical manifestation may be extraordinarily elusive. Whatever the enabling circumstances of invention and innovation generally may be, they apply to weapons making. Among these circumstances is sure to figure the need to shake loose privileged claims on governmental power and hardened collective deals that stand in the way of any reordering of men, machines, and investment funds. Enlargement of the means and manpower available for the war effort requires the people in charge of the central state apparatus to have means and excuses to draw on large amounts of soldiers, workers, and capital. The success of this resource mobilization is in turn likely to depend on the taming of locally based oligarchies or intermediate elites who might otherwise impose a stranglehold on crucial resources, as they so often did in the history of the agrarian empires. The capacity to keep open the direct line between the heights of the state and the material and manpower base of the war effort is likely to require a reform of the governmental structure. Such a reform demands a shaking up of the same rigidified collective bargains and liens on governmental power that stand as obstacles to continued innovation in the production system.

The reform of society also relates indirectly to the conditions of enlarged mobilizational and technological capacity. Advances in mobilizational and technological capabilities require changes in the organizational foundation and practice of warfare. These changes in turn put pressure on the formative arrangements of the surrounding society. At a minimum, established social divisions and rankings must not be so inflexible and comprehensive that they preclude the existence of any open space on which organizational experimentation for the war effort may take place. The members of the fighting forces must be able to deal with one another in ways not already predetermined, for the most part, by the habits and hierarchies of the society in which they live. Even these minimal conditions of organizational reform are likely to cause trouble for important features of social life.

Warfare may seem to require unthinking obedience and ruthless command. In many combat experiences, to be sure, the mass of the army remains subject to this brand of control. Nevertheless, wherever the need for maneuver and subtlety becomes paramount, the conduct of military operations must take a different turn. The alternative fighting style is entrusted most often to elite units that spearhead an offensive, sustain a defense, or handle the most advanced equipment. When the war effort is waged at the frontiers of technological and mobilizational opportunity or when the fighting forces fade into a broader movement of popular resistance and mass mobilization, these same qualities of the elite units must extend to the entire conduct of the war.

In all such situations, it is vital to combine operational flexibility with maintenance of an overall structure of coordination and control. This structure must be upheld even in conditions so violent and confused that both informed guidance by the commanders and ingenious initiative by the subordinates may seem all but impossible.

The more closely you examine the operational imperatives of this way of fighting, the more they seem to resemble the defining elements of a flexible practice of economic production that softens the contrast between task-defining and task-executing activities. Call this military approach the vanguardist style of warfare. The fighting units must not act according to the wooden rules of drill manuals. They must, on the contrary, be ready to identify and exploit the shifting opportunities of the battlefield. But neither can they depend on an unformed trust in one another and in their leaders or in a spontaneous sharing of emotion. For the thrust of battle must be able to continue even at times of despondency and fright. The vanguardist style of warfare must allow for divisions of responsibility in the context of overall guidance. It must be capable of absorbing ever more complex information and machinery. The alternative to rigid rule following and unchecked trust is the development of revisable operating procedures, sustained by a hierarchy that combines, at every level, supervision and coordination from above with initiative and discretion from below. The cumulative effect of these organizational ideals will be to undercut any rigid contrast between task-defining and task-executing jobs in warfare, though not to undercut them in a way that renders the command democratically accountable to the soldiery.

The impulse toward such an operational style often contrasts with the continued prevalence of a very different way of ordering collaborative effort in the production system or even in the ordinary combat units themselves. The army, like the society around it, may be organized according to an amalgam of coercion, exchange, and dominion. But these elements may combine in different proportions to generate different approaches to battle: the army as a communal group bound together by leadership and trust, or the army as an elite of individual fighters with minimal coordination, or the army as a coerced mass of frightened soldiers forced into combat. Or, by some combination of all these, the army may become a group of armed client-followers of their warlord. All these styles of warfare are likely to prove ineffective in a situation of advanced weaponry and massive resource and manpower mobilization.

The most likely alternative to the vanguardist approach to war is the military version of a stark contrast between task definers and task followers, a contrast regularly accompanied by rigid distinctions among the task-executing jobs themselves. The alliance of discretion and supervision in a situation of constantly reviewable operating procedures gives way to the maintenance of a firmer distinction between the task definers and the task executors. Thus, in the great armies of the mid-twentieth century, the vanguardist approach to warfare remained confined to elite armed, air, or commando corps. Similarly, the more flexible interplay of conception and execution in industry flourished in the forward areas of industrial innovation such as the manufacture of custom-built machine tools.

It is easy enough to understand why the vanguardist style of warfare usually remains the exception rather than the rule. It requires the greatest skill and intelligence on the part of the entire fighting force. It cannot easily become widespread in a society in which all the ordinary models of collective effort are cast in another mold. It represents a threatening countermodel. It therefore tends to aggravate the tension between the organizational bases of warfare and the arrangements of the host society.

But, given that vanguardist warfare usually remains exceptional and disturbing, why should it nevertheless persist, with ever increasing tenacity, as violent struggle becomes more terrible in its tools and its stakes? The answer lies partly in the requirements for taking advantage of technological and mobilizational opportunities. The significance of this point can now be linked to my earlier remark about the sense in which a war situation represents an exemplary instance of society forcibly thrown into a circumstance of indefinition.

The extreme moment of shock in battle presents in heightened and distorted form some of the distinctive characteristics of a whole society involved in war. These characteristics in turn represent a heightening and distortion of many of the traits of a social world cracked open by transformative politics. The threats to survival are immediate and shifting; no mode of association or activity can be held fixed if it stands as an obstacle to success. The existence of stable boundaries between passionate and calculating relationships disappears in the terror of the struggle. All settled ties and preconceptions shake or collapse under the weight of fear, violence, and surprise. What the experience of combat sharply diminishes is the sense of variety in the opportunities of self-expression and attachment, the value given to the bonds of community and to life itself, the chance for reflective withdrawal and for love. In all these ways, it is a deformed expression of the circumstance of society shaken up and restored to indefinition. Yet the features of this circumstance that the battle situation does share often suffice to make the very boldest associative experiments seem acceptable in battle even if they depart sharply from the tenor of life in the surrounding society. Vanguardist warfare is the extreme case. It is the response of unprejudiced intelligence and organized collaboration to violence and contingency.

In the conditions created by world history, mass politics, and industrialized economies, and under the double need to survive military challenges and to meet expectations of welfare, every society becomes a little like the country at war and even like the unit in the moment of combat. For this reason a study of the relation between destructive capability and its enabling social circumstances can help uncover the ultimate social bases of worldly success. It does so, however, from a perspective that also limits and disfigures insight.

The preceding pages present a fragmentary scheme of problems and ideas for discussing the relation of military power to its social conditions. Complete this scheme by reconsidering it from the vantage point of the felt need for reform and the reformer's dilemmas. For this purpose, consider the characteristic situation of a country threatened by a rival state that has already seized on underexploited technological and mobilizational opportunities through revolutionary changes in the organizational and social bases of warfare; say, for instance, the European powers as they faced Revolutionary and Napoleonic France.

The people in charge often misunderstand the implications of the military threat in one of two contrasting ways. Sometimes, the rulers and the reformers of the threatened state think that a mere technological transplant – often just buying the best weapons – will be enough. At other times, they imagine that the response can be effective only if it involves a revolutionary assimilation of the threatened society to the threatening one. In this latter view, only the total change of, say, Prussian or Japanese society along the lines of revolutionary France or bourgeois Europe, respectively, could allow them to stand up successfully to the danger from abroad.

The first misunderstanding involves a failure to grasp the crucial connections among technology, operational styles, and resource or manpower mobilization. It therefore also fails to plot the joint implications of these connected changes for the reordering of state and society. The other mistake – when it is not just the revolutionary's effort to turn military crisis into transformative opportunity – amounts to the freezing of all these linkages. It fails to grasp the extent of their variability. Therefore, it does not understand how they really work. As long as there is time for reform, there is also time to find a way of minimizing the subversive impact of reform on the established order. The truth does not lie in an imaginary middle between these complementary errors; the precise nature of the constraints and opportunities varies in each case. There are few technical or operational advances decisive enough to be threatening that justify the first mistake. There are none so shattering as to justify the second. (If the Aztecs had had time to come up with a military force capable of resisting the Spanish, they would also have had time to combine their newfound military potential with social and governmental institutions very different from those of the invading power.)

The minimalist strategy of restricting the subversive impact of military reform has its long-run costs whenever the aim is to keep as much of an established hierarchical ordering as seems possible and prudent. The new style of weapons employment, operational activity, and resource or manpower mobilization will be the outcome of particular compromises with dominant interests of the surrounding social order. Rulers will simply reject the military reforms that threaten to disrupt the existing state and society. But the next round of military challenges will spell trouble for these rigid settlements. It will subject them to a test they might have met more readily had they been less exclusive and less devoted to the perpetuation of an existing social design.

The most significant lessons that the study of military reform can teach us about the social basis of material advances address the relation between two contrasting theses: the idea that a temporarily successful policy of minimalist accommodation to a military breakthrough is always possible and the opposing belief that such a deal is always, in the end, delusive and dangerous. There is always room for a successful compromise between a breakthrough in military capability and an entrenched structure of privilege, rooted in a country's formative institutional arrangements. Yet the entanglement of military operations in a more or less rigid structure of social privilege repeatedly allows a state to be endangered by relatively slight improvements in the weaponry, the operational practices, and the resource and manpower mobilization of its rivals.

The expedients of the minimalist strategy resemble the ploys of a rigidified personality. A person develops personal strategies by which to deal with sources of conflict. Then he faces a slight additional stress that upsets the balance he had so precariously built. Some responses to the root experiences of fear and longing are less susceptible than others to such an upset because they depend less on a rigidified pattern of behavior and perception.

The most important of such brakes on reordering result from the prevailing scheme of social hierarchy and division. The minimalist strategy wielded by a conservative statecraft seems condemned by its very nature to this exemplary failure of flexibility – exemplary because it is only a special, aggravated instance of the weakness of every limited form of social life. What then do the politics of military reform tell us about the relation between the imperative of plasticity and the opportunities for compromise? The following analysis seeks to answer this question by three series of examples, each the occasion for an additional level of insight and refinement. The first batch of examples comes from preindustrial, non-Western societies, the second from late medieval and early modern Europe, and the third from the differing Chinese and Japanese responses to the military threat posed by the Western powers.

PLASTICITY OR DEATH:
MAMLUK, NORMAN, AND AFRICAN EXAMPLES

The Mamluks were the members of the Islamized slave armies who took over in Egypt from the faltering Ayyubid Dynasty and who held on until they suffered defeat at the hands of the Ottomans in

1517.[2] A decisive element in their defeat was their inability or un-willingness to exploit firearms to the extent their Ottoman enemies did.[3] In the battles that led to their downfall, the Mamluks paid for their failure to deploy major infantry units armed with the best firing weapon of the day, the harquebus, a primitive rifle. Instead, they relied on their traditional prize units of cavalry, armed with bow and lance. The Mamluks' use of the harquebus remained largely restricted to the despised and peripheral regiments of "black slaves." The Mamluks' failure was all the more remarkable because they had enjoyed ample warning. Their statesmen had discussed the problem at length. One of their recent sultans had tried rapidly to expand the role of firearms in the Mamluk armies, a project that seems to have en-couraged his assassins. In the final crisis, when the Mamluks were beset, simultaneously, by the Ottomans in the north and by the Portuguese along the Red Sea, they employed artillery effectively against the lesser Portuguese threat while omitting to use it where it counted most.

Why did the Mamluks prove so resistant to a change in the tech-nology of warfare that would almost surely have dramatically im-proved their fighting chances against the Ottomans? A famous study emphasizes that the reorganization of Mamluk armies and tactics around infantry units armed with firearms would have threatened the preeminence of the elite cavalry, so closely entangled in the Mam-luk experience of personal identities, loyalties, and hierarchical sta-tions. Thus the restriction of firearms to inferior elements in the army. Thus also the greater willingness to use the new weapons on the Portuguese front, both because operations in that theater were perceived as relatively less important and because they involved what for the Mamluks was unconventional naval warfare.

Moreover, the Mamluk state suffered from crucial defects in its capacity to serve as an instrument of unified, reforming action under the guidance of a forceful political will. The conquest elite (the Mam-luk slave armies) remained rigidly separated from the common pop-ulation.[4] Hence, the Mamluks found themselves in the precarious and isolated situation of a migratory ruling class that fails to merge

---

[2] The discussion of the Mamluks relies heavily on David Ayalon, *Gunpowder and Firearms in the Mamluk Kingdom: A Challenge to a Medieval Society* (1956), 2d. ed., Cass, London, 1978.

[3] For the contrast with the Ottoman use of guns, see Halil Inalcik, "The Socio-Political Effects of the Diffusion of Fire-Arms in the Middle East," in *War, Technology and Society in the Middle East*, eds. V.J. Parry and M.E. Yapp, Oxford, London, 1975, pp. 195–217.

[4] On the rigid institutional principles that reproduced the social isolation of the Mamluk conquest elite, see A. N. Poliak, "Le Caractère Colonial de L'Etat Ma-melouk dans ses Rapports avec la Horde d'Or," *Revue des Etudes Islamiques*, vol. 9 (1935), pp. 238–248.

with the conquered peoples or with its own rulers. This elite, already isolated from the country in which it lived, was internally fragmented by the fact that each Mamluk chief (*amir*) who became a sultan rose and fell with his own cohort of followers.

The Mamluk state had lived through a period of vitality and expansion. It had successfully expelled from the Levant both leftover European Crusaders and overextended Mongols. But during its later, "Circassian" period it had slid into a protracted decline. Even at the high point of its power, it had never achieved the greater solidity that became possible when a conquest elite managed to merge more successfully with the conquered peoples, as the Ottomans had done. So it suffered in spades from the entropic dissolution and the periodic crises characteristic of agrarian empires. Seen from this angle, the rejection of firearms was simply the capstone of a long process of fiscal starvation, economic degeneracy, and governmental weakness. But it was not, for all that, unavoidable; the occasional attempts to reverse it seem to have come close to success on at least one occasion.

The failure to exploit the technological opportunities of new weaponry and to devise the means with which to mobilize resources and manpower more broadly had similar causes: the failure to change the organization of government and the relation of government to society. This omission aggravated a series of missed opportunities; the conquest elite had refused to change for the sake of worldly success. This inveterate refusal culminated in the rejection of firearms. For the new weapons threatened this elite's settled habits and self-conception in a peculiarly direct way.

One of the practical effects of the tightening constraint on self-transformation and on the mobilizational capabilities of the state was to make the Mamluks hostage to any significant shift in the technical means of destruction. If the encounter between the Ottomans and the Mamluks had taken place somewhat earlier, before the spread of firearms to the Levant, the Mamluks might have done much better. They might also have had a better chance if the confrontation had occurred somewhat later. For then effective handguns would have been available for use by cavalry in motion. In the history of society, as in the life of an individual or even the evolution of a biological species, the failure of plasticity is the characteristic way of delivering yourself into the hand of chance.

My second example extends the inferences suggested by the first. It is the experience of the Crusader principalities and especially the Latin Kingdom of Jerusalem in dealing with its Syrian Seljuq adversaries. The Norman knights who, together with Frankish and Provençal allies, established minikingdoms in the Levant after the First Crusade came from one of the most spectacularly successful migratory ruling classes in all world history. They brought European "feudal" institutions with them to the Holy Land. There, the Normans ultimately suffered total defeat at the hands of their Seljuq enemies.

Their defeat pleases as much as it instructs. After all, only a little earlier Normans had founded in Sicily a kingdom that enjoyed a brilliant though brief summer as one of the most institutionally inventive and precocious of European states. In England they became the core in the ruling elite of a country that, centuries later, was to pioneer the North Atlantic breakthrough. Slight changes of choice and circumstance equalize the peoples of the world before the same ordeal of worldly success. Although the experience of the Crusaders' principalities antedated by far any sign of European industrialization and showed the triumph of a non-European people over European intruders, it exemplifies principles at work in these later and larger confrontations.

The counterpart to the Mamluk failure to adopt firearms was the Crusaders' inability to change their operational style of warfare. They fought in the characteristic manner of the European knight: the loosely organized cohort of individual, heavily armed and weighted warriors, who expected to carry all before them in the shock of a cavalry assault with the spear. Theirs was precisely the stratagem that had been made possible in early medieval Europe by the combination of the horse, the lance, and the thrusting power based on improved saddles and stirrups. It was the very tactic that had been doomed in Europe by the plebeian units of massively formed pikemen. In the Levantine theater, its nemesis was the Seljuq light cavalry. Aside from its numerical superiority and its broader logistic and popular suppport, this cavalry could exploit many elements of movement, surprise, and indirection in warfare.[5]

The Seljuqs' superior mobility provoked the Latins to try to protect themselves by surrounding each horseman with foot soldiers. The result was to aggravate further the immobility of the Norman and Frankish forces, made all the more vulnerable by their fruitless quest for invulnerability. The Seljuqs could thus capitalize on the same tactical style that seems to have played so important a role in the final campaigns of the Indian notables against the tottering Mughal state.

There was also a striking counterpart to the Mamluks' larger failures in the mobilization of resources and manpower. The transplant of a European feudal army to a hostile, non-European environment had a paradoxical effect on the ties of vassalage that bound the Latin knights together. In the atmosphere of unremitting hostility and

[5] See Raymond Smail, *Crusading Warfare, 1097–1193*, Cambridge, Cambridge, 1956, pp. 75–83.

warfare, the Norman and Frankish cadres closed in upon themselves. They hardened bonds that in the more open European situation retained an element of flexibility. This closure added to their isolation, already heightened by ethnic and religious differences from the surrounding population. In the end, the knightly class became a full-fledged caste, defined by governmental dominion, economic parasitism, religious distinction, and legal entitlement.[6]

Yet in order to meet the perils of their situation, the Latin Kingdom of Jerusalem and the lesser Crusader principalities would have had to have taken the path of radical institutional invention and self-transformation. They would have had to have developed the incipient countertendencies at work in their situation: namely, an enlarged role for the orders of fighting monks that had sprung up along the frontiers; an increased emphasis on the coastal towns, on maritime trade with Europe, and on naval protection; and, ultimately, the gradual creation of a unified Norman–Frankish–Syrian society in the Levant.

There was a direct as well as a less immediate and more far-reaching connection between the failure to carry out such a transformative program and the military predicament of the expatriate European host. Neither the Crusaders nor their Seljuq enemies could count on help from the baffled, outraged, and suffering rural populations of the area. But the Seljuqs, by devices that will soon be mentioned, managed to capture the loyalty of the city dwellers and ally themselves militarily with Turkoman nomads. From the latter they got auxiliaries and reinforcements; from the former, crucial support for their campaigns in the field. The Latins, by contrast, could never venture for long from their urban strongholds without fear of losing them.

The earlier, modern European examples showed the paradoxical but unmistakable links among the exploitation of the technical and operational opportunities of warfare, the development of military organizations based on principles in conflict with those that informed the surrounding society, and the appeal to the masses by those who commanded the state and its armies. The Seljuq experience reveals the analogous form that these interdependencies might take before the appearance of industrial economies and the spread of mass politics.

Consider the tendencies of Seljuq policy under the leadership of Saladin, the conqueror who finally took Jerusalem in 1187. Under his extraordinary guidance, the Seljuq conquest state in its relation to the larger Syriac society had continued to develop along lines that

[6] See Aharon Ben-Ami, *Social Change in a Hostile Environment: The Crusaders' Kingdom of Jerusalem*, Princeton, Princeton, 1969, especially pp. 60–71.

dramatically increased its capability for mobilizing resources and manpower. It had done so despite the failure of the Seljuqs, unlike their Ottoman successors and conquerors, to blend more intimately with the conquered populations. The Seljuq state combined an ardent, visionary leadership with the emergence of institutions for centralized rule. Both these accomplishments were set in the context of a less intentional and still more influential process: the sense of a common Islamic cause induced by the beliefs and slogans of a holy war. The ideology of the European Crusade revived and partly transformed the Islamic idea of the sacred war.[7] This extended conception of a sacred union provided a foundation for alliance between the Seljuqs and many elements of the Syriac population. It helped make possible Seljuq reliance on the loyalty of the urban population. The achievement of a proto-nationalism and even a proto–mass politics gave the Seljuqs the means with which to mobilize manpower and resources on a larger scale and enabled them to pursue in the field an operational style of admirable suppleness.

To counter this accomplishment on its own terms, the Latins would have had to have executed a program of institutional invention and collective self-transformation far more radical than the one that brought victory to the Seljuqs. The Europeans, after all, started from a position of greater isolation and smaller numbers. Events taught them the lessons that would be taught later to the Mamluks and did so in a form that depended less on margins of technological advantage than those that the Mamluks had to face.

The sense of the two experiences discussed up to now can be further put into perspective by a third situation: the relation among different kinds of West African states, with different types of weaponry, in the generations immediately preceding outright European rule. The significance of this third example is to emphasize the relativity of military technology. An apparently superior armament does not have the radical, subversive implications we are inclined to attribute to it unless its production and use are integrated into the broader social and spiritual conditions highlighted in my earlier comparisons.

In this West African area, there were at least three distinct varieties of states coexisting during this proto-colonial period.[8] There were the peoples with only the most rudimentary and decentralized governmental institutions, peoples pushed back increasingly to the

---

[7] See H.A.R. Gibb, "The Achievement of Saladin," *Bulletin of the John Rylands Library*, vol. 35 (1952–1953), pp. 44–60, at pp. 53–55.

[8] My discussion of the West African experiences owes much to Jack Goody, *Technology, Tradition and the State in Africa*, Cambridge, Cambridge, 1971, especially pp. 39–56.

marginal frontier zones and still committed to the bow and arrow as their major weapon. There were the states of the grasslands, characteristically ruled by a conquest elite of horsemen. This ruling class usually maintained a broad-based collective solidarity and allowed the highest offices of state to circulate among its own major segments. The basic weapon was the cavalry with the lance. Then there were the centralized kingdoms of the coastal forest areas, like Akwamu, Denkyira, and Dahomey.

In this third type of state, the governmental structure was more likely to be organized around the central power of an autocratic household with wide ranging powers over the supervision of European trade. The fundamental weapon was the gun.[9] But few firearms were produced in these countries. Weapons came from Europe in exchange for African slaves and raw materials. These weapons were then put into the hands of dependent armies of slaves and prisoners, placed at crucial defensive positions around the geographical power centers. (If these dependent guards had revolted, they might have reenacted something like the Mamluk experience, with the handgun replacing the cavalry. But they would have been even less able to face the industrialized European intruders than the Mamluks were to deal with their Ottoman enemies.) The centralized state found reasons and occasions to tighten its hold on power and armies through its control over weaponry and over the trade that made weapons available.

Although the centralized monarchies appeared to possess a weapon far superior to the cavalry of the savanna, this superiority was almost entirely illusory. The illusion is exposed by the relation of these gun-using kingdoms to both the European and the grassland states. When the Europeans decided to impose their rule, they had little trouble shattering the coastal monarchies. At the time that these autocracies retained their independence, they proved unable to conquer the peoples of the savanna. Instead, they coexisted with the savanna peoples in a condition of relative military balance. The gun trade was kept by the careful coastal rulers from going inland. The tsetse fly and the trees kept the cavalry from fighting along the coasts.[10]

The underlying circumstances of economic weakness and mobilizational blockage negated the potential technical advantage of the guns. All these countries – frontier, savanna, and forest states alike – shared a comparatively primitive agrarian base: a low-intensive agriculture, undertaken for the most part with hoes rather than

[9] See Ivor Wilks, "The Mossi and Akan States, 1500–1800," in *History of West Africa*, vol. 1, eds. J.F.A. Ajayi and Michael Crowder, Columbia, New York, 1976, pp. 413–414.
[10] See Jack Goody, *Technology, Tradition and the State in Africa*, p. 55.

plows. Unlike the large and ancient agrarian empires of other parts of the world, these societies could hardly experiment with even rudimentary industrial production. The centralized forest kingdoms therefore remained at the mercy of European governments and gun merchants. Moreover, the coastal kingdoms would have to undergo a radical transformation in order to mobilize more broadly their own resources and manpower for fighting and production. The praetorian guards of enslaved gunmen in the service of an autocracy's short-run interests were a narrower base of support than a large and solidaristic ruling elite of mounted knights.

In all these instances – Mamluk, Norman, and African – success clearly turns on self-transformation. The distinct circumstances of the rival powers may require more self-transformation from one contender than from another: the Levantine Crusaders would have had to undergo a more radical reform of their collective life than their Seljuq enemies. Moreover, the material circumstances of the contenders may be so disparate that no amount of short-run self-transformation will suffice: by the nineteenth century, the coastal monarchies of West Africa never had a chance against the European powers. But the requirement of self-transformation is relentless because it means that, in the long run, practical imperatives and visionary challenges will have a similar effect. There is no aspect of a people's collective life that may not have to be abandoned for the sake of meeting a practical challenge, just as there is no aspect they may not have to jettison in order to deal with the visionary appeal in politics. Consequently, the different forms of social life that exist in the world are always less real than they seem: the differences among them subsist on a containment of conflict. If the nations of the world were exposed to constant practical and visionary conflict, none of the differences among them would have any permanence. This does not mean that the peoples would become alike; it does mean that the marks that distinguish their identities would constantly shift hands and that other marks, never before dreamt of, would suddenly appear. Each people would be in the situation of a philosopher who never slept, never died, and never deluded himself but always thought his ideas through to the end until they began to come apart again. Struggle amounts to an awful thinking, its discoveries remain limited only because its course is interrupted.

The art of self-transformation for the sake of developing practical capabilities seems to have a similar content in the most varied historical circumstances. The Mamluks and the Normans suffered defeat because they failed to open up and readjust the organizational and social contexts of warfare. The Seljuqs succeeded because they did just that. The West African coastal kingdoms used an extraneous technological advantage to avoid having to change radically. But they could neither go on the offensive against the savanna states nor prepare themselves to resist their European patrons and trading partners.

In all these instances, success seems to have required the dissociation and recombination of available models of the organizational and social context of military activity. To have succeeded would not have meant, for the Mamluks, becoming like the Ottomans; it would have meant creating an order that never existed before. To possess the alien, you must change it.

In all these instances success appears to have demanded a closer partnership between the working masses and central government and an ability somehow to translate this association into a structure of collaborative effort in warfare. But it is not clear, from these examples, whether such an effort requires or excludes any particular range of organizational and social solutions to the problems of warfare or whether the influence it exercises is, in any sense, directional.

The remainder of this chapter goes on to develop these initial loose suggestions and insights in two settings. The first series of examples draws on several turning points in European military history, problems and solutions that preceded industrialization and that helped define what the initial Western versions of an industrialized economy and war machine would be like. The next group of examples deals with the response of two nineteenth-century non-Western states to the threat posed by Western powers that had already gained an industrialized military capability.

PLASTICITY AND COMPROMISE: EUROPEAN EXAMPLES

My examples from European history are drawn from episodes bounded chronologically, on one side, by the disintegration of the medieval style of fighting and, on the other side, by the rise of mass mechanized armies, supported by industrial economies, in the nineteenth and twentieth centuries.[11] Despite the broad sweep of time during which they took place, these events show an amazing unity of persistent themes and reciprocal effects. They represent turning points in warfare under the double pressure of expanding scope and developing weaponry. At each crucial juncture, the major attempts made to seize on the technological or mobilizational opportunity

[11] Like all who write on military history, I owe much to Hans Delbrück's *Geschichte der Kriegskunst, im Rahmen der politischen Geschichte,* Berlin, G. Stilke, 1900–1936, especially part 3, "Neuzeit." Another major source of help and inspiration is William H. McNeill, *The Pursuit of Power: Technology, Armed Force, and Society since A.D. 1000,* Chicago, 1982, especially chaps. 3 and 4.

directly influenced one another. They also helped shape the social terms on which industrialization and quickened economic innovation would occur in its initial European or North Atlantic versions.

The dominant style of warfare of medieval Europe, as most characteristically developed in the core areas of feudalism, was the horde of ever more heavily armed mounted knights, fighting individually, with the support of foot soldiers and archers. The major military technology had, for many centuries, been the shock of the cavalry charge with piercing iron weapons. Improved stirrups and saddles had given this shock its force. The manpower and resources for fighting were not continuously available to any central authority. The knights, with their own arms and auxiliaries, were bound by ties of loyalty and exchange to come together under specified conditions for bouts of fighting that were rarely more than sporadic.

This combat unit fought with a minimum of tactical flexibility and coordination. Its fighting style oscillated typically between two modes: the compact mass of the cavalry charge, usually followed by individual hand–to–hand combat. From the start, both variants of this approach suffered from a lack of operational adaptability. As the mounted knight began to confront improved weapons – steel-tipped pikes and primitive firearms used by foot soldiers – he responded with heavier armor. As a result, he became increasingly immobile. He exemplified the futile search for isolated invulnerability at the cost of maneuver and teamwork. Thus, the overall effect of the attempt to achieve protection against new weapons was the further degeneration of a mode of combat already deeply flawed.

Clearly, this was an approach to warfare inseparable from a highly restricted stock of weapons and a sharply limited way of mobilizing men and resources for battle. It allowed for little organizational depth or tactical subtlety. It could not be expected to survive beyond the circumstance of disintegrated governments and disordered markets that had encouraged its original development.

There was however, no single way of waging war that was sure to displace the cohort of armed knights. From the very start, there were alternative emergent lines of development, even in the preference for different kinds of weapons. At least two distinct routes were taken, over the same period of European history, in the struggle against the high medieval style of warfare. Each route exploited technological and mobilizational opportunities that lay beyond the reach of an army of mounted knights bound together by feudal ties. Each was therefore sufficient to deal a knockout blow to the armored knight of the High Middle Ages. Yet neither route proved capable of meeting the next round of technological and mobilizational opportunities without undergoing a radical transformation of its own.

The first line of antifeudal military developments could be called the standing army approach, although I use the term more broadly and loosely than its conventional application would warrant. It was characterized by a regular army of foot soldiers drawn from the peasantry of an emerging territorial state, placed under the supreme command of a monarch–warlord, and provided with improved weapons. At its most solid, such an army consisted of wage-earning soldiers drawn from an independent yeomanry and capable of combining for battle and maneuvering on the field in a way that allowed sudden concentrations of force and enabled different weapons to reinforce one another. In particular, the more powerful missile weapons, longbow – or muskets - could be allied with the shock of the infantry. This combination in turn permitted the development of defensive–offensive tactics in place of the wild attack that a feudal army had to undertake in order to engage at all.

One early example of this challenge to the high medieval style of warfare came at Crécy in 1346, where the tactical and organizational superiority of Edward III's army seems to have been at least as important to the outcome as the effectiveness of the Welsh longbow.[12] Another instance came a century later at Formigny, where the French were this time the victors and the culverin, a medieval fieldpiece, replaced the longbow as the missile that softened up the enemy for the annihilating strike. Charles VII's army was, in fact, among the earliest prototypes of the standing army. It deployed resources and manpower on a vastly enlarged scale, and it united missile weapons with concentrated infantry and cavalry shocks.

Despite its initial successes, however, this fighting style could not easily absorb the impact of a widening mobilizational scope of warfare. The gathering of manpower and resources for the war effort remained open to one of two threats. Oligarchies, entrenched in landowning, trade, or government, might starve emerging central governments of funds and recruits or set the terms on which material and human resources were available. This tendency repeatedly reasserted itself throughout European history. It was superseded only when politics became mass politics and wars became people's wars – from the campaigns of revolutionary France to the world wars of the twentieth century. When the central monarchs, who were also the commanders and creators of the new standing armies, attacked their oligarchic adversaries, they risked being crushed by aristocratic reaction or overtaken by the popular agitation they themselves had incited. The danger of runaway popular rebellion was almost always more remote than the risk of oligarchic domination, given the typical

[12] See Herbert James Hewitt, *The Organization of War under Edward III, 1338–1362,* Manchester Univ., Manchester, 1962, pp. 28–49.

accommodation between sovereigns and oligarchies in absolutist states. It could nevertheless materialize wherever the rural and urban masses had managed to keep a vibrant communal independence and the ruler was determined to make common cause with them against the magnates of the realm. The struggles of Erik XIV of Sweden supply an example.[13] Despite its extraordinary escape from the periodic governmental and economic collapse that Chapter 1 of this book described as reversion to natural economy, Europe had not broken completely free of the ancient quandaries of statecraft in the agrarian empires.

The technological opportunity generated by the continuous development of firearms could also not be easily absorbed by the early examples of standing armies. Effective handling and evasion of firepower and its coordination with shock tactics required skill and subtlety. An army adept at such practices could not be organized internally as a microcosm of the surrounding society, with its set hierarchies and divisions, nor could it operate effectively by the same crude juxtaposition of personal or family initiative and coerced obedience that characterized most of the society's productive activity. It was not enough to get your hands directly on soldiers and funds without having to rely on the good offices of independent oligarchs. It might also become necessary to inaugurate a form of organization that would stand as a disturbing countermodel to the most common forms of coordination and subordination in society at large. The earliest successful versions of standing armies arose in circumstances in which the level of technical development of firearms had not yet made acute these organizational, operational, and tactical demands of more advanced weaponry, while an exceptional domestic and foreign situation had allowed a truce in the struggles among state-building monarchies, realigned aristocracies, and working masses.

Call the other route to the subversion of high feudal warfare communal resistance. Its distinctive characteristic was the deployment of massed square formations of free peasants or town dwellers, bound together by communal ties and by a shared commitment to resist foreign overlords, and armed with clubs and poles (first pikes, then halberds) that could be used to unseat the charging knights. An early crude variant can be seen in the mauling that Flemish burghers gave to French knights at the Battle of Courtrai in 1302, where the people's weapon was a club more primitive than its Aztec counterpart and the tactical exploitation of the marshy ground proved essential to

[13] See Ingvar Andersson, *A History of Sweden*, Weidenfeld, London, 1955, pp. 147–149.

victory. The more advanced version of the same approach was the sixteenth-century Swiss phalanx, deployed triumphantly against Austrian knights.[14]

Defense combined with offense, and anticavalry shock weapons, like the spear and the halberd, with missiles, ranging from the crossbow to the handgun. The resisting popular communes of town or country provided the manpower for combat. The approach to army organization and operation that put these technological and mobilizational opportunities into effect drew on a preexisting experience of communal life. The need to give combat on this new basis in turn strengthened and diversified the forms of collaborative organization in Flemish and Swiss popular life.

But the armies of communal resistance, and the societies that established them, could not readily meet the tests of expanding mobilizational and technological opportunities in warfare any more than the early versions of the standing army. To compete with the resources and manpower available to the emergent large territorial states, the zones of popular resistance would themselves have had to create central state institutions, capable of ruling over large territories and populations and of acting decisively in the struggle against foreign powers. Such an experiment in state building could hardly have been achieved without bold institutional reforms that would have amounted to a major collective self-transformation. Even the access to technological development in weaponry was not easily open to the warfare of communal resistance.

There needed to be a developed state structure able to sponsor firearms production in partnership with manufacturing and technical cadres. Once the weapons were available, there had to be an organizational, operational, and tactical style capable of exploiting them fully. The fierce collective loyalties of massed formations were no substitute for specialization, coordination, and supervised discretion. But the countries that supported the communal armies were often mountainous or peripheral areas, where feudal institutions had never fully developed or had broken down. Often – although this could not be said of Flanders, Bohemia, or northern Italy – they were also lands that had failed to develop a more varied commercialized agrarian and manufacturing economy. Thus, the communal-resistance approach offered few pointers for an army able to translate weapons breakthroughs into operational inventions.

Not every obstacle to increasing levels of military capability applied in every instance of communal resistance. But the difficulties were usually serious enough to require a major change in the organi-

---

[14] See the detailed discussion of the *Landesknechten* in Eugen von Frauenholz, *Das Heereswesen in der Zeit des freien Söldnertums*, 2 vols., Beck, Munich, 1936.

zational and social bases of communal resistance. The sustaining institutions of the early forms of popular warfare needed to be combined, one way or another, with some of the strengths exhibited by the new standing armies of the large territorial states.

You can detect a movement toward such a combination among the Hussites of the early fifteenth century. The armies of Jan Žižka repeatedly showed an ability to fight at the mobilizational and technological vanguard of warfare although Tschernembl's call in the Bohemian War Council for mass recruitment remained largely unheeded.[15] No fighting force of the Europe of that time was more subtle in its organization and tactics. None could count on more varied and vital economic support. Yet the Hussite state gave a vastly larger role to independent popular organization than did the territorial monarchies. Its destruction was brought about by its own internal dissensions against the background of unified foreign opposition and of the difficulties attending experiments "in one country." The most farsighted military reformers and political propagandists in the north Italian city-state republics also understood that radical changes in the organizational and social bases of the popular militia were necessary to resist French, Spanish, and papal armies. These changes had to go all the way from the establishment of an Italian confederation to the bold coordination of small combat units, armed with varying styles of weapons.

The internal transformation of the standing army approach might produce a similar outcome. The territorial monarch might carry his struggle against the magnates to the point of transforming his whole national standing army into a popular militia based on grassroots collective organization by independent rural and urban proprietors. Erik XIV of Sweden came close to forming such a militia, and similar tendencies recurred throughout sixteenth- and seventeenth-century Swedish history. Alternatively, the state structure might begin to fall apart as oligarchic struggle escalated. The more broadly based armies called into existence by the civil strife might then gain a popular momentum of their own and threaten to bring down the country's whole structure of ordered hierarchy. Thus, in the course of the English Civil War, the New Model Army almost got out of hand and jeopardized the country's basic institutions.

At the start of the seventeenth century, then, both major modes of antifeudal warfare – the standing army and the communal militia – faced obstacles in creating and exploiting technological and mobilizational opportunities for greater destructive capability. But there was a significant difference of timing in the major difficulties

---

[15] See J.V. Polišenský, *War and Society in Europe, 1618–1648*, Cambridge, Cambridge, 1978, p. 64.

faced by each of these modes and in the practical benefits each might bring. In the long run the communal resistance solution might prove more responsive to a total war that engaged resources and manpower on a vast scale and extended the vanguardist style of operations to ever wider segments of the fighting forces. But in the short run the communal resistance approach required the invention of institutions and beliefs that would allow strong, stable states to be directly and willingly sustained by large numbers of more or less organized small-scale proprietors. The development of the standing army solution, in absolutist and aristocratic Europe, might fail to cut through the constraints of oligarchic privilege and mass coercion, constraints that, in the long view, could prove fatal at still higher levels of techno-logical and mobilizational intensity in warfare. But in the short run a standing army was likely to require less redefinition and disposses-sion for already entrenched powers than a popular militia, wherever kings, landowning aristocracies, and big time merchants already held sway. Any attempt to compensate for its short-run disadvantage as an overall European solution would have required the defenders of the communal resistance direction to translate as quickly as possible their long-run advantages into short-term gains in mobilizational and technological capacity. The path-breaking quality of the Hussite forces suggests the feasibility of such a translation.

In any contest between alternative organizational and social bases for a similar level of practical capability in production or destruction, victory depends partly on the ability to appropriate aspects of the rival solution and to make them subordinate parts of one's own approach, thereby changing or even inverting their entire political sense. To succeed, small republics and peasant or urban collectivities committed to the path of communal resistance needed to develop large confederations, technical or managerial cadres, and permanent specialized forces. The monarchic creators of standing armies did the opposite. Faced with the difficulty of recruiting and funding such armies without an all-out struggle against the national aristocracies, they tried to turn the strengths of the communal armies to their own benefit. They attempted this reversal by transforming the popular armies into mercenary units in their own service.

The mercenary corps recruited by military entrepreneurs served as a way to incorporate the new popular formations, with all their strengths of operational style and combined weaponry, into the na-tional army. Yet because these units were in every sense an alien corps grafted onto the social body, they posed little threat as a coun-termodel of association. It is a stratagem that has been employed throughout history, often in areas of statecraft far removed from military reform. During the Köprülü reform period, for example, in the late seventeenth-century Ottoman Empire, Albanians played a major role as staffers in state administration. Because of the sanctity they attached to the oath of friendship, or *besa*, they could be counted on at a time when most patron–client relationships in high administrative circles had dissolved without giving way to an alternative organizational structure.[16]

At the outset of the Thirty Years' War, the dominant mode of warfare in Western and Central Europe had become a restricted version of the standing army pioneered by war leaders like Charles VII of France or Edward III of England. Precisely because of the difficulty of maintaining the precarious conditions that would allow direct access to a broad, popular base of manpower and capital, most large territorial states had to make heavy use of mercenary armies combined with coerced levies of peasants. These were initially temporary fighting units hired or raised for limited periods of time. The extraordinary, one-shot financial burden drastically limited the possibilities of manpower and resource mobilization for warfare and delivered would-be warlords into the hands of cagey bankers.

Moreover, the nature of these armies had a constraining influence on their ability to exploit the technical advances in firearms and to coordinate firepower with shock. This point is borne out by the compulsion to deploy rigid mass formations in order to guarantee discipline on the part of coerced peasants or short-term hirelings. The result was to undermine offensive and defensive mobility in the field and to prevent surprising, concentrated blows with missile and shock tactics.[17]

Consider the widespread popularity of two ineffective firearm maneuvers. One of them was the use of the cavalry charge with a wheellock pistol. The firing of the shot into a compact mass of enemy pikemen and musketeers often became the end rather than the beginning of the cavalry charge, whose value as a shock instrument was thereby entirely lost. In the infantry battalions, a parallel development took place: the musket was used less as the preliminary to a shock attack with pikes than as the main instrument of battle. Infantry combat degenerated into inconclusive encounters between opposing musketeers. Siege warfare became the best proving ground for the newer weapons.

There is a recurrent tendency in the history of warfare to see in a technical advance an alternative to maneuver and engagement rather than an occasion for them. Thus, the Ottomans in the eighteenth

---

[16] See William H. McNeill, *Europe's Steppe Frontier, 1500–1800*, Chicago, Chicago, 1964, pp. 134–135.
[17] See Gustav Droysen, *Beiträge zur Geschichte des Militarwesens im Deutschland während der Epoche des Dreissigjährigen Krieges*, Shlüter, Hannover, 1875, especially pp. 10–11.

century looked for safety to enormous, unwieldy artillery pieces whose imprecision made their paralyzing tactical effects all the more unjustifiable. During the Vietnam War of 1960–1973, the Americans habitually used the helicopter as a weapon with which to land an overpowering number of troops directly into a combat theater.[18] They disregarded what the British had already discovered during their counterinsurgency operations in Borneo:[19] that a transport vehicle must not be made into an excuse to lose the advantages of tactical surprise in a futile quest for instantaneous, unbeatable concentrations of force. Although such operational mistakes are understandable, given the horror of combat and the fascination of invulnerability, they were greatly aggravated in early modern European armies of brutalized peasants and lackadaisical mercenaries.

The circumstances surveyed in the preceding pages suggest a context for understanding seventeenth-century military advances. In essence, these advances consisted in the attempt to develop the standing-army route in a way that came closer to its earliest bold prototypes than to its more recent degenerate forms.[20] The aim, in the minds of the most innovative leaders, was to exploit technological and mobilizational opportunities for warfare through reforms in the organizational and social bases of the war effort. But it was essential that such reforms stop short of a radical transformation of state and society. The armies produced by these changes were the most effective fighting forces in Europe until the day of the national levy, the people's war, and the industrialized war machine. Yet they, too, had severe limits, and during the eighteenth-century era of limited dynastic wars they too underwent a degeneration encouraged by the intricate series of compromises on which they had originally depended. The boldest architect of this new military style was Gustavus Adolphus of Sweden. Its earliest fragmentary models were the Spanish tercio and the infantry battalions organized, at the turn of the century, by Maurice of Nassau.

My account of these changes begins by focusing on reforms in the nature of armies: their innovations in structure and recruitment, operations and tactics. Then it suggests how these developments in the organizational basis of warfare enabled the innovators to enlarge and exploit technological and mobilizational opportunities. These advances in destructive capability could not be initiated or maintained

---

[18] See Robert B. Asprey, *War in the Shadows: The Guerrilla in History*, Doubleday, Garden City, N.Y., 1975, vol. 2, pp. 1412–1414.

[19] See Walter Walker, "How Borneo Was Won," *The Round Table* (Jan. 1969).

[20] See Michael Roberts, "The Military Revolution, 1560–1660," in *Essays in Swedish History*, Univ. of Minnesota, Minneapolis, 1967, pp. 195–225; Geoffrey Parker, "The Military 'Revolution' 1550–1660 – A Myth?" *Journal of Modern History*, vol. 48 (1976), pp. 195–214.

without deliberate reforms and unintended shifts in other aspects of state and society. The compromises struck in the course of making or tolerating these changes in turn imposed limits on the capacity to develop and deploy military power. The particular accommodations at each point along the way were not predetermined by basic institutional arrangements of power and production or by the class relations these arrangements helped sustain. Yet such settlements, together with many other compromises in many other theaters of practical or visionary conflict, exercised a formative influence on whole societies. They influenced the social terms on which economic progress would take place.

Wherever possible, the army became a permanent organization. If it was staffed by mercenaries, they were to be hired without limit of time. If it was raised by conscription, the landowning oligarchies were to be given special responsibilities for enlistment in their own areas (e.g., the Prussian cantonal system) and special rights to monopolize the officer corps. The Swedish method of direct recruitment from a class of independent smallholders with state-protected farms remained an exceptional solution: it most closely approached a revolutionary partnership between sovereign and people.

Whatever the manner of enlistment, war finance became more secure. The most common institutional background to this development was a bargain that included at least three terms: the corporate representation of the tax-paying estates; the active commitment of state power to defending their preferential access to governmental office, land control, and commercial advantage; and agreement by the estates to help provide the money and manpower for war. A similar deal brought central governments and oligarchies together in the financing of armaments production.

Within this context of support, the operational style of armies could be more readily reformed. More effective central command combined with increased discretion and flexibility. On the one hand, drill, marching in step, and uniforms created the background of common discipline. On the other hand, the ordinary soldier was turned into something of a technician and a tactician. Infantry formations were progressively divided into smaller groups, able to disperse and converge rapidly in the field and to take advantage of the mutually reinforcing effects of different kinds of weapons. Thus, in Gustavus Adolphus's new army the operational unit was the battalion, a mobile combat group of pikemen and musketeers, with their own light artillery. Firepower could be used as a prelude to shock by light cavalry and pikemen, and maneuver could regain its prime strengths of concentration and surprise.[21]

---

[21] See Michael Roberts, "Gustav Adolph and The Art of War," in *Essays in Swedish History*, pp. 56–81.

These advances were not achieved at a single leap. The Spanish tercio remained an unwieldy and relatively inflexible formation, while the much smaller combat units inaugurated by Maurice of Nassau and his mercenaries habitually preferred evasion to engagement.[22] There were many occasions and pathways to reach the similar tactical results. The tactics that Cortés used to such stunning advantage against the Aztecs were essentially a commando variation on the procedures of the tercio. Yet they progressed in the same general direction as the Swedish operational innovations, tested almost a century later at Breitenfeld.

These developments in the support and conduct of warfare made it possible both to foment the production of new weapons and to work out their tactical implications. The lighter and faster-loading muskets and the more mobile field artillery introduced in the course of the Thirty Years' War were the products of tenacious partnerships between governments and manufacturers. They were also among the first results of a process of accelerated technical innovation in which cadres of tinkerers and practical scientists learned to understand machines: to establish a limited catalog of machine parts and principles of construction. The parts could be placed in divergent combinations and the principles be given analogous uses across a broad range of contexts, from clocks and church bells to handguns and field artillery.[23] But these technical breakthroughs would have been squandered for military purposes in an army incapable of rapid maneuver, interlocking specialization, and the simultaneous development of both command discipline and on-the-field discretion. The same set of improvements in the army's recruitment, structure, and fighting style enabled its masters to use more heavily and effectively the resources and manpower of large territorial states in a period of brutal state struggle.

The essential social basis of these military achievements was the type of accommodation with domestic elites described earlier. Its most developed form appeared in the armies of Brandenburg–Prussia, given the more exceptional character of the Swedish state at the zenith of its military power. The example of Prussian military organization is striking as a source of insight into the constraints that respect for oligarchic interests imposed on military capability, for Prussia was the most successful military power in prerevolutionary Europe.

Without compromises similar to those made in Brandenburg–Prussia – or still more radical departures, like those tested in Sweden and Bohemia – the organizational basis of warfare, with its corresponding operational implications, could not have been transformed,

---

[22] See Werner Hahlweg, *Die Heeresreform der Oranier und die Antike*, Junker, Berlin, 1941, pp. 33–38.

[23] See Carlo M. Cipolla, *Clocks and Culture, 1300–1700*, Norton, New York, 1980, pp. 39–40, 50–51.

as it was, in seventeenth-century Europe. European armies would have remained temporary collections of resentful peasants and floating mercenaries, incapable of being trusted with greater tactical discretion and technical responsibility. War finance and recruitment would have continued hostage to unreconciled oligarchs. Armaments production would have lacked sustained support and guidance. Yet such deals had limiting effects on the long-range maintenance and development of military capability.

Some of these effects were exercised directly on the opening and exploitation of technological or mobilizational opportunities. Governmental sponsorship of weapons research and manufacture was rarely more than episodic. Despite examples as precocious as the Venetian Arsenal and rope factory and the manipulation of the Venetian funded debt, these reformed European states lacked the institutional means with which to maintain a steady level of investment flow into weapons making. Any attempt to forge these means might quickly draw states into the management of economywide investment decisions and into clashes with the commercial oligarchies. Thus, in his navy-building efforts a reformer like Colbert could easily get caught in a position that fell between the stools of independent governmental responsibility for production and effective governmental partnership with willing investors.

The danger of strangulation that beset the armaments industry held more generally for war finance. The funded debt and the organized representation of estates in local and national assemblies certainly helped turn public finance into an ally rather than an enemy of private banking and entrepreneurship, but these mechanisms were quickly overstrained in periods of intensified warfare. Any fragility in the financial system might turn marginal stress into major crisis. Thus, the relatively modest French involvement in the American War of Independence became part of the sequence of events that laid the ancien régime open to violent destruction. Again, the effort to widen the sources and methods of finance might require a more far-reaching change in the structure of the state and the character of its relations with particular social classes.

Similar compromises had a constraining influence on manpower mobilization. Here the effects were even more complex and subtle than in the instances of arms manufacture and war finance. The mere effort to guarantee a steady flow of recruits presented the state with unpalatable dilemmas. Take the experience of Brandenburg–Prussia itself. In its early phases, the canton system multiplied reasons for grassroots conflict and corruption. To satisfy their recruitment obligations, military captains and estate owners would try to conscript peasants exempt under the law, who would in turn defend themselves by resistance, bribery, and desertion.

On the other hand, if the central government intervened to fix clearly the rights and responsibilities of each estate, as it did under Frederick the Great, the result was to freeze the entire social order in a manner reminiscent of the regime of Diocletian in the late Roman empire. This solution had its own disadvantages. The hardening of the relationship of each social rank to the state and, through the state, to every other rank diminished the room for conflict and innovation in every area of social life. It also kept the peasantry in a condition of institutionalized subordination that made it a permanent internal enemy of the government and a sullen, resentful participant in the state's military endeavors.

This last point brings out the more intangible aspect of the constraint on manpower mobilization implicit in the seventeenth- and eighteenth-century strategies of compromise. Rulers could hardly count on a populace that felt no commitment to the military fortunes of the state. Popular commitment would have required popular trust, and such a trust would not easily flourish unless overweening oligarchies assumed a more limited and, above all, a more self-effacing role. A change so fundamental could be imagined and achieved only in a circumstance of protracted struggle over governmental power and private privilege.

During the latter part of the seventeenth century and most of the eighteenth century, the advances in military structure and method that had been achieved during the Thirty Years' War suffered a characteristic involution on several fronts. Each aspect of this decline was decisively encouraged by the compromises underlying most of the innovations in the first place. One sign of this fallback was the triumph of rigid, linear field tactics. This development is particularly revealing because it shows the wastage and perversion of technological breakthroughs achieved after the operational reforms of the early and mid-seventeenth century. The invention of the socket bayonet made it possible to dispense with the protective pike, making the effective combat units shallower and more flexible. The production of lighter, more mobile field artillery enabled supporting firepower to advance more rapidly in pace with the infantry line and to combine the missile with the shock. The development of the more rapidly reloading flintlock musket gave the infantryman greater autonomy and made him less dependent on protective fire during reloading. Such changes reestablished the tactical advantages of the shallow line. Yet these advantages were almost lost by the rigid, mechanical formations favored by the tacticians of the late seventeenth and the eighteenth centuries.[24]

---

[24] On the tactical and operational implications of the weapons mentioned here, see David G. Chandler, *The Art of Warfare in the Age of Marlborough*, Hippocrene, New York, 1976, especially pp. 28, 75–78.

The soldier, however, could not easily be made into a more autonomous technician and tactician when he still remained a mercenary or a conscript without any vital commitment to the state, when he still took every opportunity to break ranks, hide, or desert, when his relations to his own officers were still modeled on those of the peasant to the landlord and the lackey to the master, and when he still lacked exposure to organizational responsibility and mechanical dexterity.[25]

Another aspect of the setback was the strangulation of tactics by logistics. Armies easily became tied down to fixed supply centers and vulnerable to the capture of such bases. There was more to this dependence than limitations in the technology of transport. There was the difficulty of establishing a broad enough base of financial support to fund multiple supply points during intense or protracted warfare, and to do so without entering into destructive conflict or deadlock with the tax-voting oligarchies. The supply story had another side as well. A people's army, like the French revolutionary force, might turn its logistic weakness to tactical advantage by commandeering resources on the spot. But the armies of the eighteenth-century European monarchies could not easily make such a move without seeing their soldiers become pillagers and thus turning the civilian populace into an indignant adversary.

The direct and indirect constraints imposed on the development of military capability by compromise strategies were far less influential in naval power. The navy remained what the mercenary army had once been: an alien body, separated from the main life of society, which might serve as a field for organizational experimentation without jeopardizing the central institutions of power and production. Its needs for manpower were relatively limited, and its advantage for commerce was obvious (though not obvious enough to Dutch and French commercial elites). Naval tactics, which could not easily fall into the rigidities of lockstep land warfare, provided an early model for that more subtle relation between command and discretion that was to be so spectacularly developed in twentieth-century armored combat. All these factors encouraged development of naval technology. And the Western naval advantage was crucial in determining the precise terms of the initial encounters with non-Western powers in the Orient. The whole course of events in Japan, for example, might have been different either if the Western invaders

[25] Compare the description of the peasant-soldier situation in Otto Büsch, *Militärsystem und Sozialleben im Alten Preussen*, Ullstein, Frankfurt, 1981, pp. 21–50, with the tactical and operational ideals advanced by a military reformer like Scharnhorst in his "Three Essays on Light Troops and Infantry Tactics" (1811), a translation of which is published as an appendix to Peter Paret, *Yorck and the Era of Prussian Reform, 1807–1815*, Princeton, Princeton, 1966, pp. 249–262.

had lacked their naval edge or if the Japanese had proved capable of an early and decisive land invasion.

The next rounds in European military history confirm the points that have already been made. The armies of revolutionary France compelled the European powers to enter the next great wave of military innovations. The appeal to the people permitted a degree of operational flexibility that made it possible to capitalize on the most recent developments in armaments and to broaden the resources and manpower actively engaged in warfare.

Once again, there was a wave of relatively successful accommodations. No simple contrast holds between pioneering countries and reluctant latecomers. For example, conscription in revolutionary and Napoleonic France was limited by the conscript's option of buying himself out, a sop to the propertied classes that Prussia did not allow. Once again, compromises exacted a price in military capability at every level. Once again, the particular series of concessions and advances helped shape the formative contexts of power and production in Western societies. Within the West, the pattern of compromise was an element in setting the social terms of industrialization and the outer limits to mass politics. Outside the West, it laid the basis for the fateful Western advantage in destructive force and for the brand of state and economy to which elites and peoples in other parts of the world were forced to respond. These other nations, I have repeatedly argued, would be faced with the imperative of dissociation: the need to disengage practical capabilities from the institutional foundations on which these capabilities had originally rested in the core Western countries. But the point of departure – the reality offered up for dissociation – was the outcome of particular struggles in several realms. The quest for military power was simply one such domain. These struggles, fought out in different settings over different issues, were not the same fight in different disguises, nor can they be understood as episodes in a relentlessly unfolding transformative sequence. Nevertheless, they had similar features that reveal a general characteristic of society making: what we learn from them connects the analysis of practical capabilities and of their enabling circumstances to a general political understanding of society. Before these lessons can be worked out, however, the analysis of the European examples must be pushed a few steps further.

In the total wars of the twentieth century, the technological and mobilizational intensity of warfare repeatedly threatened to churn up the social order. For the defeated, it did so by shattering the state and discrediting its most visible masters. For all belligerents, it delivered this threat through a complicated series of wartime pressures: the need to assume an increasing measure of control over investment and manpower policy, the maintenance of full employment with its attendant risks to workplace discipline, the introduction of new forms of joint decisional responsibility by workers, managers, and officials and, most notably, the universal sense that so incalculable a horror as total war would have to be compensated for by creating a society that, in every respect, belonged more fully to its ordinary workers and soldiers.

The technological and mobilizational demands of intensified warfare also made demands on the organizational practice of armies. Wherever the innovations in decisional structure and operational style went furthest, they offered a countermodel to the organizational style prevailing in most of the production system. The most telling of these departures from organizational orthodoxy occurred in the development of tank warfare.

When the tank was first put to use during World War I, most official military thinking confined it to a subsidiary role. Some thought of the tank as no more than a trench-crossing vehicle, an additional siege weapon. Others went further. The tank would provide firepower to support infantry advances in the face of enemy barrages with automatic weapons; it was, once again, the missile supporting the shock. Lighter and faster tanks would serve as the mechanical counterparts to cavalry: they would protect exposed infantry flanks and undertake scouting missions. These conceptions of tank warfare required few radical changes in the relations among the army's branches, in its command structure, or in its operational style. The technological development was, on the contrary, used to preserve arrangements and procedures (like the infantry charge) that had been jeopardized by other technical inventions (such as the machine gun).[26]

The more insightful understood that the tank might mean much more. It could become the weapon of an entirely distinct branch. The establishment of tank units, however, was just a beginning. The capabilities of the tank division could be fully exploited only by a new structure of communication and control. Even some of the most famous tank commanders of World War II failed to grasp this requirement. The junior officer in charge of each tank crew had to be able to exploit sudden opportunities for rapid and deep penetration or envelopment. He could not be held to a fixed, preconceived plan nor reduced to the role of intermediary between the men who gave orders and the men who carried them out. If, however, central guidance failed to counterbalance this discretion, the tank force would

---

[26] See Field Marshal Lord Carver, *The Apostles of Mobility: The Theory and Practice of Armoured Warfare*, Weidenfeld, London, 1979; Edward N. Luttwak, "The Strategy of the Tank," in *Strategy and Politics*, ed. Edward N. Luttwak, Transaction, New Brunswick, New Jersey, 1980, pp. 295–304.

disintegrate and lose its power of concentration. There had to be a voice to say where to concentrate and how to coordinate the armored attack with covering air support. (Airplanes could do for tanks what a more retrograde military mind had expected tanks to do for infantry.) Nevertheless, the commander had to move around in the midst of battle, and his plan had to be constantly revised in the light of the opportunities seized and the obstacles encountered by individual tank crews.

At its best, this approach to tank warfare illustrates the vanguardist style of production and warfare. It is a way of waging war that weakens the distinctions between task and execution, and between taskmasters and executors. The self-revising plan in the protracted battle became the heart of operations. If all branches of the army had adopted similar procedures, the entire war machine would have provided a countermodel to the organizational and operational approach that continued to prevail in industry. Given the overwhelming convergence of interests, preconceptions, and habits threatened by any such extension, this countermodel was likely to take hold only where its practical advantages were immediate, unmistakable, and indispensable. The economic and governmental arrangements of the rich Western democracies in the latter half of the twentieth century would have been fundamentally different if such vanguardist forms of collective effort had been allowed to penetrate the mainstream of industrial and military organization.

PROVISIONAL CONCLUSIONS

The episodes from European history discussed in the preceding pages already suggest some provisional conclusions about the enabling circumstances of destructive capability. These conclusions in turn serve as a partial model for an understanding of the general relation between practical capacities and their organizational and social bases. Thus, these claims must be read twice: first, as an account of linkages within the military setting; and second, as the outline of a view of the relation between the transformation of society and the development of productive or destructive powers. Each of these conclusions, however, is so hedged in by qualifications and ambiguities that its value can be determined only by casting still more widely the net of analysis and comparison.

As armed conflict reached greater degrees of intensity in the course of European history, the effort to develop or exploit technological and mobilizational opportunities generated pressures for a change in the organizational and social basis of warfare. When you consider these pressures and the responses to them in a broad historical sweep, you discover that, despite many setbacks and diversions, they seem, on the whole, to have moved in an identifiable direction.

In the social basis of warfare, the movement of change was toward the subversion of all predetermined social hierarchies and divisions that would constrain the ability of government to mobilize resources and manpower for war and to lay claim to the loyalty of its citizens. This movement did not spell egalitarianism or democracy in the state and the economy. But it did mean that no independent oligarchies could be allowed for long to interpose themselves squarely between the heights of governmental power and the access to men and capital. Even rights and privileges that helped define the formative contexts of power and production might have to be shifted around quite radically, at least during the high points of the war effort. As the age of total people's wars dawned, these subversive pressures increased. The society and its government had to be so ordered that some semblance of truth could be given to the pretense that the state's violent struggles were everybody's business.

In the organizational basis of warfare the direction of movement ran toward the development of a command structure and an operational practice that did not merely reproduce the relationships of clientage and coerced dependence in the surrounding society. In structure and style, the fighting force would have to be a cyst of organized collective effort that defined specialized responsibilities and methods of coordination capable of resisting the test of battle. As the violence and the technical subtlety of warfare mounted, the most advanced branches were pressed to adopt an approach that sacrificed all fixed distinctions between task making and task following at the same time that it preserved a structure of control and coordination.

The social and organizational movements reinforced each other in message and effect. Without some disruption of the surrounding social hierarchies, the crucial organizational reforms could not be introduced. The established structure of privilege sharply constrained governmental access to recruits and funds. It also limited the schemes of collaborative effort readily available in the society and ultimately transferable to warfare. In its own organizational structure and operational procedures, an army could not easily remain an inverted picture of society. Either the familiar routines of everyday life would end up penetrating and deforming the military organization, or the army's own underlying principles would invade other areas of collective effort. The influence ran in the opposite direction as well. Without organizational reforms the increased engagement of resources and manpower made possible by a shake-up of entrenched privilege was likely to be wasted.

The direct causal links between organizational and social transformation were accompanied by a more inclusive parallelism. The maximum readiness for war would presumably be achieved in a society in which the entire social order was infused by the spirit and habits of flexible, rationalized collective labor. In civilian settings, you might have much more popular accountability and institutionalized conflict than could be tolerated in a tank battalion. But you would have the same constant availability for the recombination of units, the joinder of supervision, coordination, and discretion, the merger of task making and task following.

Many of the decisive military reforms taken here as examples anteceded their civilian counterparts, and were explicitly understood as responses to technological and mobilizational opportunities in warfare. An important methodological conclusion follows. The formative institutional arrangements of the emergent industrial economies resulted either from conflicts that occurred in nonindustrial and even noneconomic settings or from disputes about the core zone of industrial organization and investment. The struggles that took place in these distinct areas obeyed no master plan. But our chances of giving any general explanation of events like the North Atlantic industrial breakthrough depend on the discovery of significant analogies of structure and theme and ties of reciprocal influence among the different military, economic, and administrative, realms of social life.

At each major turning point in military history there were alternative organizational and social routes to the development of destructive capability. Some of these alternatives – like the communal resistance and the standing army options at the time of the disintegration of high medieval warfare – were unequally subversive in their organizational and social implications. Moreover, every time a country faced a military force based on a complex of organizational and social reforms that seemed to require a radical reordering of society, its rulers could discover a less radical way to achieve a similar level of military capability.

At first, these alternative accommodating solutions appear to be no more than stopgap measures. They place a heavy mortgage on the future by restricting a country's responsiveness to the next round of mobilizational and technological opportunities. But this view is too simple. The successful compromise is not just a way to hold off the next steps in some already preestablished long-run sequence, based on necessary relationships between practical capabilities and their enabling circumstances. It is the point of departure for a somewhat different long-run sequence. How different is not something that can be said beforehand or in the abstract, but only piecemeal and provisionally. Thus, the conflicts over the organizational and social bases of practical capability – military or not – are much more than accelerations or delays in travel along a mapped route. They both open up unsuspected paths and relocate the points of arrival.

The periods of most rapid innovation in the organizational and social bases of armed conflict were all eras of intensifying warfare. They culminated in the idea and the practice of the total people's war. The characteristic moments of involution were those, like the latter half of the seventeenth century and the greater part of the eighteenth, when absolutist rulers waged wars for limited aims and in cold blood.

The goals for which these limited wars were waged had no ultimate, self-evident importance. There is no determinate logic of state interests that transcends the conflict of interests and visions within rival countries. Every appeal to such a logic serves, in context, a particular set of social alliances and visions. The logic of state interests may be understood in varying ways. Even on the same understanding, it may be compatible with different solutions.

It is also true that the social climate of limited wars favored costly rigidities and illusions in the concrete operational aspects of warfare. My eighteenth-century examples were the inflexibility of linear infantry tactics, the logistic strangulation of maneuver, and the consistent avoidance of combat. But when all is said and done, limited war encouraged economy in the use of means, clarity in the definition of ends, and careful control over the proportion of means to ends.

The same points hold in reverse for the total people's wars of the twentieth century. The aims of such conflicts must at least appear to bear some relation to collective goals whose authority ordinary workers and soldiers acknowledge. Entire organizational and social systems of warfare are thrown into the furnace of relentless reordering. Anything for success. But the dynamic of violence and hatred gains a life of its own. It disorients the calculus of means and ends. Ultimately, it threatens to interrupt any intelligent process of organizational or social innovations and to confuse any notion of why the war was waged in the first place. It creates circumstances in which the desperate gambles of all-out battle and domestic dissension overtake the sequence of deliberate experiments.

Here, then, in summary are the conclusions to be drawn from this discussion of European military history. A state, in order to survive in the struggle against its deadly enemies, must succeed in loosening up and reordering the two crucial linkages in the relation of destructive capabilities to their enabling conditions: the linkage between technological and mobilizational opportunities and the immediate organizational, operational, or tactical setting of warfare and the linkage between this setting and the broader institutional framework of economic and political life. Over the long sweep of modern European history, the successive rearrangements of both connections appear to have a powerful directional thrust. Throughout much of modern experience rearrangements of the first link have moved toward reconstructing practical activity as teamwork among task definers and task executors. At the extreme, in the vanguardist sectors of warfare and production, these rearrangements have even undercut the contrast between task-defining and task-executing jobs. The readjustments of the second linkage have helped weaken rigid social roles and hierarchies; at a minimum, they have loosened the stranglehold of privilege over governmental power and enlarged the areas of social life open to organizational experiments.

Several considerations, however, counterbalance the sense of a directional movement. For one thing, this apparent evolutionary march does not coincide with any particular vision of democratic accountability, egalitarian redistribution, and individual emancipation. Its content is almost entirely negative. The axis of movement points toward an increased social plasticity whose true nature and implications should be defined more precisely. Successive approaches to this goal can take concrete social forms utterly opposed to our ideals. But these anti-ideal outcomes may still share a common basis with ideal goals that we do entertain: a greater loosening of the constraints imposed by a rigid order of social division and hierarchy on collaborative effort for practical ends, whether in war or peace, whether in large organizations or outside them. This possible, cumulative movement allows at every point along the way for alternative realizations of the new order and for successful compromises with the old one. It flourishes in situations of aggravated conflict whose special characteristics, however, give the achievements of military reform a quality of randomness, precariousness, and obscurity. Heightened social and organizational revisability may also take utterly different institutional forms. Although any particular set of constraints on this revisability will prove dangerous sooner or later, we cannot expect any particular group of institutions or even of procedures to be the perpetual motion machine of social innovation. Moreover, we can rarely dismiss renovating reforms and the clever compromises they enshrine as no more than doomed efforts to delay an inevitable progression; they create an alternative future.

These qualifications to simple progressivism shade into one another. The overabundance of paths to increased destructive (or productive) power shows that no ideal program can be sure to be on the winning side. Nevertheless, programs for social reconstruction that do hold fast to a particular fixed scheme of hierarchy and division are sooner or later cast off indignantly as both practical embarrassments and moral outrages.

We achieve the deepest insights into the connection between military power – or, more generally, any practical capability – and its favoring social conditions when we put the progressivist view in its place without rejecting it altogether. (By progressivist view I mean the thesis that the demands of material progress point in the same direction as liberal or socialist ideals of freedom and equality.) The progressivist view is at once true and not true. An adequate account of the enabling conditions of practical capabilities identifies the precise relation between its truth and its falsehood.

These conclusions help us understand how an economic order capable of being pulled apart and recombined with other institutional arrangements could have been put together in the first place. As the whole world began to industrialize, the initial Western versions of an industrial economy and an industrialized war machine were placed on organizational and social bases different from the ones that continued to sustain them in the West. And even in European and American history itself, there were significant though limited variations in the institutional context of industrialization. The form taken by the production system resulted from conflicts in a series of theaters only loosely strung together, some of them remote from disputes over the style and consequences of industrial organization. Military history gives us the example of one such theater, somewhat removed from the core area of economic organization.

Once industrial economies had appeared, the power to destroy became ever more closely bound up with the capacity to produce. Yet the capabilities of production and destruction were never the same. Separate organizations wielded them. They had distinct if connected histories. The military compromises influence, and are influenced by, the economic solutions. If, for example, the flexible, vanguardist style of organization remains confined to a restricted region of one of these two fields – the industrial and the military – then it is that much more likely to be restricted in the other.

There is another and more general way in which the inferences this study draws from military history fit into an argument about the institutional conditions of military and economic success. We come out better able to see and to describe how limiting influences coexist with a potential for variation. We begin to enlist the imagination of what did not happen in the understanding of what did.

Each of the points made here about the history of destruction translates into a thesis about the history of production. The analogy holds for the analytic scheme of relations among practical capacities and institutional arrangements, for the theme of a directional thrust to military and economic history, and even for the qualifications that make this theme more limited, more precise, and more truthful.

Consider, for example, one of the many qualifications to the directionality thesis: the ambiguous effects of all-out war on the development of destructive powers. One requirement of quickened economic or military advance is a periodic shaking up of vested rights. This upheaval characteristically requires that government-promoted reform from the top down converge with some form of mass mobilization from the bottom up. If this twofold assault on established arrangements is too violent – if, for example, it depends on war and revolution – it will be very rare, very chancy, and very destructive. Society will oscillate between long periods of relative stagnation in which state-protected privileges and collective deals crowd out experiments in the organization of production and brief interludes in which much is destroyed before anything can be created. To perpetuate the practice of innovation, societies must replace such drastic and violent swings with a more constant liquefaction of deals and privileges. They must invent the structures that make structures easier to change.

THE LIMITS OF COMPROMISE:
CHINESE AND JAPANESE EXAMPLES

The themes discussed up to this point in the context of European conflicts can now be reexamined in the larger setting of world history. This new stage in the analysis focuses on the problem posed by the confrontation of an already industrialized and militarily powerful West with non-Western peoples. The examples I use to explore this issue are the different responses of nineteenth-century China and Japan to the Western military threat.

The European episodes provided an occasion on which to understand how something capable of disaggregation could have been assembled in the first place. The combination of productive capabilities, forms of work organization, and larger aspects of state and society that seemed so naturally stuck together in early Western industrialism could nevertheless come apart. The account of their initial combination must therefore be compatible with the later discovery of their separability. The mode of analysis that is brought to bear must show how limitation combined with variability in the making of the initial Western versions of industrialism; the necessitarian connotations of explanation must be weeded out.

To this end, it is useful to analyze developments in an area somewhat distinct from the core zone of the production system. We can then understand the profile of Western industrialism as the result of conflicts that not only had uncertain outcomes but that took place in somewhat different areas of social life, over somewhat different issues, and therefore ran a somewhat different course. The histories of productive and destructive capabilities are, for each other, the most important neighboring regions.

The series of examples I am about to discuss pose the same problems in reverse. In the typical situation, a non-Western country faces a Western power's destructive capability already combined in certain ways with a productive power and with certain organizational and social conditions of both production and destruction. The question for the threatened country then and for the student of society now is: How can we understand the reconstructibility of such a system once it has already been constructed? If reconstruction is possible at all, it has to begin somewhere. One of the most likely places is military organization and production for war. The reason for this likelihood is simple. The military threat cannot easily be disregarded: it is urgent and it is brutal. But the rulers and elites faced by such a threat do not want to recast their entire society in the image of the foreign intruders. They lack the capacity, the time, and the will for such faithful emulation. Count on them to dissociate if they know how.

A purpose of the earlier European discussion was to suggest a more general understanding of relations between practical capabilities and their enabling conditions. The job was made easier and the conceptual scheme simpler by taking examples from a period in which military capability remained more tenuously tied to military power than it became after the emergence of industrialized economies. Now, in the next series of examples, when the military threat is posed by industrial war machines, the organizational and social bases of productive and destructive power begin to merge more fully into each other. As a result, the view of the conditions favorable to the development of productive and destructive capabilities begins to lose its distinctiveness from the ideas used earlier to explain the European escape from the closed circles of an agrarian society. This convergence prepares the way for a more general account of the institutional conditions of collective worldly success.

My primary aim in comparing the Chinese and Japanese responses to the military threat from the West is not to examine why, in the short run, Japan was more successful than China. The criteria of success are, in any event, elusive even when they are confined to the realm of worldly wealth and power. If you compare China to India during the nineteenth century, you find that, despite military and diplomatic humiliation, China remained relatively impervious to foreign governmental and commercial penetration. The treaty port cities in China failed to become, as they had throughout much of India and Southeast Asia, the bases of countrywide military domination and economic disruption. If you extend the comparison with Japan a half-century ahead, the inferences of Japanese success no longer seem as striking. Although the material standard of living in Japan continued to be much higher, the Chinese failure, in the earlier period, to come up with a workable accommodation to Western military and productive techniques set the stage for a more drastic Chinese transformation of Western industrial models. Not worldly success as a whole but the enabling circumstances of military prowess lie at the forefront of my comparison. But because the armed confrontations already take place against the background of industrialized economies, the conditions of military power can no longer be kept even provisionally and relatively separate from those of economic capability. Thus, the Chinese and Japanese examples extend our vision and deepen our insight into the two linkages that stand at the center of this stage of my argument: the connection between practical productive or destructive capacity and the marshaling of its technical and organizational instruments and the connection between these instruments and the larger reshaping of state and society.

Consider first the situation of Chinese military capacity as it stood at the time of the 1910 revolution or, for that matter, of the disastrous 1895 encounter with Japan in the Korean theater. There were formidable constraints on every significant aspect of Chinese military force: the production of firearms and warships, the mobilization of resources and manpower for warfare and weapons making, and the actual operational capacity and organizational strength of the armed forces.

China had pioneered in the early development of firearms. The gunpowder invented in the tenth century was already propelling explosive projectiles in the thirteenth century. But the monopoly controls over armaments production established by the Chinese state since the time of the Han Dynasty, the characteristic concerns of the Confucianized officials in a self-centered agrarian empire, and the existence of long periods of relative peace all worked against the rapid development of firearms. So, in a more far-reaching way, did the absence of an industrialized economy and of a continuous interaction between experimental science and mechanical technology. During Ming rule (1368–1644), the inferiority of Chinese firearms to European ordnance became unmistakable, and the Chinese themselves recognized it as soon as they saw the first Portuguese weapons, in 1520. They bought these arms and, with foreign help, tried making them on their own. They used them to stave off the Manchus. The Manchus in power used them successfully against the Russians in 1685 and 1686. But by the time of the first Opium War (1839–1842), the Chinese guns and artillery were fatally inferior to their British counterparts, and Chinese naval power remained insubstantial.

The immediate background to the establishment of arsenals and rapid development of armament production in the period after the Opium War was twofold: the suppression of the dangerous popular rebellions of the Taiping and the Nien and the threatened intrusion of foreign military power, whether from Europe and the United States or from Japan. The response to the Western threats interfered with the reaction against the Japanese. The degree of reliance on foreign financial and technical help accepted for the sake of crushing the popular rebellion proved to undercut Chinese military independence in any confrontation with Western powers.

The reforming statesmen, lower officials, and comprador intellectuals who took the initiative in arsenal making and military reform were realistic. They understood that rapid firearms and naval development were vital to the security of the state, that the steam-powered machinery, the techniques, and the organizations employed in the arsenals would have transformative implications for the entire Chinese economy, that the necessary productive initiatives and military policies would require wider administrative, fiscal, and social reforms, and that it was impossible to foresee the outer limits of the impact. Many of the reformers nevertheless seem to have expected and hoped that the "self-strengthening" reforms would leave the basic hierarchical order of state and society untouched.[27]

By 1875, the major arsenals at Shanghai, Tientsin, and Nanking were producing at full capacity and a national maritime defense policy had begun to emerge. Administrators and industrialists soon carried over to other fields of manufacturing the forms of governmental sponsorship and merchant management in enterprises pioneered in armaments production.[28] The arsenals, and their periphery of related industries, represented a real beginning in military power backed by industrialization. But they suffered from the limitations imposed by the wider social and governmental context. The major responsibility for these constraints lay in the failure of a weakened government to cut through the costly bickering among different categories of managers, merchants, and officials; to assemble the needed workers and funds; to suppress the privileges of some and grab the money of others; to identify the dissident, ambitious, and enterprising elements of the elite that might serve as the instruments and beneficiaries of such a policy; and to keep out of foreign adventures until the Chinese state was ready for them. Certainly the conflict with Japan put a strain on the arsenals they were unprepared to handle.

The arsenals themselves were a promising although abortive start. But the larger financial and manpower basis of military force and industrial experimentation remained entirely inadequate. One sign of this inadequacy was the weakness of central control over local military power. In the course of the desperate struggle against the popular rebellions of the mid-nineteenth century, the local elites,

---

[27] For an analysis of the initial phase of the late Ch'ing military reform efforts, see Mary Wright, *The Last Stand of Chinese Conservatism: The T'ung-Chih Restoration, 1862–1874*, Stanford, Stanford, 1957, pp. 196–221.

[28] See Thomas L. Kennedy, *The Arms of Kiangnan: Modernization in the Chinese Ordnance Industry, 1860–1895*, Westview, Boulder, Colo., 1978, especially pp. 152–154.

already well encased in the apparatus of the state, had come to lead and master the militias that were the country's major source of military manpower. This stranglehold on manpower that might have been used by central reformers for military or productive purposes was closely allied to the fiscal starvation of government. Although the total burden of the land tax was relatively high, an extraordinary amount of it stuck to the fingers of local officials and oligarchs or got spent for relatively unproductive uses. The burden fell most heavily on the minor tenants and proprietors who had become the mainstay of the agrarian economy. Yet the funds were largely unavailable for investment in military or civilian industrial plant and in the recruitment and provision of centrally controlled armies.

Late imperial China lacked a numerous, self-confident cadre of entrepreneurs, institutionalized opportunities for industrial and military innovation, and rulers committed to elicit mass support for reform efforts. In such a circumstance, neither military forces nor industrial enterprises could easily become areas where soldiers or workers dealt with one another and with their superiors in untried ways. The characteristic development was not the emergence in the internal life of the military or industrial organization of a countermodel to the surrounding society. It was instead an unguided mixture of residual forms of peasant solidarity and deference with the rough-and-ready discipline of trying to get a strange new job done, one way or another. Much later, the Communists would self-consciously exploit the self-defensive organization of the peasantry as a basis for military organization while gradually drawing peasants into a different structure of hierarchy and belief. The failure to produce a similar organizational experiment at the earlier moment of military and industrial reform exacted a high price. It resulted in armies that could not be counted on to fight in small units with high measures of operational discretion, coordination, and flexibility and in an industrial labor force that worked most effectively when it was allowed to remain a collection of ingenious, self-taught artisans operating newfangled machines under a single roof.

The constraints and the opportunities of Chinese military development in the closing decades of the empire were part of a larger struggle over the control and uses of governmental power. The late Ch'ing state emerged with few advantages from its bout with the mass insurrections and the foreign intrusions of the mid-nineteenth century. The relationship of the landowning, mercantile, and official cadres to one another and to governmental power was an especially important element in the story. By the late Ch'ing, the Chinese elite of landowners, officials, and merchants was sufficiently unified in its perceived interests and active beliefs to monopolize in its own favor the powers of the state and to unite aggressively against any force that might threaten its privileged access to central and local government. But it was also diverse enough to deny broad-based support to any reforming clique that proposed bold realignments for the sake of essential continuity and national salvation. The pressure to defeat the popular rebels had led high officials to deliver effective authority over local military forces into the hands of local gentry leaders. The decadent corporate forms of village life had been largely replaced by these new, militarized and gentry-controlled forms of local organization. And the reformist movement toward local self-government had itself become something of a cover-up for the manipulation of local administration by landlords and merchants and for the further blurring of the lines between grassroots government and grassroots oligarchy. The state was cannibalized in its foundations.

Other aspects of the situation come to light when the focus shifts to the dealings of this oligarchy with the rural masses – smallholders, petty tenants, and agricultural laborers – and with the dissident intellectualized elites that flourished in the country's larger cities. In both instances, the early years of the republic clarified the facts and their implications.

When you consider the extent to which ground-level administration had been captured by a relatively unified ruling and possessing class with deep local roots, it seems surprising that the late Ch'ing saw so little of what I earlier described as reversion to natural economy. In fact, petty tenancy and proprietorship continued to account for a major and even increasing part of agrarian production. All sectors of the population participated heavily in market activities.[29]

The explanation lies in the consequences of the earlier interplay between the reform of governmental structures and the deepening commercialization of the economy. The state, under the impact of successive encounters with the steppe peoples, had gained the institutional means with which to guarantee a minimal local presence and to save itself from fiscal starvation and administrative impotence. At the same time, the elites had been progressively redefined in ways requiring their active participation in both markets and administration. Their characteristic forms of dominion over the rural masses worked through, rather than around or against, governmental and market institutions. This fact illumi-

[29] For an analysis of the final state of the money-based agrarian economy in China before the establishment of communist rule, see Ramon H. Myers, *The Chinese Peasant Economy: Agricultural Development in Hopei and Shantung, 1890–1949*, Harvard, Cambridge, 1970, especially pp. 288–291. Studies like Myers's confirm the vitality of a broad range of large-scale and small-scale holdings. But they also depict the technological stagnation that usually attends the gradualistic, nonconflictual escape from reversion cycles.

nates the importance of various forms of "parasitic landlordism" and manipulations of the tax burden.

Although this was not a formula for full-fledged economic and governmental collapse, it did mean that the masses of town and country were robbed of the legal facilities and economic occasions for recurrent self-organization. Nothing is more telling in this respect than the functional replacement of the corporate forms of village organization by gentry-controlled local militia.[30] If the communal structure of local popular life survived, it did so because the gentry leader was also a lineage head or because in moments of economic and military crisis, the village continued to close ranks self-defensively. In such a circumstance, collective popular organization, when it could emerge at all, readily took covert or adversarial forms. This underground, oppositional militancy encouraged secret societies and inspired countermodels of community and hierarchy during its periods of successful resistance. The breathing space in which working people could organize collectively had always been some partial distinction between state administration and local elites. Whenever this distinction vanished, the laborers and petty proprietors and tenants were in trouble. Their chances for nonviolent organized militancy diminished.

Another aspect of the situation was the relation between the dominant, locally based, economic and governmental oligarchy and the more Westernized and footloose elites that sprang up in the larger cities. Because these dissident elites had no deep link with the bases of power in the countryside and the smaller cities, they had little commitment to the preservation of the established social order. Their vague nationalism and leftism became the crucible for republican agitation and national resistance. This activism played a major role in the Communist advance at a time when the peasantry had shown itself unresponsive, when leftist putschism had been undercut by Soviet vacillation, and when the politics of national unity against the invader provided an invaluable shield for building revolutionary armies and popular support.

Thus, China witnessed a far-reaching paralysis of state power and the denial of opportunities for recurrent popular mobilization. All the particular aspects of constraint on the development of military capabilities can be traced back to this more fundamental circumstance. Like every real situation, however, it was full of dimly perceived and barely missed opportunities. There were any number of moments at which an alliance of reforming statesmen and discontented gentry, officials, and intellectuals might have seized the state

[30] See Philip A. Kuhn, *Rebellion and Its Enemies in Late Imperial China: Militarization and Social Structure*, Harvard, Cambridge, 1970, pp. 211–223.

and disentangled some of its powers from the hold of locally based oligarchies. The most striking of these occasions during the late Chi'ng was the Hundred Days reform of 1898. It was not written in the stars that the young Kuang Hsü emperor and his reforming coterie would be defeated and destroyed by the reaction organized around the Dowager Empress. Reformist takeovers might in turn have been combined with different measures of appeal to mass organization. The wave to the masses might have failed to initiate an outright plan of radical reform, but it could easily have become an incident in the effort of besieged reformers and putschists to stay in power by hook or by crook.

During the same period, Japan provides an example of far more successful development of military power than China. The analysis of the contrast helps illuminate the enabling conditions of force and wealth in a period when the means of both production and destruction have already become industrialized. At the outset of this second pendant in the comparative analysis, however, it is illuminating to see how much each country's experience was shaped by the other's.

One of the most important causes of Japan's ability to hold off direct Western domination was China's failure to do so. The Western imperial powers were tied up in their Chinese adventures as well as in a spate of largely unrelated internecine struggles, from the Franco-Prussian War to the American Civil War. The Opium Wars (1839–1842, 1856–1860) in China gave warning to the most farsighted Japanese leaders of what awaited countries that failed to submit to the ordeal of transformation for the sake of wealth and power.

Later, Japan's worldly success, translated into imperialist attacks, became decisive for the form of China's own transformation. The national resistance to Japanese occupation became the arena for the struggle between Communist and Nationalist forces and the school for a new relationship between the working masses and the political nation. The resistance period therefore left its mark for all time to come on Chinese society. It became the occasion for China's fitful reach toward a disaggregation of the North Atlantic models of industrialism far more drastic than any yet realized in Japan.

The reciprocal interferences between the histories of these two peoples at the moment of their encounter with Western might serves as an initial admonition about anything that can be said in a comparative analysis. Whatever larger truth we may infer from a comparative analysis of these Chinese and Japanese experiences depends for its force on such seemingly extraneous circumstances as the physical proximity of the two lands: the particular way in which the land masses happen to have been disposed on the surface of the planet at the time these historical collisions were occurring. One of the tests of historical realism must be the ability to acknowledge the disorder introduced by all such random connections and to recognize that this disorder is not confined to some limited aspect of experience but penetrates every aspect in different ways. Any insight with a true claim to generality must reconcile its vision of emergent reality and possibility with its understanding of the relentless and fateful accumulation of loosely related circumstances and choices.

Consider, to begin with, the defining elements of Japan's military capability at the times of the Sino–Japanese War of 1895 and of the Russo–Japanese War a decade later.

The initial basis of this capability was the armaments industry. Even more than in any Western country, industrialization in Japan was spearheaded by mechanized, factory-based arms manufacture. During the closing years of the Tokugawa regime, initiatives had already begun to proliferate in the crucial vanguard areas of foundries, weapons production, and shipbuilding. The actual or anticipated pressure of Western encroachments was by far the most far-reaching motive for these efforts. The first reverberatory furnaces built for iron processing were set up by the Tokugawa government and by the powerful domain governments of Satsuma, Mito, and Saga. A still greater number of domains (*han*) participated actively in the construction of shipyards.[31] After 1868 the Meiji government dramatically expanded its industrial initiatives in all these areas.[32] Even the textile industry – the first large industrial sector not directly related to military aims – began under governmental auspices. Only later were the industries sold into private hands. Although the immediate occasion for their sale was fiscal pressure on the state, the decision also reflected the crystallization of an alliance and a program. Reactionary and popular forces had been put down, and enough of a consensus among realigned bureaucratic and business groups had been established to make direct governmental management of industry dispensable and embarrassing.

Many of these late nineteenth century industries ran at a loss when first established. The major source of investment funds came from the land tax, which underwent a significant change in definition and allocation through the reforms of 1873–1874. The use of this source of finance, together with the obsessive study of Western engineering and science, gave the Japanese armaments industry a degree of independence from Western capital and assistance entirely lacking in China.

[31] See W.G. Beasley, *The Meiji Restoration*, Stanford, Stanford, 1972, pp. 123–124.
[32] See Kajinishi Mitsuhaya, "The Birth of Heavy Industry in Japan: With Reference to a Re-Examination of the Meiji Restoration," summarized in *An Outline of Japanese Economic History, 1603–1940*, eds. Mikio Sumiya and Koji Taira, Univ. of Tokyo, 1979, pp. 201–203.

Certainly the existence of a large agrarian surplus was vital to this policy. In this sense, the military buildup reaped the benefits of the earlier escape from periodic reversion to natural economy that had taken place during the early Tokugawa. Nevertheless, the total tax–rent burden on the actual cultivators – petty tenants or proprietors and agricultural laborers – seems to have been, on the whole, higher in both Meiji and Tokugawa Japan than in late Ch'ing China. The Meiji seizure of central government, the further advance of local landlords, and the repressive demobilization of the peasantry were all crucial to the investment strategy that prevailed.

The second foundation of Japanese military power, alongside the armaments industry, was the establishment of a mass conscript army. Again, the breakthrough depended on a definition of the state's basic character and supporting alliances. It was necessary to defeat the strong samurai groups who resisted the conscript army as a threat to their power interests and self-definition. The resistance of these groups sparked confrontations that mixed the recruitment issue with the struggle over the abolition of samurai stipends and the debate over the invasion of Korea.[33] Again, the danger of popular rebellion had to be quashed. The raising of a conscript army presupposed a minimal degree of control over insurrectionary movements. Once such an army had been raised, it could in turn be used to terrorize the people. But the threat of rebellion within the ranks persisted, as shown by episodes like the 1878 mutiny of the Imperial Guard. The new masters of the state owed their success in transforming the military structure of power to not having had to face all these dangers simultaneously. For this reprieve they could thank their luck as much as their cunning.

A third and more intangible boost to Japanese military capability was the gradual development of an organizational structure, in the military, industrial, and administrative enterprises, that reconciled the achievement of high degrees of effectiveness with two other aims in apparent tension with each other.

One of these goals was to minimize the disruptive impact of the new organizational arrangements on the hierarchies and habits of the reordered society and the reformed state while exploiting the op–portunities that Japanese forms of corporate solidarity and hierar–chical deference might create for industrial discipline. The protracted though declining vitality of corporate village institutions through the Tokugawa period provided an initial apprenticeship in joint, super–vised activities within large organizations. The system of commer–cialized agriculture combined with petty handicraft provided large

---

[33] See E. Herbert Norman, *Soldier and Peasant in Japan: The Origin of Conscription*, Univ. of British Columbia, Vancouver, 1965, especially pp. 43–47.

numbers of people with an experience of skilled labor in primitive manufacturing. It also deepened an agrarian economy that helped finance industrialization.

The other, contrasting purpose in the development of organizational life was to minimize the need to invent structures radically different from those that were emerging in the West. Few leaders of the governing classes were willing to take chances with an organized complex of men and machines radically different from the military and economic enterprises that had already broken in upon the country; any drastic redesign of organizations or technologies would take time, entail risks, and require imagination. The contrast between the desire to avoid social disruption and the uninterest in bold organizational invention was diminished by the sharp divisions between task-defining and task-executing jobs within the Western models. It was also moderated by the way in which Japanese dispositions could be used to deal with the weak points in the Western schemes, and most especially with confrontation and resistance inside the enterprise. The equivocal fusion of contract, community, and domination could be extended more readily because it did not have to pass directly from the agrarian to the industrial setting. The many corporate bodies that flourished in an increasingly commercialized economy allying agriculture to petty manufacture supplied facilitating links.

Such circumstances, however, failed to produce an easy marriage of Japanese and Western styles of organization. There were brutal struggles whose outcome long remained uncertain, as evidenced by the conflicts surrounding the Factory Act of 1911 and other waves of violent labor unrest.[34] For the new rulers of the country and their allies in business and bureaucracy, success in these struggles was unthinkable without a minimum of consensus among themselves and a willingness to use every repressive and financial weapon at the disposal of government. The outcome, which came to look so natural in retrospect, was in fact constantly jeopardized by the dissensions of the leading circles in Japanese society and the desperate attempts of workers and agitators to find an alternative future.

The military capability whose elements I have just described resulted from two interwoven lines of development. One of them was the association established among the restored state, the realigned elites, and the working people. The other was the relation of the empire to foreign powers.

To understand the first of these two sequences, you need to dis-

---

[34] See Stephen S. Large, *Organized Workers and Socialist Politics in Interwar Japan*, Cambridge, Cambridge, 1981, pp. 40–50; Andrew Gordon, *The Evolution of Labor Relations in Japan: Heavy Industry, 1835–1955*, Harvard Univ. Press, Cambridge, 1985, pp. 116–121, 211–235.

tinguish the ambitions and alliances that produced the Meiji Restoration from the content of governmental policy in the aftermath of the Restoration. There is no direct inference from the former to the latter. Many of the groups most important to the overthrow of the Tokugawa regime suffered defeat and disappointment in the factional struggles that took place from the very moment of the *bakufu*'s downfall. No one could safely predict the identities of the winners and losers in this contest from the events that had led up to the Restoration or for that matter from any deep-seated features of Japanese society.

In the late Tokugawa, at least two major social groups remained only very imperfectly integrated into the structure of the state: the middle-level or village samurai and the more enterprising landlord–entrepreneurs of the commercialized agrarian and handicraft economy, who were largely excluded from the immediate benefits of participation in state power. The entrepreneurs were harassed by governmental regulation without being broken or tamed by it. The samurai were cut off from the *bakufu* structure without being systematically deprived of the means for doing violence. Both these groups provided vital support to the Restorationist movement. Neither had any ready counterpart in China, where the relatively tight entente of officials, landlords, and merchants had ensconced itself more deeply and uniformly in the structure of local administration and military force. Besides, the domain governments had a greater autonomy as bases of power than the regional Chinese authorities. The Japanese elites, as a whole, had a keener awareness of national distinctiveness and vulnerability than their Chinese counterparts.

But the content of the crucial reforms in the first decade of the new regime was another matter. That the reshaping and administration of the land tax would favor landlords over small tenants might have been expected from the forces at work before and during the Restoration. But the destruction or redefinition of samurai privileges was the work of men anxious to keep the financial and military resources of the state from being immobilized by a stipendiary caste. These men expected and got from their victories in the quarrels of the early Meiji era (1868–1912) a wider margin of maneuver to revise the organizational settings for production, administration, and warfare in ways that wedded national and oligarchic interests.

The seizure of the state, the use of the agrarian surplus to finance militarily oriented industry, and the careful avoidance of premature military adventures permitted a growing measure of independence from foreign control. Each such advance in national autonomy in turn enlarged the state's options in redefining the country's relationship to world alliances and the world economy.

By all these means, governmental power was disengaged from an order of privilege so confining that it would have blocked any sequence of trials and errors in the search for the enabling conditions of military and economic power. Yet the wealthy and powerful retained a continuing identity; the defeated in the internecine quarrels of the new regime won a chance to survive and prosper under a new identity. The realignment of the elites, the redefinition of land-tenure and land-tax arrangements, and the halting, precarious creation of a semi-constitutional regime of government and industrial relations all created a structure within which groups could redefine and reorganize themselves. This limited opportunity for recurrent collective militancy, however, was not allowed to escalate into the style of mass mobilization and institutional invention that might have produced a more path-breaking industrialized success. Power at the center, resolute, relatively available for transformative use, and capable of supporting an atmosphere of differential and limited but real opportunities for collective redefinition and self-organization – this was the essential achievement of the Meiji state, the source of its superiority over late Ch'ing China, and its primary contribution to Japan's military and industrial success.

The comparative study of these Chinese and Japanese experiences suggests two related conclusions. One of them has to do with the nature of freedom and constraint in the relation between enabling circumstances and practical capacity. The other conclusion deals with the connection between the bases of military and of productive capability and between the line of argument developed in this chapter and the view of the North Atlantic breakthrough suggested by the earlier chapters.

Do not misread this comparative discussion as an analysis of the reasons why late nineteenth-century China was doomed to fail and late nineteenth-century Japan guaranteed to succeed in their respective efforts to match the Western threat. Remember the relativity of success and failure that becomes apparent as soon as you take a longer temporal view. Consider the enormous importance of the effect that each of these countries had on the other in the course of their contrasting response to the Western powers. Bear in mind the barely lost opportunities at every crucial juncture in the events.

It is true that every measure of success served as a platform from which to launch further advances. In the Japanese experience, the mutual reinforcement of domestic reform and foreign autonomy had enormous importance. More generally, every step toward the disengagement of governmental power from a tightly defined structure of privilege and collective alliances, from a fixed scheme of hierarchy and divisions, multiplies options at the next round. It loosens the connection between military, productive, or administrative activities and their organizational bases and between these bases and the larger ordering of state and society. It allows a reformist or revolutionary leadership to cast about for a redefinition of these linkages that will be both effective and (to their eyes) justifiable.

But the drawing of success out of success and of failure out of failure is easily exaggerated. For one of the striking facts about any real historical situation is the frequent inversion of hierarchies of apparent achievement. Power is paralyzed by privilege and collective organization by the hardened deals and hierarchies that emerge when people think they have averted such threats to worldly success. The opportunities for transformative politics – reformist or revolutionary – suddenly reappear when government seems helpless and any major restructuring of collective alliances and identities appears out of the question.

Again, you might reasonably infer from the comparative discussion that, on several counts, Japan in 1860 was in a better position than China to achieve a limited, reformist accommodation to Western military and industrial power. The single most important Japanese advantage may have been the existence in Japan of significant, locally based elites who were imperfectly incorporated into the structure of central government and in whose eyes, society – the society that counted – was already at war with the state. China, it seems, would have been forced from the start to stage a far more radical break with its established social and governmental order if it was to have a chance at success.

Nevertheless, this judgment of relative advantage for a politics of protective reform is much more tentative than it seems at first. The more closely you study the sequence of events in China, the more you are impressed by the number of occasions on which a reformist clique came close to seizing the state. The most you can plausibly say is that, in China, such a clique would soon have been forced to appeal to a larger mass constituency than proved necessary to the founders of the Meiji state. The Chinese reformers would have confronted an elite more uniformly and deeply ensconced in the privileges of local governmental power, a more immediate foreign threat, and a more formidable task of communication and control. In this view, the Chinese reformers would have been driven to more radical expedients or else would have forfeited their chances of survival. Comparative analysis is on safer ground when it suggests that, at any level of radicalism and accommodation, the Chinese and Japanese solutions would have had to differ in the particular content of their sustaining alliances and transformative programs.

Yet vulgar historiography and social science, deep-logic social theories, and common prejudice, all join in giving a semblance of retrospective necessity to the different outcomes. We ridicule the court historians of the ancient agrarian monarchies for their kowtowing.

At least they professed to find moral insight in accomplished fact. Some even used the lessons of history to urge restraint on the powerful. Latter-day necessitarians have no such excuse.

UNDERSTANDING AND HARNESSING THE IMPERATIVE OF SOCIAL PLASTICITY

The European experiences discussed earlier in this essay focus attention on the dissociations and recombinations of institutional arrangements that allowed certain countries to exploit new organizational and technological opportunities in warfare. The later, Asian examples present the same problem from a slightly different angle. They draw our attention to efforts to dissociate some of the traits of the Western industrialized, imperialist societies from other traits: to combine Western levels of productive or destructive capability with indigenous or newly invented ways of coordinating work or, more commonly, of combining imported Western styles of work organization with non-Western governmental and economic institutions.

In both the European preindustrial and the Asian postindustrial situations, success, even survival, required the practice of an art of institutional dismemberment and recombination. This art constantly rearranges the two linkages repeatedly considered in this essay. One link joins a practical capability to the immediate organizational setting of that capability – a style of coordination in production or warfare. The other link connects a way of organizing work to a more comprehensive set of governmental and economic arrangements. The practice of institutional dissociation and recombination shakes up and wears down a society's plan of social division and social ranking; roles and hierarchies depend for their perpetuation on the stability of particular institutions. This shaking up and wearing down represents one of the major forms taken by the imperative of self-transformation in history.

The experiences of military success and failure traced here highlight a series of puzzles and paradoxes in the practice of institutional dissociation and recombination. To consider these puzzles and paradoxes is to begin the work of generalizing the argument of this chapter into a thesis about the institutional conditions of worldly success. It is to turn from the mirror of destruction to the productive activities this mirror imperfectly reflects.

The military examples suggest that the repeated practice of institutional dissociation and recombination is not a random walk. It has – at least, it has often had – a direction. Practiced long and often enough, it moves societies toward greater plasticity. Again and again, the changes that prove most congenial to the development and the

exploitation of technological and organizational opportunities in warfare or production unite two sets of characteristics.

The superior solutions turn the relations among soldiers or workers
into a visible social image of experimental, practical reason. The
workers or soldiers do not remain the passive executants of a rigid,
predefined plan. They vary the plan – and yet maintain overall coordination – in the course of executing it. As a result, they do not
stay pegged in immutable roles. The fluidity of the contrast between
task-defining and task-executing acts coincides with the softening of
the distinctions among task-executing acts themselves. Today, the
vanguardist forms of warfare (commandos, tanks, air power) and
production (high-technology industry operating with flexible production processes and nonspecific "meta-machines") represent the
practical activities that have moved furthest toward this fluidity. But
even if we go back to periods long before the emergence of these
modern varieties of production and warfare, we can distinguish
among military or productive styles by their relative closeness to the
same practical ideal embodied in contemporary vanguardist warfare
or production. We can also tell that movement toward this ideal has
generally brought success to the individuals, groups, and countries
that have achieved it.

The persistent practice of institutional dissociation and recombination also favors social arrangements with a second set of characteristics. This second group of traits has to do not with the immediate
organizational setting of production or warfare – the style of work
organization – but with the larger framework of governmental and
economic institutions within which these forms of work organization
exist. If we can discern a cumulative movement in the institutional
frameworks of our practical activities of warfare and production, it
is a movement toward solutions that do not allow a rigid set of social
roles and hierarchies to predefine the practical relations among people. The waning of the influence that any such plan of social division
and hierarchy exercises on the ways in which workers or soldiers
collaborate keeps the organization of work and exchange open to
opportunistic experiment and to the social imitation of practical
reason.

Beyond a point, the weakening of the influence of social roles and
hierarchies on jobs or exchange relations implies the weakening of
the social roles and hierarchies themselves. For the strength of a
system of social stations consists in the extent to which it imposes a
ready-made script on people's practical or passionate dealings. The
Prussian military reformers of the early nineteenth century – like all
perceptive reformers before or after them – knew that they could
not expect soldiers who were hardly more than reluctant serfs to

enact the new, more mobile tactical and operational techniques. Something had to be done to change German society.

Notice that this cumulative change in the broader institutional setting of economic or military activity requires the occasional invention of new institutions, even different kinds of institutions. It does not require fewer, less definite, or less stable institutional arrangements. It does not mean anarchy or even permanent flux. Some institutions and practices are better than others at keeping open the area of practical experimentation. In fact, the solutions that diminish the practical influence of rigid roles and hierarchies are likely to be more explicit if not more elaborate than the institutions they replace. For such hierarchy-subverting and role-loosening arrangements represent an artifact of the will imposed on inherited, half-articulate routines.

These two sets of characteristics give precision to the idea of social plasticity. Their description elucidates the thesis that the quest for collective wealth and power requires a cumulative movement toward greater plasticity in the organizational and institutional setting of production, exchange, and warfare. The imperative of plasticity requires that advances in productive or destructive powers be achieved through the subversion of fixed plans of social division and hierarchy and of stark contrasts between task setting and task following. All possible combinations have to be tried out, as quickly and as freely as possible. The only structure that can be allowed to subsist is one that offers the fewest obstacles to this principle of pitiless recombination.

No sooner do we state the thesis of plasticity with greater richness and precision than we see that it must be qualified in several ways. The preceding discussion of episodes in military history illustrates these qualifications and suggests their force. The question is: What remains of the initial thesis once we have done full justice to these reservations?

The first qualification concerns the multiplicity of relatively conservative responses that are always available. An elite can use such responses in its efforts to reconcile the imperative of greater plasticity with the preservation of the vested interests and the traditional pieties supported by the established institutional order. It is not enough for an alternative style of work organization and an alternative set of governmental and economic institutions to outdistance its rivals in the degree of plasticity it embodies. The reform program must be accepted and implemented. Besides, the struggle over alternative responses to practical challenge takes place amid institutional arrangements and widely shared preconceptions that bias the outcome of the conflict. They bias it not only by placing certain groups in a better position to dictate the solution but also by discouraging solutions that require too violent a break with inherited ways.

Moreover, the test of success that counts is the comparison of one war machine or industrial economy with its closest and most threatening adversaries. In the long run, we all die. In the short run, we die differentially. A competent conservative elite always finds that it can catch up to a rival country, or simply meet its own people's expectations, on the basis of organizations and institutions that preserve a great deal of the preexisting social order, with its roles and hierarchies and its enacted dogmas about the possible and desirable forms of human association. Thus, those same Prussian military reformers of the Napoleonic era correctly understood that they did not have to make Hohenzollern Germany into revolutionary France in order to lay the social and institutional basis on which Germany could meet the French threat. With luck and ingenuity, reformers like these can even find ways to turn to competitive advantage what seemed archaic features of their societies.

The availability of the intelligent conservative response to the imperative of plasticity reminds us of another qualification to the thesis that the search for wealth and strength has a particular institutional direction. We seem unable to discover any limited list of necessary institutional vehicles for any given measure of social plasticity. We can compare alternative sets of practices or institutions as more or less responsive to the twin aspects of plasticity distinguished earlier. But we cannot say that a given level of plasticity – or of the practical capabilities that plasticity permits – must be realized through particular institutional arrangements. We know that we cannot because every attempt to specify such necessary correspondences has been foiled by the next episode of institutional dissociation and recombination in the present or by the next discovery about institutional dissociation and recombination in the past. Thus, the successful institutional responses to the military challenges discussed in this essay simply fail to fit the patterns favored by theories that relate levels of practical capability to particular institutional systems. The most influential doctrines in the history of modern social thought have been just such theories; Marxism provides the exemplary instance.

The art of institutional dissociation and recombination does not work by selecting the best solutions from a closed list of alternative arrangements. For even if such a list exists, we do not know what it is, and our ideas about its nature and content have been repeatedly discredited. Institutional reinvention operates, instead, with the practical and conceptual materials handed down by the traditions people are in or by the traditions they can remember, recover, and study.

The influence of sequence, which so often serves the cause of the conservative reformer, also helps explain why we find less variety in the history of institutional forms than a justified skepticism about the deep-seated necessity of past or present institutions might lead us to expect. The record of experiments with the organization of military and economic activity is too messy to exemplify a table of correspondences between particular levels of capability and particular institutional systems. But it is also too tainted by narrowing obsessions and imitations and by privileged strangleholds on social resources to demonstrate the untrammeled freedom of invention that in our most optimistic moments we may be tempted to claim. It is because of the influence of what comes before on what comes after that our institutional settlements and inventions can have both an ad hoc, pasted-together quality and a surprising repetitiveness.

The significance of sequence can be generalized in a way that both qualifies further the thesis of plasticity and connects it more intimately to the experiences analyzed in this book. The general point is quite simply that the practice of institutional dissociation and recombination has a history. This history is, and increasingly becomes, worldwide.

In the course of their domestic and international conflicts the Western powers created a version of an industrialized war machine and production system that settled accounts with the mobilizational and technological requirements of warfare in a particular way. There are no deep-seated reasons why the vanguardist style of warfare could not have emerged more quickly and taken over a broader range of military activities than it did. But it seems that in prerevolutionary Europe a faster pace of radical organizational innovation would have required a lasting alliance between the people in charge of central governments and the ordinary working people. The results of a large number of conflicts, in different areas of social life, would have had to converge toward unprecedented forms of popular self-organization or revolutionary despotism.

Such innovations might have required a higher measure of institutional invention than the solutions that in fact prevailed. They might have also demanded a larger number of failures on the part of conservative statesmen, anxious to discover practical compromises between higher levels of capability and the maintenance of established orders of privilege. Nevertheless, breakthroughs of comparable magnitude had occurred before. Without them, the European escape from the closed circles of the agrarian societies would not have been possible.

Alternatively, you can easily imagine that the settling of accounts with the pressures of intensified conflict would have allowed an even smaller place to vanguardist warfare and to the subversion of established forms of hierarchy and division. The European oligarchies, relatively successful as they were, might have proved even better at accommodating a more flexible style in the war machine and production system with the maintenance of their inherited privileges. They would have had to have been bolder in turning patrons and clients, masters and servants, into managerial task definers and skilled but obedient task executors. Later, the Japanese came somewhat closer to doing precisely this.

Once the initial Western version of an industrialized economy and war machine had been set up, it influenced the immediate options available to the non-Western peoples as responses to this Western threat. Had the triumphant Western model of industrialism and warfare gone further toward the vanguardist, flexible styles of production and of fighting, the effort of the Japanese elites to disaggregate this model in order to preserve the essentials of their own privileges and their own identities would have been that much more difficult. The art of dissociation and recombination would have demanded a still greater virtuosity from conservative reformers and it would have offered still more opportunities to their adversaries among the masses or the elites. On the other hand, had the dominant Western model of industrialized armies and economies been less hierarchy-subverting and role-loosening than it was, the Chinese reformers would have had a shorter distance to go, and a greater chance of success. Reforming elites around the world would have had reason for even more confidence in the possibility of achieving even greater productive and destructive power with a minimum of disturbance to established social orders.

Thus, when we place institutional experimentation on a worldwide scale and examine its workings over long stretches of time we discover that its earlier and later moments have a relation we cannot adequately understand as the outward effect of lawlike forces. Each move in this sequence represents a transaction between the aims of people who have gained control of central governments and who are trying to impress their will on events for conservative or revolutionary purposes and the versions of workable production systems or war machines currently available in the world as models. The current forms of industrial and military organization may be ill suited to the aims of the rulers. Then, the work of dismemberment and rearrangement becomes that much harder. The people in charge, or their would-be successors, have to go further in the invention of an alternative organizational and social context for practical capabilities. This more ambitious practice may fail. It may fail because its practitioners choose unworkable solutions or because the inventors invent too slowly. Foreign and domestic enemies may do their will while the innovators try to come up with new ways of conducting production and warfare.

To appreciate the complex relation between the pull of plasticity and the push of sequence in the history of the institutional forms of warfare and production is to grasp a central, unresolved ambiguity in our collective drive for practical empowerment. Does the movement toward plasticity converge toward particular ways of organizing work and of arranging the broader institutional framework of productive and destructive activity? Or does it, on the contrary, leave us free to choose among an indefinitely large number of forms of social organization? Is it a particular fate or only the fate of a radical contingency?

We do not know the answers to these questions. We cannot tell how much built-in content the requirement of plasticity will prove to have. Nor can we console ourselves with the idea that it would be paradoxical for it to have any content at all. There is nothing paradoxical about the idea that a machine – or an institutional system – capable of accelerated self-revision may have to be designed according to precise specifications. It would not be surprising to find that people may revise such a machine or such a system in ways that make it either less open or more open to further revisions. The appearance of paradox dissipates further once we replace the vague ideas of indefinition or revisability with the more precise conception of plasticity on which the argument of this book draws.

Whatever the extent of our freedom to determine the practical forms of social plasticity, our task remains the same. The influence of sequence and the requirements of flexibility allow many different institutional combinations to emerge and to survive. We must choose the variants that also serve a more inclusive conception of human empowerment. For even if plasticity turns out to make many particular demands on us, we are still likely to have room for maneuver in choosing how and how much to satisfy these demands. A mobilizational despotism may be able to meet them. But so may a more radical democracy that fragments and liquefies claims on the resources – economic capital, governmental power, or technical expertise – by which we create the social future within the social present.

We can harness the requirement of plasticity to a higher social ideal. We can respond to it in ways that continue to lift from social life the taint of dependence and depersonalization – of servitude to rigid hierarchies and prostration to inherited roles. We can satisfy it by means that enable us to assert, as individuals and as groups, a more deliberate mastery over the terms of our practical, emotional, and cognitive access to one another. We can turn it into a foothold for our attempts to make our social contexts nourish our context-revising powers and respect our context-transcending vocation. We can give the imperative of plasticity the focus and the authority it lacks.

Chronological Chart of Islam

Year	Arabia-Iraq and the Fertile Crescent	Egypt and Syria	Persia and Central Asia	Spain and the Maghrib	Turkey	Afghanistan and Northern India
100						
200			Sassanian Empire			
300	Lakhmid Kingdom					
400						
500	Ghassanid Kingdom					
600						
650		Umayyad Dynasty				
750		Abbasid Dynasty		Umayyad Dynasty		
800		Tulunid Dynasty				
900		Ikhshidid Dynasty	Samanid Empire			
1000	Seljuq Invasion	Fatimid Dynasty	Qarakhanid Empire / Seljuq Dynasty	Almoravid Dynasty	Seljuqs of Rūm	Ghaznavid Dynasty
1100		Ayyubid Dynasty		Almohad Dynasty		Ghurid Dynasty
1200	Mongol Invasion / Il-Khanid Dynasty	Mamluk Dynasty	Mongol Invasion: Il-Khanid Dynasty	Kingdom of Granada	Mongol Invasion / Ottoman Dynasty	
1300						Tughluqid Dynasty
1400	Timurid Dynasty		Timurid Dynasty			
1500	Ottoman Empire		Safavid Dynasty		Ottoman Empire	Mughal Dynasty
1600						
1700			Qajar Dynasty			
1800						
1900						

Source: Adapted from Bernard Lewis, *Islam and the Arab World*, Knopf, New York, 1976.

Chinese Dynasties

Hsia Kingdom	c. -2000 to c. -1520
Shang (Yin) Kingdom	c. -1520 to c. -1030
Chou Dynasty ⎰ Early Chou Period	c. -1030 to -722
⎱ Ch'un Ch'iu Period	-722 to -480
⎱ Warring States (Chan Kuo) Period	-480 to -221
Ch'in Dynasty	-221 to -207
Han Dynasty ⎰ Ch'ien Han (Earlier or Western)	-202 to $+9$
⎱ Hsin Interregnum	$+9$ to $+23$
⎱ Hou Han (Later or Eastern)	$+25$ to $+220$
San Kuo (Three Kingdoms Period)	$+221$ to $+265$
Shu (Han) $+221$ to $+264$	
Ts'ao Wei $+220$ to $+265$	
Wu $+222$ to $+280$	
Chin Dynasty: Western	$+265$ to $+317$
Eastern	$+317$ to $+420$
(Liu) Sung Dynasty	$+420$ to $+479$
Northern and Southern Dynasties (Nan Pei ch'ao)	
Ch'i Dynasty	$+479$ to $+502$
Liang Dynasty	$+502$ to $+557$
Ch'en Dynasty	$+557$ to $+587$
Northern (Toba) Wei Dynasty	$+386$ to $+535$
Western (Toba) Wei Dynasty	$+535$ to $+554$
Eastern (Toba) Wei Dynasty	$+534$ to $+543$
Northern Ch'i Dynasty	$+550$ to $+577$
Northern Chou (Hsienpi) Dynasty	$+557$ to $+581$
Sui Dynasty	$+581$ to $+618$
T'ang Dynasty	$+618$ to $+906$
Wu Tai (Five Dynasty Period)	$+907$ to $+960$
(Later Liang, Later T'ang (Turkic),	
Later Chin (Turkic), Later Han (Turkic)	
and Later Chou)	
Liao (Ch'itan Tartar) Dynasty	$+907$ to $+1125$
West Liao Dynasty (Qarā-Khitāi)	$+1144$ to $+1211$
Hsi Hsia (Tangut Tibetan) State	$+990$ to $+1227$
Northern Sung Dynasty	$+960$ to $+1126$
Southern Sung Dynasty	$+1127$ to $+1279$
Chin (Jurchen Tartar) Dynasty	$+1115$ to $+1234$
Yüan (Mongol) Dynasty	$+1260$ to $+1368$
Ming Dynasty	$+1368$ to $+1644$
Ch'ing (Manchu) Dynasty	$+1644$ to $+1911$
Republic of China (Taiwan after 1949)	$+1912$ –
People's Republic of China	$+1949$ –

Source: Adapted from Joseph Needham, *Science and Civilization in China,* vol. 1, Cambridge, Cambridge.

Chronology of Japanese History

Yamato Period	ca. A.D. 300–645
Nara Period	710–784
Heian Period	794–1185
Fujiwara Period	858–1160
Kamakura Period	1185–1333
Ashikaga (or Muromachi) Period	1338–1573
Azuchi-Momoyama (or Shokuhō) Period	1568–1600
Tokugawa (or Edo) Period	1600–1868
Meiji Period	1868–1912
Taishō Period	1912–1926
Shōwa Period	1926–

Source: Adapted from John W. Hall, *Japan: From Prehistory to Modern Times,* Dell, New York, 1970.

Index

I Wish I Liked Rice Pudding

Joyce Dunbar

Illustrated by Carol Thompson

MACDONALD YOUNG BOOKS

For my mother – JD
For my parents – CT

First published in Great Britain in 1989 by
Simon & Schuster Limited

This edition first published in 1991 by
Simon & Schuster Young Books

Reprinted in 1992, 1994 and 1999 by
Macdonald Young Books
61 Western Road
Hove
East Sussex
BN3 1JD

Printed in Belgium by Proost International Book Production

ISBN: 0 7500 2825 4

I wish I liked rice pudding,

greens,   boiled turnips,   lumpy custard.

But I DON'T!

What I do like is chocolate ice-cream.

yummy!

I wish I liked
staying in on
rainy days

tidying up

be careful!

sitting still

going to
bed early.

But I DON'T!

What I do like
is splashing
in puddles.

I wish I liked
frilly frocks

socks that slide down
into my boots

scratchy sweaters

tight tights.

But I DON'T!

my favourite!

What I do like
are my baggy
striped pyjamas.

I wish I liked

the dog next doo[r]

bossy boys

horrid Henrietta

Uncle Alfred.

But I DON'T!

But I do like
my best-friend Effie.

I wish I liked
feeling sick

falling off
my bike

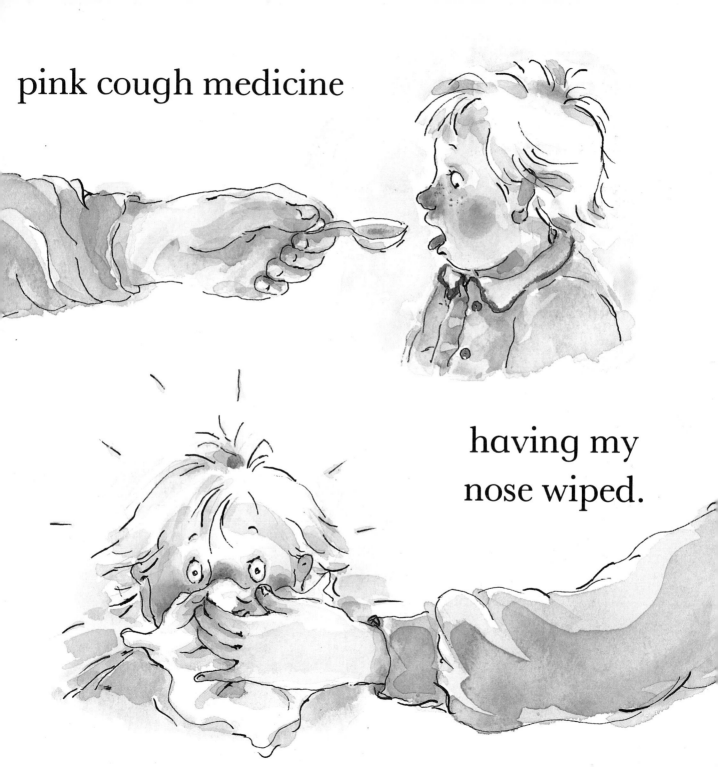

pink cough medicine

having my
nose wiped.

But I DON'T!

What I do like
is a cuddle from
my Mum.

I wish I liked
my tangly hair

my snub nose

my gappy teeth.

But I DON'T!

Never mind . . .

My Mum and Dad do!